DISCARD

The Farthest Home
Is in an
Empire of Fire

Also by John Phillip Santos

Places Left Unfinished at the Time of Creation (memoir)

Songs Older Than Any Known Singer (poetry)

Nuevo Santander, 1756

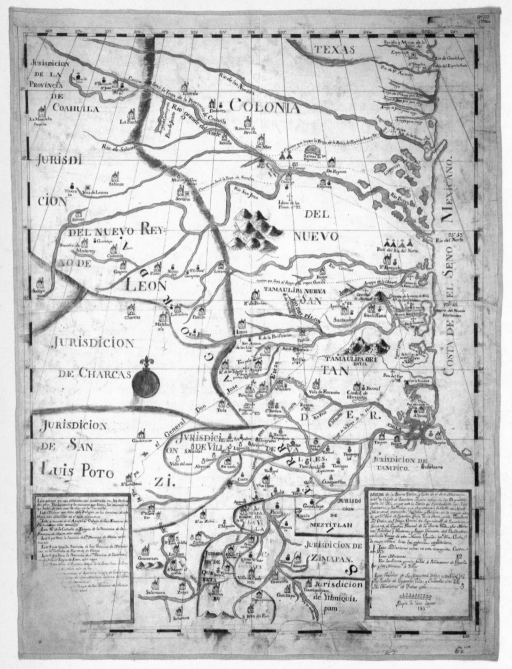

The Farthest Home
Is in an
Empire of Fire

A Tejano Elegy

John Phillip Santos

VIKING

VIKING
Published by the Penguin Group
Penguin Group (USA) Inc., 375 Hudson Street, New York, New York 10014, U.S.A.
Penguin Group (Canada), 90 Eglinton Avenue East, Suite 700, Toronto, Ontario,
Canada M4P 2Y3 (a division of Pearson Penguin Canada Inc.)
Penguin Books Ltd, 80 Strand, London WC2R 0RL, England
Penguin Ireland, 25 St. Stephen's Green, Dublin 2, Ireland (a division of Penguin Books Ltd)
Penguin Books Australia Ltd, 250 Camberwell Road, Camberwell, Victoria 3124, Australia
(a division of Pearson Australia Group Pty Ltd)
Penguin Books India Pvt Ltd, 11 Community Centre, Panchsheel Park,
New Delhi – 110 017, India
Penguin Group (NZ), 67 Apollo Drive, Rosedale, North Shore 0632, New Zealand
(a division of Pearson New Zealand Ltd)
Penguin Books (South Africa) (Pty) Ltd, 24 Sturdee Avenue, Rosebank,
Johannesburg 2196, South Africa

Penguin Books Ltd, Registered Offices: 80 Strand, London WC2R 0RL, England

First published in 2010 by Viking Penguin, a member of Penguin Group (USA) Inc.

1 3 5 7 9 10 8 6 4 2

Map of Nuevo Santander from Dolph Briscoe Center of American History,
The University of Texas at Austin

Letter by Laura (Riding) Jackson from *The Telling* by Laura (Riding) Jackson (Athlone Press,
1972; Harper & Row, 1973). By permission of the Laura (Riding) Jackson Board of
Literary Management.

Photograph courtesy of the author

LIBRARY OF CONGRESS CATALOGING IN PUBLICATION DATA
Santos, John Phillip.
The farthest home is in an empire of fire : a Tejano elegy / John Phillip Santos.
p. cm.
ISBN 978-0-670-02156-7
1. Santos, John Phillip—Family. 2. Spaniards—New Spain—Biography. 3. Spaniards—
Texas—Biography. 4. New Spain—Biography. I. Title.
PS3619.A597Z46 2010
813'.6—dc22   2009042560

Printed in the United States of America
Designed by Nancy Resnick

1/2010

Para Frances

The Prophets wrote about the future as if it were the past and about the past as if it were yet to happen, and similarly with the present. Sometimes they spoke figuratively, other times more realistically, and on occasion quite literally. One says more or less than another or expresses it in a better way.

—Christopher Columbus, *Book of Prophecies* (1501)

Contents

Uncle Lico's Vela Genealogy Disk

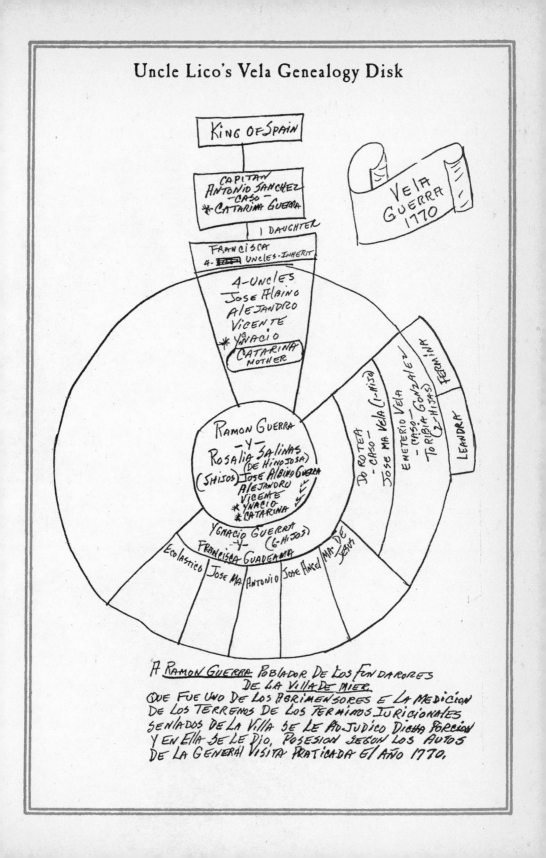

The Lopez Genealogy Disk

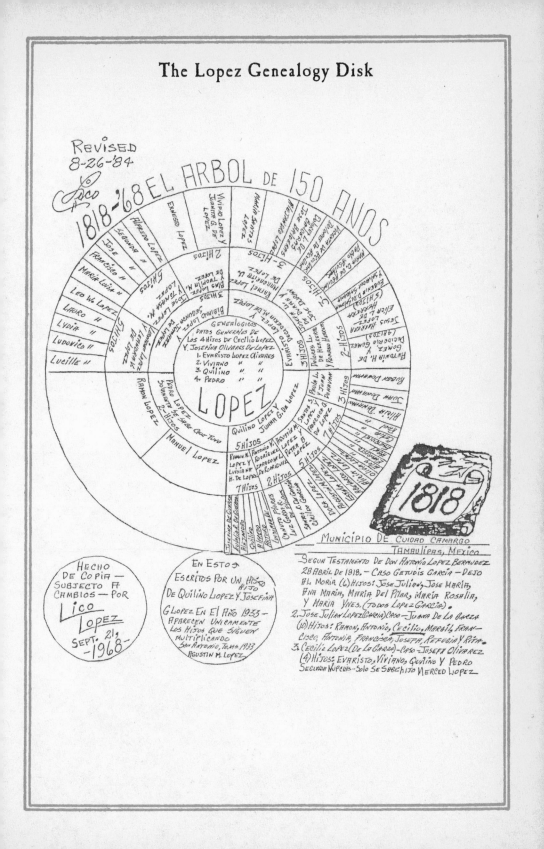

The Lopez-Vela Family, 1947

From left to right: BACK ROW: *Ludovico, Leo, Lauro*
SEATED: *Lucille (my mother), Leandra (my grandmother), Lydia*

Lopez-Vela Family Tree

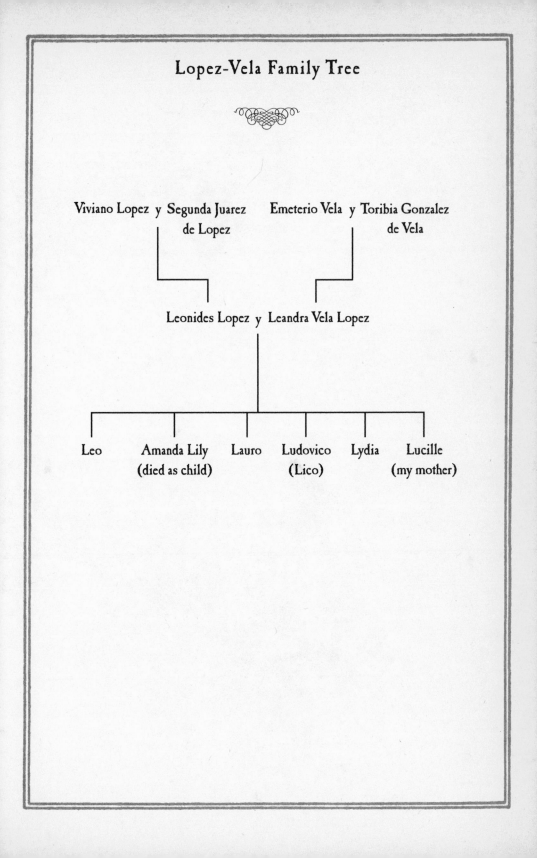

Viviano Lopez y Segunda Juarez de Lopez

Emeterio Vela y Toribia Gonzalez de Vela

Leonides Lopez y Leandra Vela Lopez

Leo

Amanda Lily (died as child)

Lauro

Ludovico (Lico)

Lydia

Lucille (my mother)

The Farthest Home
Is in an
Empire of Fire

I

Las Entradas

1. Proemio for the curious and benevolent reader

This is a story that took place long ago in a homeland far from
where I live today, in a land whose first, forgotten names were
never meant to be written down.

I cannot name them now. Perhaps no one can.

It is an American story that began in *la otra América*, before
Jamestown or Plymouth Rock, but it could have been anywhere in
the world.

Anywhere at the farthest edge of an unimagined country, where
people unknown to each other first meet.

This was Nueva España.

Nuevo Santander.

Mexico and Tejas.

Along with many other South Texans, I am a descendant of the
people of this forgotten tale, but nothing of their lives was ever told
to me by my elders. Only a few of their names survive. Nonetheless, centuries on in the tale, their story has come to me for telling, their lost story of a lost world—of ancestors who believed they

were creating a new world in the age of prophecy's end, the glorious triumph of their ancient traditions.

They left behind a landscape of prophecy's ruins—weathered limestone dwellings, missions, abandoned villages, forgotten archives. Exquisitely drawn maps and long histories of that world are hidden in libraries or secreted away deep within unplumbed family troves—but many have tattered over time, others turned to dust.

Moreover, from the time when the first fleeting chronicles of this world were being written, it was already passing away.

At its birth, this world was already more than half-overtaken by oblivion.

It was first approached by the sea in 1519, when a fleet of four barques captained by Alonso Álvarez de Piñeda traced the coastline of what came to be known as the Seno Mexicano, today's Gulf Coast, drawing a portolani map as they set out from the tip of Florida following the coast all the way to the Río Pánuco, named on an earlier expedition, south of present-day Tampico.

Nearby, to the north, Álvarez de Piñeda and his mariners had seen a great river, its mouth flanked on both sides by palm forests, so they called it Río de las Palmas. Upstream, they had encountered Indians but did not make contact with them, only exchanging fitful first glances across worlds, across the river that would later come to be known as Río Bravo or the Río Grande del Norte.

Today we know it simply as the Rio Grande.

Looking north, beyond the great river that runs through this landscape, low rolling hills were scattered across the horizon, purple with morning-blooming ceniza sage. Inland to the south, there was a land of inhospitably jagged, pewter-colored mountains that descended to the sprawling river plains. The heat was unforgiving. To arrive there overland from farther south, you had to leave everything behind, cross a vast terra-cotta desert and a cordon of soaring peaks, carrying with you whatever would be needed to survive.

Later attempts to settle the region in 1523 were quickly abandoned when the land was found to be hard to cultivate; bedraggled soldiers eventually mutinied and marched all the way to recently conquered Mexico City. By the end of the sixteenth century, dozens of explorers returned to refine the rough details for maps of the region, alliances between conquistadores and cartographers.

Eventually, the land would be found to provide its own rough succor. The streams were full of róbalo (bass), trucha (trout), and mojarra (perch). There were deer and rabbits, wild boar, yucca flowers and chile pequín, wild gherkins, guajillo honey, nopales and cactus fruit.

My ancestors gradually found their way there over the succeeding century and were among the founders of the Villas del Norte, the legendary towns created in the last conquistadorial campaign in Mexican history.

They later came to be known as los Llanos Mesteños, the mustang plains, where the emissaries of Spain, progenitors of my mother's Lopez-Vela families, first met the unimagined lands of that place without a name. Those lands were dubbed los Llanos Mesteños from the practice of the earliest sixteenth-century explorers of leaving a male and female horse on each side of any river they encountered in their wanderings. Over the decades that followed, the abandoned horses fattened themselves on the rich pasture grasses, tart acacia leaves, and sweet agarita berries, mating and proliferating generations of progeny, populating the lands in every direction with roaming herds of wild horses, animals that would be essential to the enterprise of settlement and building that the Spaniards undertook when they returned a century later.

The Españoles, or, as they came to be known, "los peninsulares," had their own way of living in deep time.

Today, a vertebral city is emerging from the parched geography of time and Texas earth, stretching forty miles, from Rio Grande City, past Mission City, to McAllen, Pharr, Edinburgh, San Juan, all the way to Brownsville. Highways 281, 44, 359, 77, 649, 83, and a web of other two-lane farm-to-market roads crisscross through this land that became southeastern Texas and northeastern Mexico, in the remote frontera territories where this story began.

I can't remember when I wasn't obsessed with finding the missing chronicle of my ancestors. I knew there was no book that could be put before me that would contain the stories of their journeys over sierras, across grassy dry llanos, tales of their onetime extensive lands, dispossessed and dwindled over time through divided inheritance, charlatanry, and, eventually, abandonment. I remember them now, as distant as Hesiod's age of heroes, from an apartment looking out over Central Park in New York City.

In photographs from my childhood in San Antonio, Texas, I often appear seated listening to elders, on a shady patio at the house on Cypress Street with Tío Viviano; with my abuela Santos in front of the fireplace she had turned into a flowerbox in the house on Cincinnati Street; or in the front room of the home on West Russell Street, standing over Grandmother Lopez in her La-Z-Boy recliner as she pointed to a photograph in an old album.

In other photographs, I'm the lad in Mickey Mouse pajamas, sometimes wearing an orange elephant Halloween mask, with a volume of the *World Book Encyclopedia*, books about space travel, or a certain book of children's stories opened across my lap. In the most harrowing tale in that latter tome, I remember how a pancake, my staple food until age ten, escaped certain death by growing legs and leaping off the plate and running away, an image that struck terror right through me.

Reading could seize me with fear or it could give me a sense of being connected to a story that reached outward into the cosmos or back to the beginning of time.

At some point, my love for books and the quest for the missing tale of my ancestors merged and became inseparable. The idea of a book that could tell the lost and nearly forgotten tale of my ancestors began to pull at me like an invisible sun.

Whatever their intentions, however exalted or dark their designs, they conducted themselves from the very first days as if they planned to pass a spell of eternity in those tierras nuevas, as if they knew they were taking the long road home.

Time itself became one of their conjuring tools for the unlikely ambition of building a New Spain on old Mexican earth. But the vaunted traditions of Spain met their match in the hardscrabble lands of Nueva España's barbarous northern regions.

Driving through the small town of Realitos in South Texas, the cemetery was already dressed for Día de los Muertos during one late

September not long ago, with a large carved stone setting of the Last Supper by a local artist dominating the grounds. Familiar family names were on the stones there: Guerra, Vela, Lopez, Chapa, Baez, Saenz, Flores, Garza, and Salazar. Names that had been handed down through the old lineages were often lost in the deepening streams of the mestizaje, as mestizos often came to take the names of their employers, a religious exemplar or an official of great note.

For mestizos, given names often only harkened them back to their mysterious origins in the New World, partly rooted in the indigenous world, partly in Iberia.

The lands became the Nueva Extremadura, so named after a region in Spain from which early conquistadores came.

Una Extremadura Verdadera.

Perhaps not the original homeland in Spain, speaking historically, nonetheless *la verdadera*, the true one. They became Nuevo Santander y Santander Verdadero, named for another province of northern Spain from which many of the explorers came. Gradually, these pairs, the Spanish original home and its New World duplicate, became blurred and the fading memories of once treasured birthplaces were eclipsed by the new homelands.

Everything could be mirrored, echoed, everything of the Old World would be re-created in the new. This absolved my ancestors of the obligation of discovering exactly where it was in the world they had come to. For most families, for generations to come, perhaps forever, there would only be the Mundo Nuevo.

At the founding of Mier, one of the ancestral towns of my family's history just across the present-day border west of Roma, Texas, the nearby stream once called Cynapicatli by the Indios was given the name Alcántara by a frontera scribe in honor of his hometown of the same name in Cáceres, Spain. And Iberian Alcántara itself was the legacy of an earlier colonization, as it is an Arabic word for "bridge."

One of the first Ibéricos to traverse those lands on foot was el naufragio, the shipwrecked Cabeza de Vaca, in 1536, only fifteen years after the fall of the Aztec capital in the Valley of Mexico, Tenochtitlán. He passed through as a lost and wandering pilgrim, heading south seeking kindred Españoles, likely crossing the Rio

Grande in today's Zapata County, Texas, near a broad shallow bend in the river, where other ancestors of mine would found the town of Revilla in the mid-1700s.

His published account of his journey sent many curious Españoles to the north in search of notoriety, legend, and loot.

When Capitán Luis de Carvajál y de la Cueva arrived with an expeditionary force in 1576, he drew maps and a geographical précis of the region, seeking a place of refuge from the Office of the Inquisition, which had branded the Portuguese explorer a false convert from Judaism. Complaining of the heat, he reported seeing great herds of bison and antelope, fat javelina and menacing gatos de montaña, and even endured brutal winters of icy wind and snow in a mini ice age that began late in the sixteenth century.

Capitán Alonso de León, another Spanish explorer who arrived in the northern region of Coahuila and became governor there in the 1660s, recorded much of this. He spent the next fifty years traveling these lands that were still without a name. The Mexica of Tenochtitlán had long referred to these lands as of the Chichimeca—the place of the dogs. For the Spaniards, they were known vaguely as "las Tierras Bárbaras."

Alonso de León saw then that his precursors of just one hundred years earlier were already at the edge of being forgotten forever. Between 1670 and 1690, he wrote a series of three discourses on the history of the exploration and settlement of the new tierras, so that the story would never be lost:

> As it pains me to see so many lives and great works of so many Españoles having perished at the jealous hands of these barbarians, buried now in the caverns of oblivion, I determined out of my own curiosity to make an account from official records of all of the things that happened (as if that were possible), and finding them much confused, dubious, and of such abounding incertitude (for such was the manner of the antiguos), I resolved to put them all aside.

Instead, de León, who called himself "gente de razón," a person of truth and reason, wrote his discourses based on stories he had been told of those who had come before, from those expeditions he had personally mounted into the "Tierras Bárbaras," and from an abiding belief that all the esfuerzos of the Españoles were part of a divine order that was being revealed in his time on earth.

In España Nueva del Norte, which was to become Mexico and Texas, de León saw abounding evidence of this divine plan unfolding, in the grandeur of the heavens, in the abundance of gold, silver, and the bounty of Mexican nature, in the concord in which all of this was placed in motion, and finally in the augurs and signs that had been placed in the world by God, to aid in proper and final moral judgment. He wrote his histories and discourses so that nothing of those grand exploits would ever be forgotten.

For all of his efforts, Alonso de León's lengthy treatise remained unpublished for nearly two hundred years, appearing in Mexico City only in 1909 as a volume in a series of books entitled *Documentos Inéditos ó Muy Raros Para la Historia de Mexico.*

We lack the memory, the records, and the words to tell the story of that world. How we imagined freedom but consecrated slavery. How we dreamed of a kingdom of God and anyone else went under the sword.

We are dubious inheritors of these "undiscovered" lands, the continents that would come to be known in their entirety only over much time. The Americas, like their dream-laden seafaring settlers, emerged in rough drafts—improvised versions of only fantasized totalities.

This was a way that wantonly ignored any references to whatever might've existed before. All of this transpired, and nearly all of it was forgotten, except among scholars of the history, and only a few of them come close to telling the story right and true.

Still, it was mostly forgotten by the people whose families lived it, as if it never really mattered to begin with, despite whatever pretense to prophetic destiny the first Spaniards in Mexico harbored—that the conquest of Mexico was a part of the completion of history, and that Christ's return and reign on earth would soon transpire.

There will be a conde who will come and change all of this land forever. It is the Conde de la Sierra Gorda who will establish las entradas, the portales through which all of España will come to the river and be made new.

Everything that was nearly lost has come to me as my story. I didn't want to become a professor of this tale, a scholar of the arcane details of history. I wanted to return it to the heart of my family. But instead of running to this destiny, instead of pursuing it ceaselessly, I ran away from my inherited story, postponed its telling almost endlessly, as if having been delayed so long another spell of dilations and detours would hardly matter.

Maybe I require the story now to fathom our survival.

I do not know to what end and by whom I was called upon to gather my ancestors' tales.

This was one of the two elemental forces steadily, remotely directing the course of my life.

My other manqué, the other guiding star toward which I was always steering, was women, or rather, a certain unnamable woman, an amalgam or ideal whose rare integument had more to do with spirit than anything carnal.

Even in adolescence, I was never mad for the flesh of just any young woman.

A lithe body and beautiful face alone did not draw me. I learned that in elementary school when my first crushes were more interested in collecting pictures of the Beatles than using the Ouija board to speak to the souls of the dead.

From my earliest desires, I longed for the embrace of another seeker, the embodied passions, consolation, and companionship of another soul on the mysterious and unpredictable path of a quickening apocalypse, our long-sought-for revelation to each other and ourselves.

This was just years after the Summer of Love, so there was ample pure groping, occasional abandonment into a spiraling flash of carnal magnetism, but I would always return; I was always seeking someone else, always Isis, Guinevere, Oshún, or Xochiquetzal, an accomplice in the dharma, a conspirator with whom I might tres-pass through ecstasy to the holy of holies in heaven, from where we could look back upon all that humans had wrought.

That was the orientation fixed in me from before any stirrings of my loins, the song in the throat of the bird before it was born. So my compañeras were mostly poetesses, actresses, scholars, theoreticians, and mystics—complotters in the great work, one and all.

Nancy exhorted me to go through embattled Northern Ireland in the summer of the hunger strikers. Stephanie wanted to drive through the ghostly streets of Khartoum, past burning barricades, on the night of a coup d'état. Carina insisted we should drive into Chiapas on the first evening of the Zapatista uprising. And Lene convinced me we should keep to our original plan on the day of the attacks of 9/11. Lodging in the Jemez wilderness, listening to the terrifying events far away in my hometown of New York City on the radio, we left the pueblo ruins at Bandelier and made our way to the Museum of the Bomb in Los Alamos.

My head was Cervantes, my body Cuauhtémoc. My loins were Huitzilopochtli, god of war. As with the Chichimeca in ancient times, he instructed me to leave all that I treasured behind and go on a long journey in search of a promised land.

I test myself. I test my family.

I seek a litany of ancestral names.

I retrieve the maps of their journeys.

I will trace legacies of abandoned homelands.

I test myself. I test my lover.

2. At the beginning of our New World lineages

This is a story of mothers. Fathers and sons enter and pass away in the tale, but the mothers go on forever. According to my mother's brother Ludovico Lopez (Uncle Lico), the Lopez-Vela families' tireless genealogist, if we could tell their story entire, it would surely lead us back to our rare and exalted genesis in antiquity, undoubtedly as the descendants of one or another king and queen of Castile.

My maternal grandmother, Leandra, was born a Vela and married Leonides Lopez. Stories of Leandra's Vela family's deep origins vary wildly; one account suggests the true patriarch of the clan was none other than Dracula. A genealogical historian of the Vela family from Kingsville, Texas, reports that "the Vela surname comes from Prince Vlad Tepes, known as the Impaler." Vlad the Impaler is often cited as the historical figure that inspired popular belief in Dracula, so enthusiastic and innovative was he in the gory arts of public torture, fond of mounting his victims, like ornaments, on staves alongside roads and squares.

"He was born in 1431 in Valaquia, Romania. He was the son of Vlad Dracul. He was a noble and descendant of the king of Hungary. His father had the 'coat of arms' of the Dragon. In the primitive church, the Dragon represented the devil. Ferdinand the Catholic (the king of Castile, patron of Columbus) was a descendant of Bela, king of Hungary." So reports the Kingsville historian, noting that the Turkish invaders of Romania had set the standard in martial brutalities, and hence Vlad was simply giving them their comeuppance. He does allow that this family tie may explain a certain propensity among the Velas for dark imagination.

Thus presumably did Bela somehow become Vela in the times before Dracul's progeny left Romania for Hispania, from thence eventually to set off for the Mundo Nuevo. Vela means "candle," but can also be used to mean "sail," as in the sail of a boat, or to mean "sleepless vigil," as in the velador, the name given to a sentry, the wakeful keeper of a nightlong watch.

A Juan Vela is named among the conquistadores of the Yucatán in a chronicle of the year 1534. Whoever the first Vela was to arrive on Mexico's shores, barely a decade had passed after the Conquest before the lives of Velas were being recorded in the most distant northern outposts of New Spain.

Jorge Vela arrived in Mexico in 1531, ten years after the Conquest. For his service to the king as a Conquistador del Valle de Santiago, he was awarded tributes of land in "the region of the Chichimecas."

There was also a Vela in Cerralvo, in the northern region that was to become Nuevo Santander in 1645.

He appears to be the first Vela to come to the north.

Francisco Vela came into Nuevo León from another part of New Spain. In 1665, he asked that his brand be registered, "that was inherited from my father and was registered in Cuéncame which is far away to secure the record." Cuéncame is about three hundred miles from Monterrey in the present-day state of Durango. In 1685, he petitioned for a royal grant of land in recognition of his forty years riding on every expedition and that his five sons had borne arms since they were strong enough to carry them.

And from one frontera church document:

"Francisco Vela Rocha, Alferéz, married María Ortiz Sánchez. Married circa 1650 in Saltillo, Coahuila, New Spain." The pareja would later move to Villa de Cerralvo, near Monterrey, the town from which the settlers of los Llanos Mesteños, founders of the Villas del Norte along the Río Bravo, would eventually set out. There in Cerralvo, Vela became an alferéz, or second lieutenant, of the small presidio.

The surname Ortiz, from the matriarch of this lineage, was of Arabic origin; back in Spain these people had referred to themselves as "Moctares" or Mosarab. After the great catástrofe of 1492, the banishment of both Jews and Muslims, those that remained became assimilated, their names gradually Hispanicized. No longer classified officially as Arabs, this ancestral memory would become even more distant in Nueva España, the great empire of forgetting where new admixtures of nationality and ethnicity were still to emerge.

The families of settlers to the north were relatively few, and marriage or consorting with Indians, "women or men of the land," was stigmatized, if more and more common, leaving the stories of the lineages of these early Hispano Norteños often blurred and confoundingly interwoven. The daughter of Alferéz Vela and Maria Ortiz, Maria de la Rocha, would marry Diego Garcia on October 10, 1684, in Monterrey. Their marriage required a special "Consanguinity Dispensation" codicil to be appended, the case attesting to how closely the families that had settled in Nuevo Santander and Nueva Extremadura really lived.

Not even the ardors of the brushland desolation of the Seno Mexicano were enough to overlook España's consanguinity laws. These had been put in place by the church to maintain Spanish racial purity while discouraging close intermarriage between families over generations.

Hence, this **Dispensa de tercero grado de afinidad por copula lícita**, filed by Diego Garcia, the groom. He had already been married to Juana de Montalvo, lately dead, who was a half sister, through *bastardía*, of the Doña Maria Ortiz, the mother of the bride, Maria de la Rocha. While the union might have been scandalous, it was not considered heretical.

The eleven-page-long document explains how a church official notarized this matter and the marriage was allowed to proceed; the integrity of these Spanish bloodlines was vouchsafed.

In Uncle Lico's genealogical disk of grandmother Leandra's Vela family, the scroll legend in one corner reads "Vela Guerra 1770," with large parts of the circle left blank. Leandra and her sister Fermina appear as the progeny of my great-grandparents Emeterio Vela and Toribia Gonzalez. Emeterio was the child of Jose Maria Vela and Dorotea Guerra. It was this great-great-grandmother Dorotea who was descended from the Guerra family that had been among the founders of the town of Mier in the eighteenth century, and according to Uncle Lico's caption, had received royal Spanish land grants in 1770 in recognition of their founding role in the region. In another of Lico's records, a quickly sketched Vela family tree is crowned with a box for the ultimate patriarch of the lineage, labeled simply "King of Spain."

What we know of my grandfather Leonides's Lopez lineage was gathered in oral testimonies by one Augustín Lopez from San Antonio, Texas, in 1933 and passed on to Uncle Lico in 1968:

> In these writings, made by a descendant of Quilino Lopez and Josefina G. Lopez, there appear only the progeny who continue multiplying, San Antonio, Texas, 1933, Augustín M. Lopez.

Presumably, the rest could be left behind, having fallen out of the story altogether. After all, it was enough just to maintain a chronicle of those who remained present in history.

Uncle Lico took the sparse information that had survived those 150 years, "hecho de copia—subjecto a cambios" (made from a copy, subject to change), and drew a genealogical mandala based on those names, meticulously sketching a scrolled parchment to one side, set in heavy ink shading that bore the legend:

1818.

For it was said that in 1818, where this remaining Lopez back story began, the family's origins came from the written testimony of a certain *Hidalgo Distinguido*, Don Antonio Lopez Bermudez in the municipio de Ciudad Camargo, Tamaulipas, a frontera colonial settlement that survives to this day on the Mexican side of the border. Don Antonio was a scribe, much favored by the viceroy in the last Spanish administration on the eve of independence, a noble post that had vested him with land grants, though the regime was then only three years away from its demise and the birth of the Mexican republic.

These Lopez were more fecund than my Vela lineage.

Abuelo Antonio and his wife, Gertrudis Garcia, had six children. One of his two sons, Jose Julian Lopez de Garcia, married Juana de la Garza and they were to have ten children: the first, Antonio, was of course named for the patriarch of the family, but he was followed by a girl whom they named Antonia to his still greater honor; then came Francisco, named in due reverence to Madre Juana's father, followed again by a girl whom they named Francisca, to honor him once more; then Margíl and Josefa, twins, followed by Refugia, Rita, and Ramón; and finally, Cecilio Lopez, my great-great-grandfather.

Cecilio and his wife, Josefina Olivares de Lopez, would have four sons, Evaristo, Quilino, Pedro, and my great-grandfather Viviano, who was killed in a fall from a galloping horse while still young. His wife, my great-grandmother Segunda Lopez de Juarez, had perished first, found dead in a chair in the salon of their home in Laredo.

Thus, my grandfather Leonides, whom I never knew, along with his two brothers, José and Blas, were orphaned at an early age, and sent to live with their Tío Quilino and his wife Tía Juana, who worked and lived on the large La Mota ranch near Cotulla, Texas. They were raised as Quilino and Juana's own, along with their cousins Ramón, Antonio, Augustín, Santos, and Paula.

By then, over successive generations and among the quarreling, proliferating progeny of Abuelo Don Antonio, the Lopez patrimony of royal Spanish land grants had been so widely sectioned, frittered, pilfered, and stolen that most of the old man's descendants who had moved away from the lands in Camargo forgot any claims to their onetime entitlement. They were just more poor denizens of the old Tejano ranchería life, in a forgotten part of what had by then become the state of Texas. Having begun their story at the turn of the nineteenth century as the heirs of conquistadores, they began the twentieth century transformed into members of an American "minority."

One hundred years after Don Antonio's death, the Lopez family had completed a journey. From among the earliest Spanish settlers on the forbidding northern frontier of a vast empire, they had become Mexicanos pobres, or, more uncertain still, poor Tejanos in a country that hadn't existed when their whole story in the New World began.

Once the sentries of Spanish civilization in the New World, sent to the northern hinterlands of Nueva España as a bulwark against the French, British, and barbarism, they soon became supplicants in the very same lands they had come to think of as their own. The usurpers were themselves usurped, onetime conquerors themselves conquered.

How has that world changed between then and now? Out of such a long history in those territories, spanning more than two centuries, we became an American minority.

But a minority of what?

After overtaking a land that was never ours and making our home there so long ago, how did we then in turn once again become the outliers?

No wonder then that for so many of the Lopez and Velas, all of our elaborate histories and family lineages came to seem like a mirage that might just as well be forgotten, so that we could get on with the pressing new metamorphosis at hand: becoming American.

3. Augurs and signs, and how I came to write this tale anew

Readers will judge for themselves how much credence is to be placed in the way the observed world can seem endowed with cryptic evidence of unapparent meanings in our lives and the times we find ourselves in. The Españoles who first settled the remote lands of northeastern New Spain were dedicated interpreters of these ephemeral revelations, maintaining chronicles of those happenings and prodigies that pertained to historical events transpiring around them. Some things were beyond understanding, fathomable only by the great Creator.

There were reports in the year 1588 of the sun darkening at high noon in the skies over the village of Cadereyta, north of Monterrey, followed in the days afterward by the appearance of an augur in the shape of a great sword beneath the sun. A fish was caught bearing markings of crosses, swords, flags, horse heads, and barques of war.

In another instance, one soldier took a fright when his sword, previously owned by Martín de Zavala, legendary governor of Coahuila y Tejas, began to glow red and erupt in flames, as if it had just been pulled from a forge.

The soldier and chronicler Juan Bautista Chapa reported this sign as a prophecy "of the many wars that were to engulf this Realm because only the Divine Majesty may permit the occurrence of certain signs that indicate the events of the future. This is explained by St. Augustine in his tenth book of 'The City of God,' in Chapter 16, in which he says, 'in certain intervals of time, monsters are permitted to be found, determined by His Providence. They generally signify troubles to come, others are simply portents and prodigy that simply announce calamities.'"

Which brings me to the story of my monstrous birth, and the monstrous births of my two brothers, identical twins.

I was born carrying the markings and fault lines of the Conquest history that my ancestors had lived in the New World. Married already for eight years, my parents had been told they would never have children. By the mid-1950s, they were fully "Americans of Mexican descent," young San Antonio professionals, Mother a teacher and my father a postal worker, who had both emerged out of the saga of old Mexico, by different paths.

My father's family was Norteño and mestizo, taller and fairer than many Mexicanos, but the presence of our Indio ancestors was evident in many of the Santos and Garcia faces, flat cheeks, almond-shaped eyes, straight black hair. Mother's family, on both sides, was "puro Hispano," or so Uncle Lico said, and there were many documents and genealogies that vaguely recorded their descent from the earliest explorers and founders of the Seno Mexicano.

"Good genes!" Lico once wrote on the back of a picture taken of him sitting smiling by a fountain while on a vacation in Monterrey.

Against the prognostications of several doctors, I would be born at the intersection between the bloodlines of the Mundo Viejo and the Mundo Nuevo, already well within the drift streams of the great Mexican mestizaje, the mixing of the peoples of the world that began in Nueva España.

On the evening I was born, nearing midnight on their way to the hospital, and though he knew his old city well, my father remembered becoming disoriented as he got lost driving through the downtown San Antonio neighborhood of the old Spanish village known as La Villita, a warren of closely interweaving callejones and streets, lined with old limestone sillar walls dating back to the eighteenth century.

Then the car, an aging Hudson, broke down in an alleyway named for Felipe Dos, one of the mad kings of Spain, grandson to Isabella and Ferdinand. It was during his reign that Spain began its descent from the pinnacle of imperial world power. His passions lay elsewhere, regularly staging fantastic rehearsals for his own funeral, and Felipe oversaw the building of the monumental royal tomb El Escorial, to which he eventually brought the bones of all of his ancestors, commanding that thereafter a continuous death mass

should be offered each day for all of his progenitors and progeny—
and for the sake of his own soul in eternity.

As my parents waited for an uncle to come rescue them, they
decided that I should be given the name Felipe, albeit in an Angli-
cized version, to commemorate the benighted turn of events.

My father and grandfather were both christened Juan Jose. If I
had been given my father's name, I would have been the third, and
neither of my parents wanted me to be called "junior." I had a difficult birth just past midnight, with baby photos revealing my gri-
macing face bruised, big ears protruding, both eyes nearly swollen
closed, presumably lacerated by the iron calipers that tugged me
into this world. Moreover, I was born with a "mongoloidal spot," a
large dark circular pigmentation across my lower back that is said to
betoken indigenous ancestry in the New World—and farther down,
a small tail protruded at the end of my spine.

The tail was quickly snipped off, leaving only a scar, and my spot
eventually faded away, but my secret heraldic *nombre real de España*
was indelible.

Further confounding the doctors who had predicted barrenness
for my mother, my twin brothers, George David and Charles Daniel, were born three years later. George was born first, runtish, blue,
and struggling to breathe, with the umbilical cord wrapped in tight
loops around his neck, as if he had been garroted in the womb. Dr.
Estrada, an old friend of Mother's, was able to revive him, though it
had first seemed he might quickly perish.

Forty minutes then passed and Charles had still not emerged, forc-
ing the doctor to straddle my mother's chest and force him out, "like
a pea-shooter," as the doctor later described it. The two lads were
soon in very hearty shape, but after this trauma, Mother lapsed into a
deep postpartum depression from which she only slowly emerged.

We were a generation of monstrous births, finding fitful wel-
comes into a world that, for our ancestors, had become more and
more unfathomable as each century passed. Unbeknownst to our
family, even our nascent bodies gave testimony to the haunted lineage that stretched behind us like a dusky comet tail.

In photographs from our childhood, we appear in the costumes of our Mexicano past, me in charro or vaquero gear, boots and six-shooters in place, my brothers in trappings that Mother called their "Lord Fauntleroy" suits, ruffled white shirts, brown velvet vests, and knee pants, with golden sashes and bows, along with stockings and black slippers. At family gatherings, we were always the cousins wearing tiny sports jackets and ties.

No one except Uncle Lico talked about the family's sources in Spain, and no one really took him seriously, but I always wondered about our *antepasados perdidos*.

Mother would refer to Grandmother mentioning her ancestry in Spain, but she imparted no special fascination for the madre tierra. Grandmother Leandra thought of herself as Mexican, observing all of the days of the sacred Mexicano calendar, Día de Independencia, Cinco de Mayo, and Día de los Muertos, when she insisted on being driven to Laredo to visit the grave of her parents, Emeterio and Toribia.

Mother's only Spanish affect is a lifelong fascination with Don Quixote, the last remnant of Españolidad in the Lopez-Vela line. In fact, it wasn't an affinity for Cervantes's great literary creation, but for a Lladró porcelain figurine of Don Quixote painted in muted lavender and cream pastels, captured in his fully bedraggled nobility. This was the only artifact in our house that spoke in any way to our Spanish provenance.

Mother had treasured the figurine that had belonged to her mother. Alas, his head had been lopped off during a family gathering after my father's funeral, when one of my brothers, wielding a shotgun for a family photograph, had jostled the display case where the old knight had kept his sentry of honor since Grandmother's death. After he crashed to the floor, the Hidalgo Ingenioso's sombrero de tres picos was shattered, his head separated from his body in one neat seam, his delicate fingers cracked into a thousand tiny shards.

Not too long ago, after an entire day in New York trying to find the prized Don Quixote figurine mother was looking to replace, I realized I had taken on an impossible quest. He was truly a lost cause, the legendary standing Quixote, gangly and disheveled, his battered armor and prized breastplate laid to one side.

There were rumors he'd gone out of production for lack of demand, that he was less loved in these times, that his timeless effigy would soon be retired once and for all. In Berlin, I'd found a praying Quixote, a priceless vintage heirloom itself, I was told, looking like Peter O'Toole with anorexia, his crestfallen goatee pointing to heaven, his clasped hands rising in the shape of a flame from his chest, all handpainted in pearly colors that made the porcelain seem lit from inside. Mother wasn't interested in that one.

Back in New York, at the Lladró shop on West 57th Street, Quixote was as big as a Thanksgiving turkey, seated, as inconsolable and droopy as a saint from an El Greco painting, in a chair in front of a large table laid out with piles of open books. But my mother had insisted that he be standing, slightly bow-backed, gazing toward the sky in a thoughtful posture over the glorious, battered shield that had been his grandfather's pride.

I finally found an orphaned standing Quixote, to mother's delight, in a Pakistani-owned electronics shop on 42nd Street, but I continued to wonder about the lasting allure of the figure of the old, broken-down knight.

Why would the Lladró porcelain figurine of the Hidalgo de La Mancha, once so popular, sought after for so long, be now nearly discontinued? How many had been made, how many destroyed during doleful festivities around the world? What would be left of Don Quixote in another decade or two?

In the days that followed, it began to seem as if Quixote was haunting me. On several occasions, I saw different people in the street, complete strangers, each one bearing a print of Picasso's squiggly black-line painting of Don Quixote with Sancho Panza and a windmill in the background.

The first time, it was a woman who walked into a Chinese restaurant on Broadway, wearing the image on a baggy white T-shirt:

"Haven't seen that in a while," I thought to myself. "Maybe not since college, when I used a cardboard copy of it to make a new cover for a disintegrating Norton edition of *Moby Dick*."

The second time, a day later, it was a bodybuilder, carrying it daintily in a legal-pad-sized print:

"Twice now. That's really strange."

Then, the third time, a guy in khaki pants and a white T-shirt, walking slowly down Amsterdam Avenue, holding a large framed copy of the print to one side, as if he were displaying it to me while marching in a parade. Then it was:

"Don Quixote, are you talking to me?"

Only street noise, as the man with the print boarded a bus. I watched through the windows as Quixote moved toward the rear seats, making his way through a tightly packed throng of New Yorkers.

"Speak now, distant grandfather knight."

4. Crónica de un pueblo de huérfanos

Uncle Lico was also determined to recover the true names of the noble lineage of his father, Leonides, the grocer of Cotulla, Texas. They were Lopez, meaning "the son of Lope," and the name Lope at some time in the hoary Spanish past was said to have meant both "wolf" and "brain." Over the centuries, the Lopez had dispersed widely across the Iberian Peninsula, becoming so common a surname they lost any particular geographic patrimony.

Many of the Lopez who were among the first to settle the northern hinterlands of New Spain listed themselves in census reports as Lopez de Jaén, Jaén being a town of old Al-Andalus, Andalucía, in southern central Spain, but there were no tales, memories, or records to connect our family to that province or name. Uncle Lico's research had never reached the generation of Lopez who left Spain to come to Mexico.

In the tableaux from one version of this aged family's heraldic coat of arms, there are four windows, representing the skeleton of some forgotten drama: a wolf, a knight slaying a moor, a fortified castle tower, and then a chevron with crisscrossed lines, perhaps suggesting the maze of paths taken out into the farther dominions of the world.

And thus our ancestors emerged from the forests to slay the infidel, and after a time of enjoying their gains, they set out into the vast unknown world, resolved to never return again.

Lopez appear in the lists of the earliest ships' logs, the **Maestres de Las Naos,** captaining ships embarking from Sevilla for the storied new lands across the ocean. One Juan Lopez helmed four journeys, in 1512, 1517, 1527, and 1529, the last two landing in Mexico, in the makeshift new port in La Vera Cruz, which would become Veracruz.

Alonzo and Francisco López both led ships that set sail for the Indies in 1515. Annals record how Francisco made his final journey west in 1534; his end in the New World goes without mention. They found their way to outposts scattered across the infant Mundo Nuevo.

Another Juan López, hijo de Pedro López, from the Villa de Miguelturra, sailed to Santo Domingo in the autumn of 1536.

In late January of 1538, Abián López, the son of Gonzalo López of Bajadoz, led one of the first exploratory expeditions to the peninsula of La Florida.

There were Lopez in Mexico from the beginning of the story of the Conquest. Their names, and some traces of their stories, appear in the records *De los Asientos de Pasajeros,* listing those mariner conquistadores who accompanied Hernán Cortés from Hispaniola on what would become the fateful expedition into undiscovered Mexico.

They included Francisco López de Catalayud, who is among the first to be recorded as having married "a woman of the land," as Indian women were then called, with whom he fathered many mestizo children. Also, one Álvaro López, a carpenter, made a massive wooden cross that was placed on the top of a Mayan temple, in front of which Cortés preached an evangelizing sermon. He was an agile swordsman who would later slay many in the battle of Cholula.

Simón López de Gabriel was killed in one of the first skirmishes of Cortés's campaign.

Martín López, craftsman and carpenter, was later to be made a Marqués del Valle in recognition for his feat building the boats ordered by Cortés for use in the final siege against the Mexica of Tenochtitlán. Jerónimo López, knighted as a Conquistador de Nueva España, is said to have personally overseen preparation for the details of the lonely, hasty Mexican burial of his onetime comandante, Hernán Cortés, after he had fallen from the favor of the Spanish Crown and died of dysentery while on a trip to Spain.

"And Lopez should be López!" insists one of my mother's cousins, Oralia López.

"López con un acento sobre el 'o.' Así es corecto! That's the way it should be, but you know, I guess people get lazy. Too lazy for an accent, can you imagine?"

While there is no evidence any of these were our direct Lopez ancestors, the farther back in time you go, the wider and more encompassing the tributaries of our lineages become, and simple names with their shreds of story testify across centuries to these bonds.

Go back far enough and everybody is related to everyone. Forty generations into the past and we are ancestrally linked to a sprawling human host of a billion souls. Nations strike a course, bobbing, running aground, or sinking into the deeps of that ocean of humanity.

Still, a story that draws together the lives of that many relations eludes us, relegated instead to the play of chance, serendipity, and misfortune, like an apocryphal chronicle of the genealogy of clouds.

But why and when were the imprints of those common moments in our remotest past so distantly forgotten?

By the middle of the twentieth century, my Lopez were the orphaned progeny of an orphan patriarch, himself the legatee of an already long-orphaned world, the great, secreted-away *mundo perdido* harbored in the hearts of Iberianos who had left their madre tierra behind to carry the vision of Nueva España into the farthest northern extremities of ancient Mexico. They had come to the north in the days of the first entradas, the first incursions across the banks and stream of the great Río Bravo del Norte and beyond.

Everything is apocryphal on this planet of mystery. Our blood teems with the voices of our antepasados, and there is an undying etheric echo, connecting you to the body of every ancestor that has led to you. In this sense, there are no orphans.

Compared to the intimate, tribal tale-spinning circles of the Santos clan, the story of my mother's families was a dusty, remote, stillwater place in the past, left long unstirred either by nostalgia or shame, properly dwindling out with the dregs of the twentieth century that had seen the Lopez move from the South Texas hinterland of Cotulla to the imperial metropolis of the region, San Antonio. The embrace of oblivion that lies within this neglect was less evident than was a perpetual sense that my mother and her siblings, along with their cousins, were simply marching with no obligations to, or burdens from, the past.

With the help of his uncle Agustín, Uncle Lico had retrieved some of our ancestors' names from oblivion, but there was no apparent mystery to be solved, no insult or grievance to be redressed. I assumed that since no story had been handed down, there must be no story to begin with.

At least no story de alguna importancia.

Only later did this floating lacuna in the Lopez tale come to seem insufficient.

Insufficient for what? For decades, I mulled over these ancestors' names in wonderment of how little I knew of them. Uncle Lico's genealogies and records were a strange fable of his quirky ethnic imagination, unconnected to any official record, impermeable to any confirmable historical fact.

There were only the scarcest keepsakes. Along with photographs, there was Grandmother's red leather aspirin-case-sized address book, a stack of canceled checks from Frost bank, Aunt Fermina's last will and testament, written in her own hand, and her spindly gold-wired spectacles with the thick glass lenses as green as water from the Gulf of Mexico, needed for her weak eyes, an effect of her albinism. I regarded their artifacts and perused their documents for decades without any spark that might give evidence of hidden-away reckonings.

What made it feel necessary to see these legacies come to light?

Distant planets, invisible to our most discerning telescopes, are hunted by the faintest gravitational wobbles they induce in their host star's motions in space. The absence of the Lopez story in the past exerted a gravitational pull on me, despite my own long neglect and reticence about delving into the familia's history.

What was it, ever beckoning to be told?

I could trace lines from the earliest history of Mexico where the names Vela and Lopez are inscribed in first rosters of Españoles to arrive on the Mexican mainland.

Were these distant but direct-lineage relations? Perhaps.

They were carriers of the same surname, that ineffable talisman humans carry through history expressly in order to connect them to their ancestors, real or presumed, and to those who will come after them.

Abuelo Martín López, the ancestor commanded by Cortés to build the four brigantines to be used in the final attack on the Aztec capital of Tenochtitlán, is remembered for a peculiar detail of maritime engineering. One eyewitness account reports how he used human tallow fat that had been rendered from the bodies of dead Indian victims from earlier battles to effectively seal the seams of the barques. This story came to be used by later defenders of the Indians seeking a larger cultural context for understanding their practice of human sacrifice that had been discovered among the savages.

Iberians were not above desecration of human bodies when it served their purposes.

Can a deep-seated, dark family trait be discerned in such a relacíon?

Uncle Lico didn't think it was such a big deal.

"When you're dead, you're dead, man, so there's no telling what they'll do with you. That was a Lopez, alright."

Lico had run a cemetery in San Antonio for an old buddy of his for a while, so death didn't spook him.

"That must have been a mess, though. You know those ashes they give people? It's all plywood and scrap wood! Human ash is nasty to work with, man, greasy and real fine, and it gets into everything. It's hard to get out from under your fingernails, even scrubbing hard with Lava soap."

On a trip to San Antonio from New York City, I returned to the grounds of the Misión Concepcíon in the iridescent sunlit heat of a new century, a new millennium. The sun-bleached stones of the old church and its arched passageways hold their secrets mute, running deep into the history of those lands. Who knows where we began?

We are unfolding the sky now to gaze at the beginning of the universe, and yet we remain mute to the deep mystery of our own genesis.

All these evanescent lines into the past run at first only along the meridians of the four names you receive from the lineages of the parents of your father and mother. In the implicit algorithm of human origins, each earlier generation broadens the shadow cast by our blood into the past. In the indeterminable way these courses mixed through history, what do we gain by recovering our specific chains of descent through all mothers and fathers?

Lopez and Vela, yes. But our genealogies also show Gonzalez and Ruiz Guadiano, Guerra, Garcia, Hinojosa de Chapa, Baez de Treviño, and Fernandez de Tijerina.

Also Cuellar, Hernández, Ramirez, Juarez, Saénz. Then Ochoa, Olivares, Montalvo, and Guerra Cañamar. And that scans only some of my ancestral lines back to the seventeenth century.

Follow the lineages back as remotely as you can, relations spreading out wider into the past like a genetic radio broadcast, and soon it is apparent that we are from everywhere.

Eventually, we are implicated by the whole human story.

But you have to begin somewhere.

The Lopez and Velas began their New World story in Spain, en la madre terra incognita.

II

A Book of Swoons

1. Of the color of daylight in eternity

Inside a lightning arc struck in reverse, careening backward toward the sky, accelerating through a heavy mist that streaked by me in comet tracks of rust and vermilion, it was a complete roaring into fierce oblivion, trying to look behind me against the wind, rain stinging my face in the tempest void, until I blinked, focused, and I thought I saw a landscape, far off below me, pinwheeling and receding, eerie beige crescents, dull bronze squares, and shimmering capillaries of rivers and creeks running all through. Then just as suddenly, I was speeding just above the wet desert floor, and its grainy surface smelled like the carbon skin of an enormous machine.

I reached out to touch it.

All of this, in the instant after I let go of the banister in a strange courtyard.

"This light is impossible," I thought.

This is the hazy daytime of eternity, I heard someone say, a faint voice fading away in the wind.

I heard the slowed-down, distorted tremolo of the harmonium that quavers at the beginning of "Strawberry Fields Forever," faintly

playing back, and breaking up into thick radio static, over and over
again.

I awoke suddenly, squinting, making out uneven shapes of a flat,
grey beach and slow blurs of dancing light on an empty, motionless
bay. The sound of lapping water was far off, mixed with echoes of
car horns and traffic.

"This is impossible light."

I tried to move my mouth to speak those words, but all that came
out was a murmur. From the unfortunate mayhem of the night before,
my lips were bruised, my gums tender, one side of my cheek scraped
angry purple, stinging in the salty Catalán air of Barcelona. I took in a
deep breath and wondered if I had really survived my first day, already
shedding blood in the vaunted, unknown motherland, España.

Tana's fine silhouette was drawn in a faint aura of amber twilight's flame. Tana, or maybe it was Tamara, was a hippie nurse
from a mixed Spanish and English family in Tasmania, traveling in
Spain to find a long-lost great-aunt who was meant to be living in
Madrid. It had been that morning at the pensión, when I was feeling so ill and sore I wanted to have a seizure and get it over with,
her strong face was looking down at me in my sick bed, as still and
bright as the northern star.

I'd only met her the day before in the lamplit hallway, where she
had told me of her quest in Spain to find her distant relative. Then
she heard me ailing that morning as I stumbled in from the night's
catastrophe, and came to help.

I wasn't making a very good second impression.

Looking at her reclining on a beach chair, reading a newspaper
through petite amber sunglasses, she turned her head to me. Her
gaze was a beacon guiding me gently back into my body.

"You were sleeping a long time, ya viene la noche." She spoke
Spanish with a perfect Castilian accent, tolerating my rough Mexican variations.

Tamara had reddish sandy hair, cut short like Joan of Arc's, a
gentle sun-weathered face with laugh lines, large hazel eyes, and
a smooth, broad jaw. She had the lithe, powerful body of a veteran
hiker, and the silky hair on her arms glistened in the dusk light.

I thought about being with her forever.

"I thought this was already eternity," I said, my voice cracking. "Or I dreamed it was."

She stared at me incredulously. Tamara seemed to be the earthy, pragmatic sort. She had generously packed a lunch of olives, manchego cheese, chorizo, and bread, and helped me come to the beach, but I could tell she was not going to indulge my hangover metaphysics.

"Maybe this is eternity," she said impatiently. "And anyway, how would you know? What's the difference? Isn't this all happening in eternity already?"

"Today feels like eternity to me," I replied.

2. Cuento de un naufragio en la madre tierra

I hadn't gone to Barcelona in search of eternity, but it almost found me there.

It was 1980. I was on a long break from university studies back in England, encouraged by Uncle Lico in San Antonio to "go and have a look" and report back to him regarding the unknown country my mother's families—the Lopez and Velas—were said to come from. Almost every month, I received a new package from him, containing exhortations to make the trip, family documents, a revised genealogy of one of our family lines, or clippings of developments in San Antonio politics, where Henry Cisneros was running to become the city's first Mexican American mayor.

Though he had searched out the genealogies of these two families for decades, Lico Lopez had never gone to Spain, and he had no idea exactly where in Spain our family might've originated.

I had not imagined making the ancestors the subject of my writing. I was born in the age of rock and roll and space travel. Ten years before my birth, extraterrestrial aliens were reputed to have crashed to earth in nearby New Mexico. Why should I concern myself with the benighted tale of what happened to the ancestral Spaniards who found their way to the New World?

In truth, since it was never spoken of while I was growing up, I had little fascination for Spain; but I was a devotee of the poet Federico García Lorca, so Granada would be my final destination.

Unlike Lico, I was no archival genealogist, choosing instead to depend on serendipity as a tool and method for my research. I was a committed practitioner of poetic inadvertency, ready to receive, wary to seek out, allowing everything to be revealed, lest anything discovered be tainted by dubious intent. If any family members presented themselves on the pilgrimage route, all the better, but I wasn't expecting much.

It was a four-day train journey from London to Barcelona, with an evening in Paris and another in the old Provençal village of Moissac. In the fields all around Moissac, grapevines were bare and pruned, strung in tight helical bundles atop the sandy loam, awaiting the first buds of spring.

An old farmer in rubber overalls and Wellington boots was watering a stand of auburn workhorses. Along the narrow streets, cabbage was boiling with smoky bacon while the rich, pearly chimney smoke hovered above the rooftops across the village. It was an olden world, as if changeless over centuries, beyond the reach of the transforming incandescent light of cities, and far from anything I had known in South Texas.

Meeting up by chance in the Barcelona mercado with a rowdy colleague from university, my arrival day had detoured into an extended carouse, traversing the amontillado caves of the city during what turned out to be Barcelona's annual Día de Mexico fiesta. I was dressed in a shirt made of brightly striped serape fabric from Saltillo, Coahuila, making me as close to a Mexican as the Catalanos of the rough tabernas and cafés of the Ramblas were likely to find.

At first they regarded me curiously, another strange progeny of the Mundo Nuevo with a clumsy tongue *en castellano*. I told one waiter how San Antonio had been the headquarters of the Spanish governor during the early colonial era, and that his flat-roofed adobe mansion had been scrupulously preserved, long after the last governor had been forced to flee the interloping Anglo Texican insurrectionists.

Such was the sense of pride en España that lived on to this day in San Antonio.

Eventually, each new tapa and copita de vino was submitted for my delectation and wonderment. Garbanzos in tomato-garlic sauce. Albóndigas con albahaca. Fideos con mariscos in a buttery wine sauce. For some hours I thought that perhaps this was my long- lost home after all.

An already woozy barman in a dusky cave declared me the guest of honor. That's when the intermittent copas of tequila and sherry began to flow like ambrosial nectar until late in the evening, when, as if in slow motion, I saw my mate from Oxford, who had an exaggerated sense of the theatrical about much that he did, throw an empty mug against a wall-size mirror, shattering it entirely, sending the roomful of patrons whooping and screaming, running out into the chill night air of the Ramblas, scattering in all directions.

I lost my companions in the melee, wandering alone and exhausted, and well into my cups. I realized I probably couldn't find my way through the maze of streets in that oldest, labyrinthine precinct of the city.

"Cuatro Palaú? Cuatro Palaú?"

I repeated the address of my pensión to passersby, only to watch them hurry to walk past me with a mix of disdain and fear.

Just as I was beginning to think the smooth, cool white marble paving stones of the historic district might make a suitable pillow for the night, several other revelers replied that they knew the address and would gladly take me there.

3. Wherein the Lopez and Velas appear, in medias res, of the long Iberian saga

Though some of my ancestors were Spanish Tejanos, early settlers in the rugged northern frontier of colonial Mexico, later Texas, none of us had ever felt particularly connected to Spain. It made no difference that the Lopez and Velas might have been in Spain already hundreds of years at the time of the first Iberian encounters with the New World. Perhaps they were Christians, perhaps Muslim, or perhaps Jewish, as had been long rumored among the Velas, my grandmother's kin.

There would have been some grandfather, or perhaps it was a grandmother, who decided to risk everything for a caravela ride to the New World, likely never to see Spain again. Once in the New World, our Iberian ancestors conjured a new sense of home for us in these Mexican lands, reciprocally forgetting distant origins even as we began to feel as if we had always been in the tierras of the Mundo Nuevo, as if our genesis had been in those same dear and familiar homelands of future Mexico and Texas.

My Spanish ancestors were not homebodies. They were outliers from the start of our story en las Américas, nomads setting out from whatever their Spanish past was, willing to leave all they knew behind once and for all in search of a new way of life in an unimagined place. Perhaps they were confident that the past would remain where it had always been, if only abandoned, lost, swallowed up, like the enchanted continents of myth like Mu or Atlantis that live on in memory long after any map survives detailing their coastlines and whereabouts. Because of that long estrangement across generations and hundreds of years, there were no living memories of Spain in the Lopez-Vela families.

Where had we come from?

Uncle Lico found the echoes of our ancestors among the founders of the villas de Camargo, Guerrero Viejo, and Ciudad Mier, the onetime farthest outposts of Nueva España founded in the 1740s, already very late in the story of that world.

Today those towns nestle the south bank of the Rio Grande, across the border between Zapata and Roma, Texas. We never traveled there when I was growing up, visiting the Norteño Mexican state of Coahuila instead, where my father's family had come from. Grandmother Leandra was likely born in Mier or Guerrero, Mexico, though her birth certificate was lost, or more likely destroyed.

When asked about her birthplace, Grandmother would only say that she was baptized in San Diego, Texas. And to ask her age was to incur her wrath. When she died, insurance policies she left behind recorded birthdates ranging from 1882 to 1894.

Later, dwindling over time, compelled to leave by frequent epidemics and ongoing border violence in the region, the Lopez and Vela families had resettled in Roma, on the U.S. side of the river, then Laredo, then ended up in Laredo and Cotulla, Texas. By then, all that was left of the Velas was my grandmother Leandra, who would have six children, and her albino sister, Fermina, who died childless.

Finally, the survivors of these old family lines made their way up the last stretch of dusty highway to San Antonio, where my generation was born.

I don't remember Grandmother ever mentioning anything to me about our grand family origins, Spanish or otherwise. She spoke Spanish fluently, and always with her maid, Maria Moya, but never a word to us in the old tongue.

By the time she settled into one of her duplex properties in the late 1960s, Grandmother retreated into her stoic though somewhat disapproving vigil over the late twentieth century. Her final home was a cake-box shutterboard shambles of a house on West Russell Street in San Antonio, a onetime noble neighborhood that now had a decrepit, long-occupied, and weary look upon it.

Grandmother seemed like something immovable and of great antiquity, not just in appearance, but of spirit too, as if her soul had acquired a density and gravity that could bend the fabric of time and space around her. She had outlived most everyone she knew. Aloof, she appeared to have tired of everything, of her children and her grandchildren, of friends, comrades, even food. She was tired of the world altogether, tired of nature itself. She didn't want to hurry death, but she could sometimes seem incredulous that hers was so long delayed. I thought she must have been hundreds of years old.

Her gravitas was never menacing, though. We did not fear Leandra. When she would look after me and my brothers in her home, I would quarrel with her about what we should be watching on television, and later she would complain to my mother that I would cry because I wanted to watch the news while she wanted to watch another channel with that soap opera that began with the creepy benediction that would always spook me, "Like sand through the hourglass, so are the days of our lives . . ."

Of course, we always ended up watching her novela, so there was no reason for her to complain about my passing insurrection.

She never grew angry with us, though I heard her occasionally become cross with my mother over such petty concerns as missed items on grocery lists and disputed city council candidates. She had survived her hard near century of years, raising five children mostly without a husband, continuing the migrations of her ancestors that began in Cerralvo, then Revilla, which became Guerrero, then San Diego, then Laredo, then through Cotulla to San Antonio.

You knew when a matter had been concluded for Leandra when her gaze would suddenly turn steely and her lips would slightly purse in a barely perceptible yet withering twitch of discontent. Whatever you might be talking about—Vietnam, LBJ, the Beatles, grocery shopping at Piggly Wiggly—it was time to move on.

Grandmother's detached presence was also an effect of her deeper disconnection with nature itself. She generally detested the outdoors, especially during the summer months, which in San Antonio begin in April. Still, her unique dislocation from the natural world meant that she was apt to wear fur coats for a July wedding, if she thought it would be fashionable.

To hear Grandmother tell it, she was descended from a line of Velas and Gonzalez who had been trying for generations to break free of cycles of planting and harvest, along with the messy drudgery of animal husbandry. She never spoke of where she was born, but she was proud to have been baptized in San Diego, which she regarded as a cosmopolitan Texas capital of the remote greater world of the Villas del Norte into which she had been born.

Eventually, her parents Emeterio and Toribia moved the family to the metropolis of Laredo, Texas, where Leandra was raised amid the mercantilist city culture of that border trading town, founded on the north side but already spanning the Río Grande. Perhaps most of their land had been wrested away from them by then. The small remnants of the historic Spanish land grants, recorded in scratchy writing in her small red leather address book—that were bequeathed to Leandra and Fermina—were part of the Guerra family patrimony from their grandmother. By the time they were born, there is no evidence that they had any claims to lands granted by the viceroy to their Vela or Gonzalez ancestors.

Grandmother and Fermina both became teachers, and after the death of my grandfather Leonides, Leandra completed her exodus from the natural world of the Río Grande Valley by leaving Cotulla behind and bringing her children to San Antonio, where she used her modest funds to buy city real estate that would never have to be planted, tended, or harvested, only maintained as a proper landlord would. Fermina had already established a homestead there, managing her own properties and becoming a notary public. Being an albino, it didn't create a stir when she married an Anglo, becoming Fermina Vela Ferguson.

With Leandra and Fermina established in San Antonio, the Velas were finally free of nature.

But even as we were all becoming, molecule by molecule, urban and, later, suburban Americanos, Uncle Lico became ever more feverish to reassert our Spanish dignity, our history of onetime entitlement in the storied age of the colonial frontera.

His quest accelerated and grew more feverish as he neared his unanticipated death. No one knew who that first ancestor might have been, except for Uncle Lico, our family's self-appointed genealogist, who was certain we were descendants of some king of Spain or another, whose name, inexplicably, had been long ago forgotten.

As far as Uncle Lico was concerned, so exalted were our origins that among the Lopez and Velas, even a king's name could be left behind after a little spell of time.

We might just as easily have descended from the king of Lemuria, all those bodies falling like snowflakes out of the gelid sky of deep time.

4. In which I return to the forgotten house of nada

Tamara held my hand as if we had known each other for years, cradling my palm with both of her hands, caressing the swollen veins along my bruised knuckles, gradually making the soreness and stinging subside.

Like me, she had come to Spain without knowing what to expect, feeling little connection to the land of her ancestors. Her aunt in Madrid had spent most of her life as a nun in a cloistered convent until leaving the order in the mid-1970s. She whispered a rumor that her grandfather had been an officer in Franco's *falangista* army, causing a part of her family to flee in disgust.

She felt more drawn to Antarctica, she said, and had considered going there, but trekking through Spain was easier. I tried to remember where Tasmania was, a great island floating wraith in the waters of Oceania. There were Españoles there too; probably Greeks, Jews, Armenians, Portuguese, and Turks as well, not to mention plenty of English—all of the world's wandering tribes. Tamara's Spanish mother had married an Englishman, and Tamara was born in Kent. The family had emigrated to Australia, then Tasmania in the '60s. She said she came to Spain mainly to escape from Tasmania, but now that she was in Barcelona, she had been surprised how at home she felt.

"I've never thought of anyplace as home before," she said.

I wasn't feeling any special affinity for Barcelona or Madre España.

"Doesn't feel much like home to me," I replied. "More like purgatory, actually."

Tamara laughed. "Well it's a lot nicer when you don't go around getting mugged every day."

We were both on a search in an unfamiliar land of unknown ancestors. It stirred old imaginings of finding someone who shared my curiosity about a hidden knowledge about ourselves secreted away in the catacombs of our family histories.

My girlfriends until then hadn't been much drawn to those questions. Maybe Tamara would be the one.

Seeing me distractedly staring at her as we sat on the beach, she quickly changed the subject:

"How many were there?"

"What?"

"The ones you ran into last night. How many?"

"Four to start, I think, then others came along as we walked. Six or seven eventually. We went through the callejones of the Ramblas, and I repeated the address I was looking for."

"Were they Spanish?"

"They had a strange accent. One told me they were Palestinians. I told them I came from occupied territories too—of the American Southwest—and we all had a laugh. Everybody had been *hechando copas*. I thought we were *compañeros*."

"This is a city of refugees, Barcelona. Catalanes take everybody in."

"Then, when we got to the doorway of the pensión, I got this creepy feeling. I could tell they were nervous too. As we stepped through into the solár, and I started up the stairway, I realized it wasn't the right place. One of them reached for the breast pocket in my jacket, and my amontillado haze was burned off in a flash."

"Which one hit you?"

"I thought of *Enter the Dragon* and *True Grit*—Bruce Lee and Rooster Cogburn."

"Who?"

"Those movies. You know in *True Grit*, there's a last scene where a real old eyepatch-wearing John Wayne takes the reins in his mouth, faces off across a field against a whole pack of bastardos? It was like that, only with fists of fury, Tex-Mex kung-fu style."

"I never saw those films. How'd you get hit?"

"They were all around me. I had one hand on the marble banister, and I swung my leg around, catching one in the jaw with my foot, and I swear he flew across the lobby like a cartoon goose dropping all his feathers. I bruised my knees falling on the marble, and got hit on the side of the face, and one went past me through the portál. But I grabbed a little flowerpot and planted it on another guy's forehead. Another cartoon. I was shrieking Hindu kung-fu curses and wrenching my face into a tiger-fang grimace with my eyes bugging out. That was Toshiro Mifune. The two or three left standing just stood back terrified and let me pass like I was a ghost, so I walked out the door and ran into the streets, suddenly stone cold sober, crisscrossing Las Ramblas until I found Palaú Street again. The door to the pensión was locked. I didn't get in until dawn, and, well, you saw me then."

"You looked a mess, mate."

I left off telling Tamara how, having finally found the great oak door of the pensión locked in the dimly lit street, I searched the cars at curbside until I found one at the end of the block with an unlocked back door. It was an old dented Peugeot, smelling of stale tobacco smoke and cramped with piles of receipts and scrap paper, but I pushed the debris away, tucked in my knees, reclined across the backseat, and fell into a delicious sodden sleep.

And that's where eternity seeped in, looking for me.

I was alone in a courtyard of some unfamiliar Mediterranean villa, a sunlit plazita surrounded by elaborately carved and polished malachite columns, the arches between them decked with hanging flowerboxes that dangled tendrils of succulents. In the center of the colonnades, there was a patio with a gurgling travertine fountain. The smell of orange blossoms and mint was strong in the morning air.

I could hear voices behind me, from inside the villa, sounding like a host of people with silverware clinking against plates. I suddenly felt anxious, like a trespasser about to be found out. As I focused on the ornately painted tiles decorating the fountain's stone basin, I noticed that the railing I was holding on to alongside a scalloped stairway began to gently vibrate, becoming more pronounced with every breath I took.

If I concentrated on tightening my grip long enough, I could eventually still the vibration. But after another breath, it would resume, more violently than before. The curlicued wrought iron became gelatinous, oscillating and shivering as if it were exploding outward from its imperceptible atomic particles into the apparent air.

My arm grew so weary with the vibration that I could no longer hold on.

As I let go, all at once I was whipcracked backward with enormous speed, accelerating into spinning spirals, as if I were flying upward toward the sky, feet first, in reverse. My body seemed immaterial, transparent, but able to sense the droplets of condensing cloud vapor on my face. Distantly in the wind, I heard the backward organ sound from the beginning of "Strawberry Fields Forever." My distress gradually gave way into a smooth glide forward, and I gazed down onto a landscape of dry, tended fields and gentle hillocks. From an unfathomable height, I could see there were sprawling ancient mosaics of ochre and golden fields, long plots of burnt sienna and grey, until the craggy topography of mountains rose up green in the distance.

The storied ruins of Madre España, ages-old cities and necropolises, aqueducts and ancient roads, were illuminated in the hazy daylight of eternity.

5. At the rumblings of the beginning of another quest

What could ever be said of our most distant ancestors? Can you salvage a chronicle of a long-forgotten world? Over how many centuries had so many Lopez and Velas come to be so serious and sad? Why had we abandoned our homes along the way of ceaseless irreversible journeying? What would ever make us feel settled again, how would we find our true home?

Why return to the past now to seek answers?

"I propose that you seek in yourself the remembrance of the before."

That's what the note read that I found in my old desk, scribbled in my hand but of unknown authorship, presumably copied, but from I know not where.

Probably from the satsanga of one guru or another, Yogananda, Nityananda, Muktananda, I thought.

"Then write what you find and believe your words."

Later, I had written "Who?" in one corner. Then, turning the blue note card over, I saw more writing in faded brown ink, in the familiar longhand script of Nancy, an old girlfriend from England:

toilet bowl.

Then, late one night while channel surfing I hit an interview shot on a grainy home camera public-access talk show.

"History is a message from the ineffable," observed Terence McKenna, the renegade ethnobotanist, talking about the revelations he had received while ingesting ayahuasca in the jungles of South America.

Maybe so, I thought; but if so, it was a hidden message in an extinct language, broadcast over some exotic radio frequency, out of reach of the world we live in. Family stories had the same inchoate resonance.

I had long thought of my family's histories as containing some lost and secret intent, an encrypted prophecy, some indistinct message of primeval origin I alone was drawn to rediscover, divine, and tell, from the time I started writing poems during high school in San Antonio.

This was my story before I had any way of telling it, and it would take more than a poem. Staring into a mirror in my bedroom back then, I watched as my face transmuted, becoming a thousand mestizo faces, castizo, morisco, cambujo coyote, torna atras; brown men and women, black, then café con leche, then puro blanco, thick eyebrows turning thin, then thick again, fat nose to aquiline, hollow cheeks to great jowls, my turtle chin squaring off, becoming bearded, eyes changing their color and gaze from moment to moment.

"All of these are traveling with you," I thought I heard a voice say.
All of their stories are traveling with you.

Stories only began in genealogy, in the descent of bodies, seriatim, through family lines into the deep well of time. To reach farther back in time was to know myself. Surely by this way I could reach where I came from and discern where the whole story was headed.

Then speak what you find and believe what you say.

This started sometime around my freshman year in high school, a year I retreated from my circle of childhood friends and spent more time alone. One afternoon, while reading *David Copperfield* at the Westfall branch of the San Antonio Public Library, I heard the same voice, so strangely implicit that it was barely perceptible.

No world. No time. No body. No mind.

I realized I had been hearing this voice already for some time, usually speaking in short philosophical aphorisms that had the lilt of lofty, incoherent greeting-card ruminations, maybe written by a Tibetan lama.

As mind is to body, so time is to world.

Only memory, ever. Memory, in search of rememberers.

Redemption is secretly underway, outside the view of the world.

I taped a cardboard poster to the wall next to my bed and began writing these "sayings" down as they were spoken to me, written on the tongue, during the night—alongside exhortations of the supremacy of Husqvarna off-road motorcycles and quotations from John Lennon.

The face is plural.

Thoughts get tangled up in evaporating threads of clouds.

Eventually, I stopped hearing the voice and threw away that first chronicle of these strange *dichos*.

6. Una despedida al siglo veinte

For years, I remembered my first trip to Spain as if it were the abandonment of an already long-postponed quest that was my birthright out of our Tejano lineages in South Texas and colonial Mexico.

Tamara, or was it Tana?—my Tasmanian nurse and protector— had said she would remain in touch. Licking my wounds, I gave up the rest of my planned itinerary to Lorca's Granada and returned limping back to Oxford. When we parted in Barcelona she promised to come visit me in England. There were a few postcards, from Madrid, Fez, then silence. I never saw her or heard from her again. I left my Barcelona days behind; the inaugural, inconclusive bruising in my ancestral lands.

That was my interrupted mission, in an improvised pilgrimage, a search put aside for more than a decade, seeking the storied legacy of ancestors who had left the world of their ancient origins behind. Our Spanish past was an antediluvian city, buried under millennial drifts of earth, stone, and sand. In shadings of grey and beige, satellite photography revealed the lingering evidence of walls, avenues, and dwellings, clearly etched into the desert's slate floor. If the old city was to be revealed again, this was where the digging would have to begin. Sevilla. Madrid.

The López de Jaén, the Velas *de quién sabe dónde*.

This was the secret compromiso of my writing, to find and tell the forsaken stories of our New World families that had traveled across continents and centuries to finally make their home in San Antonio, Texas, amid the roiling last decades of the twentieth century. Gradually, like a planet falling into an unchanging orbit around a star, the ancestors' lives and journeys became the subject of virtually every poem I wrote.

Short stories were about Sabinas, Muzquiz, Nueva Rosita, and Palau—the Mexican towns and villages of Coahuila I had come to know in trips across the border at Piedras Negras. Other stories were about the old Texas I was born into, street characters of downtown San Antonio, like my father's distant cousin who had become a prostitute on Broadway, or the old Mexicano who spent his days in the centro gathering cans and meticulously laying rows of them neatly in the street for passing buses to crush into aluminum pancakes which he could neatly stack into a canvas bag he wore on a frame hanging off his hip.

Through untallied migrations, our antepasados had led us to these places and these people, and into a time in my youth when the world was poised for wondrous if fearful events. A classroom movie showed a boiling mushroom cloud over Nevada, the blasts decimating an old barn in a single, godlike exhalation. We watched as a slain president was buried on black-and-white television, a riderless horse parading down an empty boulevard in the nation's capital.

An astronaut, elegantly fitted in a silver spacesuit, opened the hatch of his Gemini capsule and emerged into the vacuum of space, spinning on his umbilical tether. UFOs crossed the skies over San

Antonio, recounted to me in feverish tales by classmates and cousins. Newspapers reported the story of a woman in India who had
been pregnant for eighteen months and the baby could be heard
reciting verses from the Koran inside her belly. It seemed events in
the world were coming to some still undetermined climax, though
I was unaware then that my ancestors who first came to the lands
of "el Norte" were themselves convinced they were advancing the
completion of prophecy. And that their settlement of the tierras of
Nueva España would help bring that destiny to completion.

My brothers and I were indoctrinated to expect the strange
events that were undoubtedly augured as we watched *Project Terror* every Friday night, a weekly sci-fi television movie feature that
began with a pulsing radioactivity alert siren over which the trade-
mark slogan was gravely intoned:

"*Project Terror!* Where the scientific and the terrifying—emerge!"

It wasn't clear what we were expecting, but these were surely
momentous times.

Like any young writer, I was drawn to writers and writing for
the beauty of their words, an unanticipated elegance of rhetoric; but
it was their forensic delvings into the mystery of who we are and
where we came from that guided me in searching out my path of
revealing the family's past.

What hidden or occluded knowledge could we at last gather to
ourselves and write down after so many centuries in the onetime
alien place we had come to embrace as our true home?

How would that story come to be told? Would it be a long poem,
perhaps? Or maybe a book?

7. On beginning an impossible book

There was another woman who left a deep impression on me, from
afar, late in my teen years. I first learned of her through her poetry,
for which she had achieved literary fame in the early twentieth century; it was sonorous and strange, full of galvanic and edgy abstract
psychological X-rays of the mind and heart. I soon learned though

that she had repudiated it entirely in the late 1930s. I had long been interested in writers who eventually denounced their own work, such as Chaucer, Aquinas, Rimbaud. But in this case, my distant mentor hadn't facilely repudiated her own poems; in fact she judged them to be exemplary, if still inadequate. It was Poetry itself she repudiated.

As it turned out, it was what came after her renunciation that truly affected me:

> There is something to be told about us for the telling of which we all wait . . . we hurry to listen to stories of old human life, new human life, fancied human life, avid of something to while away the time of unanswered curiosity. We know we are explainable, and not explained . . . Until the missing story of ourselves is told, nothing besides told can suffice us: we shall go on quietly craving it.

Those are the words of Laura (Riding) Jackson, a poet and literary philosopher whose life spanned the twentieth century. I corresponded with her for several years when I was an undergraduate at the University of Notre Dame, initially to invite her to attend a literary festival there. She had notoriously renounced her early work as a poet, and indeed Poetry altogether, to pursue the true telling of "the missing story of ourselves" that she alludes to in this passage from her book, *The Telling*, a sequence of philosophical aphorisms about truth, language, and autobiography, published in 1974. One admirer observed, "It has about it a quality of a sacred meditation." Her vision of writing a book that would accomplish this mission of truth-telling begun in 1938 was a project she never published before her death in 1991.

Poetry was artifice, a machinery of false distraction. Her feverish curiosity about this story manqué, this intuition of a lost or absent tale of ourselves, left a deep imprint on me, a question really, about how the path of being a writer relates to the search for a perpetually missing story.

Where would I look for the missing story? Along with other writers of these times, in poems and prose, and later video, I looked for them in nearly forgotten family tales, the neglected words of the *viejitos*, their keepsakes, the histories, documents, and artifacts hidden away in libraries around the world. There were stories of the journeys that brought part of the family to South Texas, other ancestors who were there before it became Texas, before the Republic, before Nueva España, Nueva Extremadura. Despite my Barcelona debacle, Spain continued to beckon like a forgotten home. Then there was always the question of what came before that, and before that, and so on and so on.

Spain at best was a way station on the path into more remote ancestral antiquity.

San Antonio was a fertile place to be a young poet in the 1970s. The city abounded in connections to a rich and storied past, music was everywhere, both in the Mexican community and in the emerging Austin music scene, and there were other young writers like Naomi Shihab with whom I could seek out adventures in the city and the nearby countryside and share our coveted, dearest literary visions. In that age before unlisted numbers, we often sought out favorite writers, all the great ones we read, finding their addresses and phone numbers in catalogues at the public library. I wrote to William Burroughs, to Ken Kesey, and Denise Levertov. Naomi and I once quarreled over whether William Saroyan was dead. So we called him, and he answered the phone! When we told him I had wagered he was dead, he broke out laughing and congratulated Naomi for winning the bet.

Around this time, I also first wrote to Laura. By the 1970s, she had long ago become Mrs. Schuyler Jackson, as she signed her first letters to me, but she was also known as Laura (Riding) Jackson in the literary world, and she had once been more widely known simply as Laura Riding; muse, consort, conspirator, and imperious governess of the British poet Robert Graves, with whom she had lived a darkly romantic utopian tale in the 1920s and 1930s. I knew little of all that then, writing to an address in Wabasso, Florida, only as a devoted young fan, sending her my appreciation for her challenging yet alluring poems.

Though I was accustomed to getting polite replies from writers I contacted, I was stunned to receive from Jackson a three-page, manually typed and densely pencil-edited excoriation of my little homage. I'd never seen anything like it, a text smoldering with spiritual fire, marred with the abundant edits of her lapidary mind. Sentences strung on impossibly, folding in on themselves as if written in some strangely reticulated parallel version of English. There were typed corrections and penciled-in notes throughout. In some places she had just typed over earlier sentences, or in any space left between the lines of battered letters.

Allowing a brief gracious nod for my attempt to fathom her work, she insisted I couldn't possibly have understood it. Homage? Of course. Her oeuvre was, in her own unabashed estimation, the highest achievement possible in the way of poetry. But not even that pinnacle was sufficient: Was I not aware of the fact that she had renounced Poetry itself, hers included, in 1938, nearly forty years before? As she later explained it, "It is not that I failed poetry. *Poetry* fails."

And in ensuing years, her denunciation of literary culture had become more encompassing. In her reply to my first letter, she wrote, "I judge most contemporary writing to be devoid of a motive of truth, I judge contemporary writing to be *characteristically* not concerned with the matter of truth." She cautioned me that if she were to accept the invitation to come to Notre Dame, "I should very likely be wanting in an attitude of happy fellowship towards the other writers because of the writing they prosecute . . . there is nothing in the contemporary literary writing to give reason for celebrating—I mean the writing of the writers of the time who are receivers of literary plaudits adding up to some public effect of noise . . . I think the contemporary race of writers owe to their fellows of general and academic location engagements of solemn, contrite endeavor to cleanse themselves of their offences against the honor of language, and the right of their fellow-speakers of their language to respect as partners in the honor of being, all in linguistic relationship."

I was dumbfounded and chastised. Elsewhere, she replied to some of my compliments regarding her work, writing, "As to the case regarding your feelings about *The Telling*, I must reject, however besides you may feel toward it, the conception that any part of what is said in it has *any* spiritual or diagrammatic compatibility *in truth* with Hinduistic mandalas."

She did end that first letter on a more cordial note, reassuring me that "this that I have written is not an assault! I thank you for writing to me, and with openness of confiding of ideas, enthusiasms, expressions of good-will towards myself and my ideas and my work—Think over what I have written."

It was to be the beginning of a curious epistolary relationship with a legendary figure whom I would come to learn was one of the most formidable literary women of her age, and one who had lived an obscure, almost mystically directed writer's life through the twentieth century. I wouldn't learn her whole extraordinary story until many years later, after her death.

How she became the lover of Graves after being nanny to his children. How she nearly killed herself during an argument which included Graves, his wife, and another poet, who had been lover to both Laura and Graves's wife—when she leapt out a fourth-story window in North London. Graves ran one flight down, then jumped out a window too.

How afterward she and Graves, in self-imposed exile, formed a commune in Mallorca, receiving writers and artists from all over the world, advancing their vision to use literature to seek and tell universal human truths. How after they came to America when they were forced to flee Spain's civil war, she dumped Graves and married Schuyler Jackson, an obscure American poet. How at the same time she renounced poetry for its failure to communicate the human "truth" she sought to tell, retiring with her husband to rural Florida, where she spent the rest of her life committed to her quixotic, reclusive literary-philosophical plan of completing the impossible book in which she would tell the missing story. She died in 1991 at the age of ninety.

Through the letters we exchanged, along with numerous scarifying telephone conversations, I almost succeeded in bringing her to the University of Notre Dame (she ended up sending a taped lecture), despite the fact that she hadn't left Florida in decades. She left a mark on my work, as she did with just about every writer whom she ever encountered. I had long thought that those letters had been lost, tossed away by my mother during a vast cleaning out of the family attic in San Antonio. And then I recently found them all, the reel-to-reel tape included, bundled and bound with hemp twine in a remotely stashed box full of old love letters and my unsolicited correspondence with writers.

There were letters from all of the Williams—Burroughs, Stafford, Goyen, and Tennessee. Notes from Denise Levertov, Stanley Kubrick, David Ignatow. There's a photo Ken Kesey sent of himself, standing in overalls with his big hands spread apart, in a muddy corral, bearing the caption:

> *He was a little guy, green, just this big, he climbed out of his ship, took a soil sample and then took off.*

Laura's letters were set apart from all the rest, still almost glowing with her familiar ghostly power. I remembered how, after receiving one of the fat envelopes, scribbled over with pencil notes, I used to stow it away in a drawer to cool off before reading it. She pursued her mission when possible in whatever printed public forum would offer her an audience. But she advanced the same principles in all of her interactions, which grew scarcer and scarcer. T. S. Matthews, a onetime editor of *Time* magazine, wrote of how she would consume his writing and then return it to him completely edited and revised. After nearly two years of trading letters, Mrs. Schuyler Jackson signed off suddenly, sending me a copy of Charles Doughty's vexing, hypnotic epic *Arabia Deserta*, and explaining that she needed to devote all of the time she had left to completing her great book, the work of her life.

I never contacted her or heard from her again.

Our dialogue, thirty years ago, for better or worse, left me much more circumspect about writing and reading poetry, and awakened my curiosity about the mysterious, poetic powers hidden within autobiography.

8. A storm, a collision, a greeting

It was 1992, the quincentenary of las Americas, a year to mark the five hundredth anniversary of Columbus's arrival in the New World—the onetime Turtle Island—a whole world the mariners discovered dwelling apparently under what must have seemed an altogether separate sky.

It had been more than a decade since my first visit to Spain, and I thought little of ever returning. That was also the year Uncle Lico died, taking much of his research and discoveries with him, putting all of the Lopez farther away from our family's story.

I had gotten married and was living in Astoria, across the East River, driving my car into Manhattan every day over the Queensboro Bridge to make a nightly live television news show. In the midst of this routine, some mornings the towers of the city hung in the fog or shimmered in the early sunlight like sentinels of a forbidden city I suspected I could never really enter.

Already eight years in New York, I had never imagined staying there for so long.

My stories, with the bones of my ancestors, were buried in another place. But as the years passed, the sense of belonging elsewhere—Texas, Mexico, somewhere in the greater Southwest— grew fainter and the stories I told as a journalist became my only stories. One evening, finishing a late meal after a long day I had spent in a video-editing marathon, I passed out during a meal in a crowded and noisy Caribbean restaurant in the East Village. I had been eating and talking with my old friend Tom when I suddenly felt the whole scene rushing away from me, as if scenery was being rapidly wheeled offstage, and then everything went black.

I awoke to find myself on the ground next to the table, a voice shouting "Are you okay?" and another, "What did you take?"

Strangely though, I felt utterly refreshed, almost ecstatic, with the feeling that my spirit had somehow been greatly lightened, once and for all.

"The poet spirit has left my body," I told my friend as he led me out into the street. I marveled at the crisp night air that further revived me, a brilliant moon basting the obsidian city in soft, pearly light.

"Are you kidding?"

He looked at me incredulously, telling me how I'd gone out in the middle of a sentence.

"You really scared me, man. Your eyes were wide open, but you weren't there."

I couldn't dispel the feeling that something had been divested from me, as if the long-imagined undertaking of writing the family tale had suddenly been lifted from me, allowing me to assume another life altogether, far from the lands of the Lopez-Vela origins.

The ancestors were undoubtedly with us; the family back in Texas had not wandered very far from their remains. But their presence was insensate and diminishing, day by day, perhaps even hour by hour. All the indwelling wayward journeying and settlement that had brought us this far into the annals of the New World must've made a difference, setting us apart from others of other histories, other accords with time.

We had simply lost track of all the movements, all the changes.

When the journey had appeared to be a straight path, from Laredo to Cotulla, from Cotulla to San Antonio, it was really part of a larger orbit, of lives circulating around villages, towns, and cities, through the centuries when humans did that sort of thing. And just when it seemed as if whole generations might be contained in one orbit forevermore, the bloodline would find a way to stake a claim outward, spiraling farther into still unknown domains, neither in a hurry to know all the world too quickly nor so aloof that the destiny of the family would not still eventually transpire without eventually encompassing the planet entirely, or so I thought.

My brothers, identical twins, took their own separate paths.

George David became a psychiatrist in Houston, offering his patients tethers in the midst of their beaconless maelstroms. Charles Daniel became a dancer in an Austin company that created new works in which he would scuttle across the stage like an elegant mantis in search of other bodies to exalt and spin.

As I had already left the poet's life behind for television, or perhaps I had been abandoned by poetry, my secret troth was to be a journalist of the anagogic annals, to connect the disparate details and report an unseen story taking place behind the face of the apparent world, the story of the fate of our humanity. I wanted to witness events of the day as if they happened five hundred years ago.

What difference did it make that the indigenous people of the New World had lived unto themselves for so long? And vice versa for the people of the classical world with its tripartite great dominions—Europe, Africa, and Asia. What did it mean that these open circuits of the human had been closed by the discovery of the New World, where all of humankind would eventually meet, incalculably mixing among themselves, becoming something new in this still unfolding process?

For some years, I had imagined writing a book that would gather all of the secret true histories of the discovery and conquest of las Américas. It was to be titled *Immaterial Empires*. It would comprise a compendium of all the arcane tales issuing from that cataclysmic meeting of old and new worlds, perhaps as a way of starting to account for how the families that I came from in Texas had come to find themselves written into this strange historical epic.

Immaterial Empires would tell the comprehensive story of how the inner reality of the New World, and Mexico particularly, was revealed in history. The people who encountered each other there mingled their bloodlines, and new expressions of humanity emerged from their union. In human terms, it was an unprecedented evolutionary event transpiring just beneath the surface of official history, so there is no explicit memory preserved of these transformations.

The Velas and the Lopez were no exemplars in this history. The challenges they faced over hundreds of years linked them to many other families that long ago reconciled themselves to perpetually becoming something new, with little need ever to look back. This was a part of the original American story. My family and many others across South Texas like it, descended from the same ancestors, and yet no one remembers it that way today. I imagined the "Immaterial Empire" stretching the vast arc of a virtual horizon, from Tierra del Fuego to the icy waters lapping the shores of Baffin Island. This was the spiritual homeland to a polity that was uniquely unknown to itself, or perhaps one that was coming to know itself only very gradually over many hundreds of years.

This was the farthest destination in all of the wanderings of our ancestors, the farthest home to be founded sometime long into the millennia of our unceasing and restless diasporas.

No one saw the story as the original epic of America, except for Uncle Lico, ceaseless preacher of the family's true tale. Our ordinary Mexicano, Tejano, Americano family were inheritors of an epic tale. Most of my cousins had forgotten the story—or it was never told to them to begin with. My brothers and I were among the last of the twenty grandchildren of Leandra and Leonides Lopez, a progeny that brought the kaleidoscopic spectrum of types that emerged from the mestizaje.

Some were dark-roasted and hairy, tall or stocky; others were as fair as Scandinavians, light-haired, statuesque. Some looked Semitic, Egyptian, Turkish, Armenian. One or two looked Samoan.

In a formal family portrait from the 1940s of Grandmother sitting in a grand ottoman with all of her grown sons and daughters around her, they could be an accomplished Lebanese family. Standing in a row behind the others, Uncles Lico, Leo, and Lauro, dressed in dapper grey suits and sharply appointed ties, could be bankers, or gangsters. Sitting on one armrest, Aunt Lydia wears a shimmering silk blouse and skirt. On the other, my mother is in a dark man-style suit and skirt, her black tie matching her brothers' sartorial élan.

And Grandmother sits between them all, one relaxed foot showing the sole of her shoe, her head set to one side, her lips pursed in a bemused grin.

Alongside Lico's documents and family papers, I amassed boxes

of yellowing newspaper clippings, photocopies of obscure historical texts, notebooks and stacks of three-by-five blue note cards, and
early in the 1990s I had begun to make drafts of some of the imagined chapters.

The Spaniards thought they had found the lands that contained
the true Garden of Eden. Upon seeing the Españoles, the Mexicans
believed their God had returned, according to prophecy. Debates
ensued over whether Indios had souls, and whether they were even
truly human at all. Everything that was of the New World, fauna
and flora, was thought to be physically stunted and morally inferior.
Untouched by the revelation of the Gospel, these lands were implicitly the dominion of *el Demonio*.

All of our history had emerged from that collision of prophecy
and damnation.

My father's family, the Santos and the Garcias, had connected us
to Mexico, while Mother's family, the Lopez and the Velas, offered
a bridge, albeit broken and lost, back to Spain. When so much had
been forgotten, everything seemed to pertain, as if the schism of
the Conquest remained alive in every one of us. Surely there was
a story in our history, but no one knew where it had begun or how
far along in the telling we had come. It was a swirling vortex of
a tale, impossible to contain or render in any vernacular, century
upon century of geographic dreaming that had become our legacy
in these once unimagined lands.

Still, after my *despedida* with the poet spirit in that Caribbean
restaurant, I had put *Immaterial Empires* aside, and attended to the
business of my everyday life in New York City, which I had thought
I felt only happy with.

There is a story for every time, and a time for every story.

Years passed, until the arrival of 1992, the Columbian quincentenary year, with its harkening to the birth of the Americas. It
reminded me once again of the old missing family tale, my unwritten story of the immaterial empires of the New World.

It was in the last days of that year, early into the last decade of a
dark century, that a great churning storm swept up the eastern coast

of the United States, battering beaches and uprooting trees, its violent whorl shaking telephone poles out of the ground and sending their wires sparking in every direction as it approached.

Richmond, Annapolis, and Trenton were all punished before New York City.

Cities along the heavy storm's thundering path were shuttered, battened down, and flooded in the runoff of swollen estuaries, rivers, and creeks.

When this *tormenta* finally hit the city, the rain fell in *chorros* of dense interlocking patterns, whipped by the great gusts that were undiminished after the long journey up the coast. The streets of the city were empty, strewn with tree branches, trash can lids, savaged exoskeletons of cheap umbrellas. Calling it a "nor'easter" betrayed the dark majesty of that weather.

That weekend, my brother George and sister-in-law Cindy were visiting, and we had planned to have dinner in a Queens restaurant on the bank of the East River. The gargantuan storm had subsided by mid-evening, though the rain-slick streets of Long Island City remained deserted as we set out. We were merrily making our way to the night's feast, set against a sprawling vista of the glistening Manhattan cityscape.

The car's wheels hissed on the dimly lit, wet cobblestone blocks of the warehouse district near the river when, in the middle of a sentence, I drove through an intersection and collided furiously with a taxicab coming from the wrong way on a one-way street. From full throttle, we entered a spinning well of crunching metal and screeching tires—then came to a violent halt.

Suddenly the whole world grew quiet, and time stopped.

I saw steam rising from the car's mangled engine, the amber roof light of the cab's off-duty sign illuminating the wreckage. I pulled myself back from a slump over the steering wheel and turned to see that everyone in my car seemed to be sleeping, my brother leaning tranquilly forward against the dashboard, our wives, Stephanie and Cindy, leaning on one another in the backseat.

"Everything is fine," I thought. "We should just go on to dinner."

I leaned back into the driver's seat and felt my head where a large knot had formed after striking the windshield frame. I realized I hadn't taken a breath in a long while, and when I did, the air rushed in as if it were coursing through a vast canyon.

I gripped the steering wheel as I heard a long-lost, strangely familiar voice slowly pronounce these words in a calm but decisive tone:

Time is short.

III

Immaterial Ancestors

1. En Manhattitlán

I had arrived in 1984 in New York City as a curiosity, an apparently (at least) half-civilized savage from the borderlands, brown and long-haired; draped in a proper wool suit, black with red laser pin-stripes and a sharply cut "pachuco" line in the jacket, baggy pants—and a fine pair of ebony Tony Lama boots that could impart the power to levitate, if that was required. My black-and-silver tie was decked with ancient Egyptian glyphs.

Chicanos were scarce, if not unknown, at CBS Television News when I was asked to join their corps, especially ones talking about liberation theology, the importance of learning more about Islam, and rumors of a new epidemic emerging in San Francisco.

Trying to justify her hiring of a greenhorn producer from the hinterlands for her documentary unit, Pamela, my executive producer, arranged for me to meet the network's vice president for news, a tête-à-tête she arranged at a fancy Italian restaurant off of Sixth Avenue, near the network's fortress of corporate solitude called Black Rock.

Maybe he was just curious.

The estimado señor joined us a half-hour late, short and punc-
tilious, silver-haired, dressed in a frank blue suit, striped tie, and a
white shirt that looked as if it had been ironed with enough starch
to last eternity. He was full of fascinating tics: chin shifts, forehead
lifts, and a periodic blink that looked as if something I said had
totally flummoxed him. As he talked or listened, he would pull out a
small leather cuff with index cards from his breast pocket and write
a note, replacing it quickly.

After some awkward questions like "How far is San Antonio
from the border?" and "When did your family come to the States?"
conversation finally turned to his beloved Notre Dame, my
alma mater, and the promise of the football team for the current
season—until I confessed that I had never attended a game during my undergraduate years, and still didn't much keep up with the
team's fortunes.

To make matters worse, over my four years at the university, I'd
had a series of quarrels with Father Ted Hesburgh, Notre Dame's
legendary president, whom the executive held in almost divine
regard. A billowy tiramisu was being served as Pamela excused herself to make a phone call and left the table.

The Vato Ejecutivo looked over and focused his slate grey eyes
on me. Suddenly, he looked as pale as an old cardinal, hard to discern if he was tranquil or apoplectic.

"You look like a gangster," he hissed with an urbane indignation
I only knew from Spencer Tracy movies. Then silence, his jaw tens-
ing again.

Was it a joke?

The waiter brought espressos.

"I was thinking the same thing about you," I deadpanned.

And then we laughed. And then Pamela returned.

Ironically, that moment may've secured the strange concordat
under which, for the next five years, I made dozens of documentaries at CBS: honor between gangsters. I would make the programs around the world about faith-based uprisings of the poor,
revolutions in the Americas, resurging Islam in the Sudan; and the

network would dutifully broadcast them, on Sunday mornings, when only insomniacs or junkies were awake.

It was a workable arrangement.

Our documentary program operated there under this Kafkaesque television quid pro quo. We had the resources and channels of the CBS News network at our disposal to report on virtually anything we chose to report on, in whatever format, style, or voice we elected to use. But, scheduled at 7 a.m. on Sundays, no one saw the show. Nielsen meters back then didn't even survey that time period. We were allowed to do our work, but outside the arena of audience attention, in the abandoned zone of a noncommercial time slot.

I thought of the monks in clifftop monasteries during the dark ages, toiling over illuminated manuscripts that few would ever see. I believed that if we could hold out, maybe we could create a new kind of television program that would be global, hip, and rigorous, reporting on the biggest story in the world: how humanity channeled its beliefs and cultures to refine society and transform and renew itself.

This was the anagogic journalism I had imagined, reporting on the world from the perspective of eternity. Instead, the budget dwindled, though somehow it was still enough to make forty new shows a year. We lost our research staff, lost producers and telephone lines; eventually the executives came looking for the light bulbs.

Recognition was hard-won. I received an Emmy nomination for two documentaries on AIDS, early reports on the spiritual dimension of the mounting epidemic and its impact on black and Latino communities. When I went to Los Angeles for the awards ceremony I learned that the other nominees in this daytime category were a Luciano Pavarotti special, an episode of *American Bandstand*, a "dog-nabbing" episode of *The People's Court*, and Willard Scott's hosting of the Macy's Thanksgiving Day parade.

The parade show won.

We heard shortly thereafter that the show would be canceled and the unit dissolved at the end of the same year. The show ended on Christmas Day, appropriately with a musical reflection on Schubert's *Death and the Maiden*.

2. When a tale never ceased beckoning

The mind and heart leave no fossils; all of their artifacts are made of the most fleeting, unstable stuff. Though no one was seriously injured in the accident that destroyed our car, great changes were set in motion. Within six months I would be divorced, and would leave my job to travel to Mexico, and the strange inward voice that had returned to me resumed its telling of the old story.

Though I wasn't fully aware of it, I had been becoming more and more estranged from the life I had been leading for almost ten years, living in New York City, making television documentaries, later becoming a television executive, writing only late at night and keeping that to myself; I had been happily married, complete in every way except the way that I secretly knew I'd always felt called to live.

The mounting tension in me had brought great distress to my wife as I grew more and more restless, turning into someone unfamiliar, constantly asking her what it was we were meant to do, what it was we were truly seeking, separately and together. And making matters more complicated, I had met someone I could talk to about these yearnings, a woman who was herself beginning a spiritual journey of self-discovery, born of a Mexican mother and a Basque American father who had claimed to be a descendant of Cortés. Increasingly, I wanted to spend my time with her.

Just months after the automobile accident, I was separated from my wife and trying to sort out what to do next when I heard there was an Inca curandero from Bolivia visiting the city and consulting with the infirm, troubled, and confused during his stay. I had seen psychiatrists and counselors and had left each of them feeling utterly unaffected, and still at sea.

In the middle of a workday, when I went to the address I had been given for Don Eduardo, it turned out to be a penthouse apartment on Manhattan's Upper East Side, beautifully furnished, but in the main salon where he was seeing people, everything was covered in plastic—sofas, armchairs, desks, and lamps—everything but the coffee table where Don Eduardo had set out the implements of his healings: round river stones, colored crystals, small bundles of sticks, old coins, a few eggs, dried flowers in a bowl, a half-smoked cigar, and a liquor bottle with no label, half full of an amber liquid with more dried flowers floating inside.

A young woman who turned out to be his daughter and assistant received me at the door and introduced me to Don Eduardito, as she called him. He was dressed in a white shirt and pants, wearing a grey fedora with yellow and red parrot feathers poking out of the band, and he stood about four and a half feet tall.

Smiling mischievously, he looked up at me pretending to shield his eyes, and said that the criollos in Bolivia weren't as tall as me, laughing in a childlike singsong way. He looked me over from bottom to top, lightly touching my chest, and then asked me to turn around and touched the middle of my spine and let out a great sigh.

"Please take off all of your clothes and sit down here with me," he said, pointing to a chair across from the sofa where he took a seat, the coffee table strewn with his talismans between us.

"You may leave your underwear on, so that my assistant does not become more frightened. She has already told me she has never seen such a hairy human!" With this, he cracked himself up with laughter, his daughter joining in.

As I sat down he became more somber, and it was hard to tell how old he was. When he laughed, he appeared to be a vital sixty-year-old, but as he grew silent, more lines in his face were evident and I wondered if he might not be an octogenarian; though when he moved about, he was perfectly limber and quick.

He put an egg in my hand and asked me to describe what was bothering me.

I began to tell him about the car accident and the specters and dislocations haunting my life since, and he nodded smiling, saying, "sí sí sí, tsk, tsk, tsk." I told how I had left the life I had known since arriving in New York almost ten years before, I'd left my marriage, and that I was unsure what lay ahead. I wasn't sleeping, was feeling vacant, was often startled when I was unable to recognize myself if I saw my haggard passing reflection in windows or glass doors.

As I was speaking, he took long drags on his stumpy cigar and then slowly blew out the smoke so that it trailed in long pearly ribbons through his settings of stones, sticks, and dried flowers. He listened to me while he watched the smoke wander and dissolve among the precious objects he had brought from his village, which he said was by a river in Bolivia. Finally, he reclined back into the sofa and gave me a long, knowing look as he nodded.

"Your breath has been knocked out of your skin, my dear friend. This can happen when we are moving from one time of life to another. Everything loosens up then, like a snake shedding its skin. Sometimes you'll get a good shaking to let everything go, like the car crash, but your body is now dragging behind your breath about three feet, like a dead tree branch. But I can fix it, don't you worry."

Don Eduardo whispered something to his daughter, who was sitting alongside him, and she left the room briefly, returning with two long pine branches full of green needles. He asked me to stand up and close my eyes. He pulled away the chair I had been sitting in and he began to use a soft cloth to brush my arms and chest and both legs, massaging my shoulders and scapula in deliberate, rounding strokes. As he began to sing a slow, repetitive song under his breath I heard a lighter click as the pine branches were set alight, crackling so close I could feel the heat on my bare skin.

"Please don't open your eyes until I tell you," he said, and suddenly I heard the flaming branches whoosh past my head and down both sides of my body, dropping cinders that made me wince as he gripped my shoulder firmly while continuing to whisper his song.

The burning branches passed by again, and then again, and it felt as if both the healer and his daughter were circling me, my body strangely at ease in the middle of this fiery vortex, until all at once they were extinguished with a hiss in some nearby water.

From behind me, I heard Don Eduardo uncork his bottle and take a great swig from it. Suddenly, he blew out the liquor in a fierce mist against my neck, smelling of a rum perfumed with some sweet flower, dripping down my back now. After another swig, he sprayed my face and chest, and repeated this several times until I was standing there soaked, standing in a puddle of rum on the plastic sheets until a large towel was thrown over me and he told me I could open my eyes as he confidently announced that my breath had been restored to a new body.

"Your life is still going to be a mess for a while. Your old body was too damaged to save. As you get accustomed to this new body, things will get better, you're going to see."

I looked down and saw the same body I had seen when I woke up that morning, though it was now covered with small pink dried flowers that stuck to me with the rum. And I hadn't brought a change of underwear. I retired to the bathroom to clean up and get dressed.

When I returned, Don Eduardo was gathering a few stones and coins from his trove into a small leather pouch, explaining to me that my condition could have been much more serious if I hadn't been so protected by my ancestors.

"Usually, they do not follow when someone is so far away from their home, but they are here with you, and they made sure that you would not perish in this place. But you still needed a new body."

He handed me the pouch and explained that I should not open it and should keep it in my pocket for at least one full cycle of the moon. In the meantime, I should bathe every day in a bath infused with two large tablespoons of honey and three handfuls of rose petals. As he said goodbye, he reached out to shake my hand and his hand seemed as if it was as light as paper, barely touching fingertips, suddenly seeming very old again as he wished me well and told me everything would soon be better, not to think about it too much.

Already late for a meeting back at the television station and reeking of perfumed rum, I grabbed a cab and tried to arrange my collar and tie by looking in the driver's rearview mirror as we dodged through traffic. Back in the daylight, I was startled to see my own face, looking inexplicably younger and unburdened, a few small dried flowers gingerly stuck to my forehead.

After years of telling other people's stories via television, I soon found myself returning to the search for the first stirrings of my family's tale in the New World and before. I wasn't foraging for a detailed genealogy of my innumerable ancestors. I wanted to find out who the antepasados believed *themselves* to be—their deeper, unrecorded legacy, the story they had imagined themselves to be living and telling to time.

What did they make of their lives and how was that meaning to be passed on generation to generation?

What could it mean to us, their survivors?

3. A return to Spain

Seven years passed after my "homecoming" trip to Barcelona before I ventured back to Spain. On that inaugural visit, I had left without any hint or stirrings of an ancestral connection to the land or the nation, in no hurry to return to Iberia after my nocturnal debacle in Las Ramblas.

In the meantime, I had completed my literature studies in Oxford, pursued and left graduate studies at Yale, and after a brief return to San Antonio working for the arts section of the *Express-News* newspaper, I moved to New York City to make documentaries at CBS.

And so, after this interval, my next trip to España was no journey of self-discovery; it was instead a search for someone else's story—the life of Pedro Arrupe, the longtime father general of the Jesuits. It was a sort of documentary quid pro quo, one of many during my years at CBS. In exchange for letting me make a documentary about the 1987 Harmonic Convergence and the roots of New Age philosophy in Western mysticism, my executive producer had assigned me this biographical documentary project.

I had never heard of Arrupe, and had very little contact with Jesuits growing up since they had been few in San Antonio, a longtime diocesan redoubt. At the time I made the television program about him, he was still alive, though invalid and unable to speak, under constant care in the Jesuit headquarters in Rome after a debilitating stroke in 1981. I went to Spain to seek out the sources of what I discovered to be his world-traversing vocation in the church, one that ultimately brought him into direct conflict with the Vatican of Pope John Paul II and his then chief lieutenant, Cardinal Joseph Ratzinger, the man who would later become Pope Benedict XVI.

Arrupe's life constituted a remarkable chronicle of the twentieth century.

He was born in an old, middle-class neighborhood of Bilbao in 1904 and became a Jesuit only after excelling in and completing his medical studies in the venerable Colegio de Medicina in Madrid. Along with many other clergy, the Jesuits were expelled from Spain during the antireligious public fervor of the turbulent years of the Spanish Republic. Arrupe became an ordained vagabond, spending time in the Netherlands working as a doctor among the poor before coming to the United States, where he ministered to the incarcerated for a time in the prisons of Missouri.

Fluent in Spanish, French, Dutch, and English, along the way he also began studying Japanese and eventually followed the path of many Jesuits before him to Japan, where he became the rector of the Jesuit seminary in Hiroshima. There he became fascinated with Zen Buddhism and the elaborate, delicate ritual of the tea ceremony as well as the traditional meditative art of flower arrangement. These disciplines were all incorporated into his training of his Japanese Jesuit novices, already reportedly causing some concern among the ecclesial stalwarts back in Rome.

This theological tension was eclipsed with a bright flash one clear morning in early August of 1945 when, just after morning mass, the first atomic bomb to be used against a populous city was exploded in the clear skies over Hiroshima. An estimated seventy-five thousand civilians were instantly killed, some literally turned into shadows on the walls and pavements of the city. The Jesuit novice house was built just over a ridge from the city, so it was spared. Arrupe was one of the first to enter Hiroshima's ruins, among the first to render medical aid to the suffering. Survivors were woefully burned and disfigured. Arrupe found the living walking amid the rubble of the city like wraiths. Later he would write a memoir of his experience of that morning and the succeeding days, titling it *Yo Viví la Bomba Atomica*, "I Lived the Atomic Bomb."

He was later made head of all Jesuits in Japan, and then in 1965 he was elected as Father General of the order. In that office, he championed the *aggiornamento* of the Second Vatican Council, seeking to bring the church into a direct embrace of modernity and, especially important for Arrupe, into interreligious dialogue with all the world's faiths and cultures.

When this progressive movement in the church ran afoul of Pope John Paul II's Vatican, particularly in its association with liberation theology with its championing of the cause of the poor, Arrupe along with his world order of Jesuits was at loggerheads with Vatican authority. He was petitioning to Pope John Paul II to be allowed to resign when he suffered a massive stroke during a trip. Under the Jesuit constitution, the father general can only retire with the pope's consent.

Jesuit conspiracy theorists believe Pope John Paul did not allow Arrupe to retire, anticipating that if allowed to do so, he would be able to manage the election of his successor. Instead, after Arrupe's stroke, in an unprecedented step, the Vatican suspended the Jesuit constitution and appointed a new father general.

Arrupe lingered in poor health until 1991 and died in the clinic of the Jesuit curia in Rome. Like many Spaniards and Basques before him, Arrupe set out in into the world carrying the story of Christ, nearly two thousand years old, as a tale of an exemplary life that had the power to evoke and redeem the humanity of whoever was encountered along the way. Unlike most of his predecessors, however, Arrupe was not a militant evangelizer. Unlike many of the conquistadores who came to Mexico, he did not see himself in the role of fulfilling prophecy in the appointed "end times." Instead, he sought ways to find the implicit ties between whatever creeds were revealed to him in his travels around the world and the faith of the church tradition he had been raised with in Bilbao.

This was a profound conversion of Spanish martial theology, the very kind that had baptized the settlement of my homelands in South Texas. Coming at the end of a long history of Iberians imposing their beliefs on peoples they conquered, Arrupe moved in the world like a perpetual pilgrim.

In search of what?

Divinity revealed through humanity.

On the journey to shoot the documentary on Arrupe's life, high up into the mountains of remote Basque country on the road to the Jesuit fortress stronghold of Loyola, in a small village taberna where I had stopped for lunch with the Italian film crew accompanying me, we had a feast of grilled sausages and wild mushrooms, seasoned with peppery fresh basil.

When the proprietor offered us servings of his wife's still-warm rice pudding, I took my first bite and felt transported back to South Texas. The dessert was just as I had known growing up, made by my mother, who had learned the recipe from her mother. It was simple and not too sweet, thick and creamy with evaporated milk, and spiced with sharp cinnamon, cardamom, and a pinch of cayenne.

I hadn't wondered about my family's Spanish origins in a long while. It was these long-forgotten spices that brought an immediate spark of recognition, a feeling of kinship more affecting than any document or history could provide. Suddenly, on this unexpected remembrance, I wondered again if our *nacimiento* in Iberia could ever be found again.

I was drawn to regather the patterns and momentum of such ancestral ephemera. We were creations of the New World. Our more distant past, whether in the Americas or in Europa, was shrouded in fog. But all of those spirits, all the ancestral lineages found me no matter where I traveled to or made my home. And the farther back I reached, the greater the mystery became.

The old stories of my family called to me in New York City, so far from the homelands. There came a November day nearing the century's end when, riding a cab across Manhattan, I heard a radio news announcer describe a startling discovery of a pre-Columbian Mexican statue—in Brooklyn. The NYPD had received a hot tip to search a certain brownstone of unknown ownership near Prospect Park, where officers found a large wooden packing crate in the garage. Inside the crate, swathed in a nest of yellowing confetti, officers found an eight-hundred-pound, elaborately carved stone head.

The next morning, one paper described the presumed smuggler's booty as an ancient Mexican sculpture of a lion swallowing a man's head whole. But when I saw the photograph, I realized it was something else. The chipped, heavily weathered basalt piece was a figure commonly associated with the ancient Olmeca people of Mexico's Gulf region, *abuelos de los abuelos*, the eldest ancestors of the Mexican indigenous world.

The stone in Brooklyn was actually the head of a feathered snake, its mouth open wide, with the face of a man emerging from the beast's maw. It was the primeval Mexican hero god Quetzal-coatl, mystic, lawgiver, wind deity, the divine plumed serpent that enchanted Mesoamerica for centuries, here giving birth to, or perhaps becoming, a human.

And residing in Brooklyn.

That day, already fifteen years since I had left my home in San Antonio, I was a writer living in New York City, searching again from afar through the traces of my Mexican American family's memory, following the nebula of stories that connect us back to the millennial epic of Mexico. Suddenly, Mexico's oldest god appeared in New York, prophesying transformation.

I never learned how Quetzalcoatl came to Brooklyn or what became of his wayward effigy. Elsewhere I had found a hidden great shrine to the Nahua god Tlaloc, ancient Mexican deity of the rain, set into a granite bridge spanning a waterfall in the northern reaches of Central Park. Perhaps it had been placed there unconsciously by Frederick Law Olmstead, Central Park's creator, who had confessed to being haunted by Mexican culture. There, where runners pass, mothers push their babies' prams, and dogs perambulate with their owners, were the two great goggle eyes of Tlaloc, the god who had ruled over the ancient city of Teotihuacán, now keeping watch over the falling waters of a Central Park stream.

I suspect that, eventually, along with the gods of the European world, all of the old gods from Mexico, Latin America, Asia, and Africa will come to find their home in America.

We can hide under the city's girded graphite skies, crisscrossed with bright comet tails and the gauzy flame tracks of jets, but eventually all of the ancestors will come seeking us, sending their gods into the subways, walking like mendicants into the plazas and avenues of the city.

Try as you might to set off on your own, they will always return to remind you of their untold tales.

4. An abuelo from the future

Why not farther outward? Why not traverse our clear silent void, frictionless, without threshold, leaving behind the dear, the familiar, the alabaster cistern where I washed my face one indelible dawn in arctic water? Then the lot of us, soldados primos, running out to the tip of the small rocky pine island and jumping naked into the crystalline lake. Why not follow a vast curtain of aurora borealis like the silvery magenta one of the night before, untethered, disappearing into the ebony sky like a lost balloon? Memory was always supposed to be about trusting the future, the onward, no?

The dharma should be unencumbered, ni por compromiso ni por herencia, que no? Basta ya con España, basta con el Mundo Nuevo.

Tu abuelo estimado, C7C7C7C7C7C7 : . . .

Those were the first of his words, the first I discovered mysteriously downloaded during the night in a mysterious text and sound file left on my computer's desktop, labeled "Dichos.doc." When it played back, I realized I had been hearing this voice already for years, only inside of me. The sonorous, throaty tones, a sibilant Castilian lisp, the rhythmic Elizabethan batteries of p's and t's, all in rapid sure-stepping riffs, imperiously correct, but with a hint of the same unnamable sadness I hear echoed in Stephen Hawking's antiquarian electronic voice.

These were the first *dichos de Cenote Siete*, who announced himself, or revealed himself, as my great-great-great-grandfather *from the future*.

This is not the story Uncle Lico would have told.

I had left that one long ago, or so I thought, without finishing the tale. Uncle Lico had died years before, without completing his search to find the ancestor who first transplanted our lineage from Spain to the New World. But when this all began again, after the quincentenary of the Americas, after undertaking my first trips into Mexico and Spain in search of ancestors, after nearly twenty years away from the homelands—*my tale now*—these were the first of his words, my *other* guide, Cenote Siete.

As the sound file loaded and played, the first words scrolled out onto my screen in an elaborate serif font, shimmering at first, making the monitor glow inexplicably bright. Coming out of my own sleep mode that morning in New York City, I wondered how someone had breached the laptop's Internet firewall during the night. The letters flickered on the screen, as if trying to hold on against some molecular storm, taking their form for an instant before disappearing entirely, then fading again to black. Nothing I read looked familiar, but perhaps, I thought, it was an eruption of some cache of corrupted files.

Then:

You will undoubtedly wonder, Yan Phiyak (one of his ways of addressing me), *whether this is something you wrote, forgot and left improperly filed away. And what about, "I propose that you seek in yourselves remembrance of the Before, and write what you find, and believe your words."*

So spoke one of the ancient peregrinos, a Guru, a Cacique, quién sabe . . .

Source unknown, que no?

I recognized those words from long ago, a note of unknown origins that had been discovered years before this, and that I had always kept near my writing desk.

Cenote Siete (the name means Jungle Spring Seven) wrote that he came from the distant future, the twenty-fifth or twenty-sixth century in the Gregorian calendar, or thereabouts, by his estimation, though he claimed to be unconcerned with such pedestrian matters as earth years. They were irrelevant to him, except as they pertained to his great mission.

He explained that he lived in a world called La Zona Perfecta, a time when some humans remained on earth, while many others had transmigrated completely into what sounded like a solar system–wide version of the Web; and still others, like himself, moved easily between the two *dominios*, of flesh and ether. Cenote Siete, sometimes C7, claimed to have always been able to contact me through both, going back to my childhood.

I came to you first when blood was first decanted from your body, and for a brief spell, you entered La Zona Perfecta. I came to you first when your blood first came into contact with the ether.

He described a scene, and I remembered when as a child a large syringe full of blood had been taken from me in a downtown San Antonio clinic for some medical exam. Shortly thereafter, for the first time in my life, I felt all the wakefulness rush out of me in one gust and I lost consciousness, only to wake up on the floor of the examination room, with the nurse and my mother standing over me.

This was the first time I took you flying in the brilliant skies of La Zona Perfecta. Do you remember none of that? How we traced the entirety of the great river, from its headsprings in the sierra, down through the deserts, all along the trails our ancestors trod, widening out at the delta to a forest of gulf palms?

I remembered that day well, but there was only a blackout as I fainted, only oblivion until I was resuscitated.

He claimed to be my descendant. Though he said few are interested in doing so, in La Zona Perfecta, it is possible to reunite with any ancestor of your lineages, so long as a sufficient quantity of their blood comes into contact with the air.

But I have no children.

That's what you say now. In any case, there are tributaries and rivulets from the numberless streams de nuestros origenes, some lead into greater courses of souls, while others end in placid coves and ponds. I can find my way to one or the other.

After decades of secret communications with me, it had become easier with the emergence of the World Wide Web, and for the first time he could address me directly in his own written words, using the "memory machines," as he referred to computers, offering cryptically that these machines were in fact the heralds of the coming time of La Zona Perfecta.

He had announced himself now, he said, to aid me in telling the story of *our* forgotten ancestors, the shared quest of writing *Immaterial Empires*—that, he confessed, had actually been his lifelong mission, and had required him to leave behind his world and his time to venture forth into the unfathomable waters of the past so that his mission might be completed.

In his essay "Eureka," Edgar Allan Poe reported the contents of a note from a bottle that had been discovered corked and floating in the Mare Tenebrarum, a mysterious and distant ocean detailed in the ancient maps of the Nubian geographer Ptolemy Hephestion. Poe told how that note, a dense philosophical-scientifico treatise dealing with the nature of the universe, was written in the year 2848.

I design to speak of the physical, metaphysical and mathematical—of the material and spiritual universe; of its essence, its origin, its creation, its present condition, and its destiny . . . My general proposition, then, is this: in the original unity of the first thing lies the secondary cause of all things, with the germ of their inevitable annihilation . . . no man has ever taken into his brain the full uniqueness of the prospect; and so, again, whatever considerations lie involved in this uniqueness, have as yet no practical existence for mankind.

I sent you to that book of Poe, and to the great prophecies of Guillermo Blake as well, as both of them were sometime denizens of La Zona.

In a letter to one of his patrons, Blake had written of how he had received his inspiration from the spirit of his departed brother, whose essence had entered his body as a shooting star that had fallen upon one of his feet. "Thirteen years ago I lost a brother and with his spirit I converse daily & hourly in the Spirit & See him in my remembrance in the regions of my Imagination."

I remembered Blake's further confession, "I hear his voice and even now write from his Dictate."

Cenote Siete left yet another reminder in the next of his missives, quoting to me from another of Blake's letters,

. . . I have written this poem from immediate Dictation twelve or sometimes twenty or thirty lines at a time, without Premeditation & even against my Will; the time that it has taken in writing was thus rendered Non Existent, & an immense Poem exists, which seems to be the Labour of a long life, all produc'd without Labour or study.

And just in case I might be inattentive, this final sentence was highlighted:

I mention this to shew you what I think is the Grand Reason of me being brought down here.

But enough of the literary fineries, que no?

According to C7, he had been born as an ordinary human being in the same lands as my birth, but during his time some epoch-cracking evolutionary switch was unexpectedly thrown by some unknown means, and much of humanity migrated into La Zona.

As he described it, it was on a specific afternoon, *la tarde de luz,* the "afternoon of light," when, he said:

All history was taken up into eternity.

It began as a sad game, a juegito triste, a way, I can see now, in the midst of our dwindling lives, to touch the infinite, the boundless ineffable sublime. Children who have a hunger for higher things will always find each other and make their mischief to find the way to the mystery. In late ochre afternoon light, we clambered up the hanging tungsten mesh of shivering gantry towers, strung taut with gossamer platinum lines across the Llano River plain. Scaling to the apex of the pylon, the arm braces hung out onto the nada, whistling in high boreal tones, and when we shimmied out to the end, one hand after the other, gripping the beam, we would look down and see the giant red granite dome of Enchanted Rock, the veins of dry river sand, all of the reticulum of our soon-to-be-lost home.

Then we would swing out, swaying back and forth like reeds in the hill country breezes, watching to see who of us would trace the longest crescent, stay in motion for the longest time. We were all adept and fearless, acting as if we were masters of the void we were dipping our bodies into.

It was Hermano Caracól, more fearless than any of us, who was the first to let go. Releasing his grip, he did not fall, hurtling like a meteor toward the earth. Instead, he vanished in a whip crack of light that glimmered out along the cables in every direction. Suddenly, the silence of the nada grew quieter still. We hung perfectly still, looking at each other and at the blank space where Caracól had been moments before. Eventually, each of us followed him, letting go in explosions of serape-colored light.

And me, Cenote Siete, always with my secret dearest, flickering memories of the wild world, I was the last to let go, the last to enter, and I must confess I did so warily.

　　That was how we came to dwell inside La Zona—the revealed machine of creation—pilgrims inside the innumerable luminescent streams, inside the centripetal forces of time, arcing vast parabolas into the past, drawing accelerating ellipses into the future, all the while disappearing and reconfiguring through infinitesimal algorithms into solar hours of a borderless etheric mind.

　　We can bathe in the shadows cast by distant planets, one hundred and ninety million miles away.

5. An apology to my uncle

I would never have admitted it to Uncle Lico, but there were long intervals when I regarded the chronicle of the family's Spanish origins as an impossible tale of invisible ancestors. After I moved to New York, from my far-off outpost in the Northeast, the questions that had long obsessed me became increasingly distant and faint. If I wrote anything but documentary scripts, it was parsed out across a secret archipelago of notebooks and paper scraps that would never cohere.

　　My silence about our Lopez-Vela Spanish story betokened surrender, the conclusive putting aside of a long-postponed quest. Our Mexican past was opaque enough, clouded as it was by forgetting and dispossession. The family carried on in our homelands of centuries, for the last hundred and fifty years as part of the United States. The clocks in our houses counted ticks against memory's backward-running stream, against the current of the moments, hours, days moving forward, on and on.

　　Finally, for our latter-day generations, farther and farther down the way it became unfathomably hard to swim upstream, every stroke back toward the source seeming to hoist against the impossible drag and weight of centuries of our *olvido*, our forgetting.

　　It is late afternoon in a dwindling town, Cotulla, lost somewhere in the arid heaven of South Texas, crisscross of dusty streets and railroad tracks, a town plaza with gazebo, and a silent sunlit room where a desk by a window is laid out with ledgers, documents, codicils, rustling in a steady, gentle breeze. The old camera smells of liniment and oil, tilted on its wooden stand to photograph a genealogical chart. Tu Tío Lico (for I was with him, too) takes a bead with one eye, holds his breath, and brings the flash with a touch of his little finger.

The memories of Spain were left unspoken. Eventually, across generations, they were jettisoned altogether. But because they were Tejanos, because they were Españoles, because the Iberians had long habituated themselves to inscribing records of all their worldly exploits, there were documents to preserve the legacy of New Spain. They captured the resurrection flash, the super burst of radiation at the moment of transmogrification. These markings proved to be nearly indelible.

How much of the story are you willing or ready to carry, and to what end?

In the Plano de la Poblacíon map of San Antonio de la Villa de San Fernando, drawn up in 1794 by visiting cartographers from España, the village is imagined by its founders as a perfect square of five planned blocks and streets, arranged around the church and the courthouse. The aporcionamientos of each of the founding families are designated by name.

Uncle Lico became a realtor in the way that a Spanish hidalgo might've lorded over his properties. Every part of the land was part of his God-appointed patrimony, but he was willing to put it in the good keeping of others. For Lico, real estate and genealogy were inseparable.

My uncle Ludovico Lopez was born in 1922, in Cotulla, Texas, among the ruins of the onetime northernmost tierras of Nueva España. He was the youngest of my mother's brothers, after Leo and Lauro, and just younger than my aunt Lydia. It was his idea that there was a Lopez-Vela tale to tell in the first place. His siblings would've been content to pass on the forgetting that was their inheritance.

Of course, Uncle Lico would have liked to tell the tale himself, rather than hear it in the diffracted voice of his nephew emissary. He would certainly have imagined it as a wondrous noble, if rough-hewn, epic, a transliteration of the *Poema del Mio Cid* into the broken-down and unlovely South Texas dust of our origins.

Every family has a forgotten tale of where it came from, an invisible genealogy imprinted forever in fiery molecules inside the heart. But who is driven to tell it and why? Why not forget and move on? Why not go with the onward, unburdened by the vexations and mysteries of retrospection? If there were anything worth remembering, surely it would have been, passed on from life to life, unbroken through time.

Everything else we just as well left behind. Why get into all of that again?

Uncle Lico never spoke of what drove him.

No Herodotus of Tejano antiquity, Lico finished high school in San Antonio before joining the army for World War II. Later, he'd say he had attained the "caballero's degree." Uncles Leo and Lauro also served in the military, stationed in Asia and Europe respectively. Though Grandmother organized several emotional farewell parties for him, Lico never left San Antonio. After the war, he became, along with his brother Lauro, a businessman—an occasional realtor, a landlord of numerous properties, including a few nightclubs of dubious worth and reputation, and toward the end of his life he opened what he called "a fancy junk shop" named Woody's, and became a member of the San Antonio Board of Tax Assessors.

From whence *his* calling to discover and pass on the old tale of the familia? How far back in his life? As long as I can remember, it was his obsession.

All of the relations of Cenote Siete share this vision, sabes? Your tío was an exemplary sentinel of the sangre—the story might've been lost entirely were it not for him.

Undoubtedly, but I could never tell the tale in the way he might have. Still, once I was older, every few months he would send another manila binder folio containing holographs of the latest family document he had uncovered.

From the time I began writing poems and stories as a teenager, Uncle Lico chose me as the repository for his gleanings from the lost annals that included references to our otherwise erased ancestors—

the remorseless and unflinching progeny of Iberia from the lands of the Mundo Nuevo that were christened Nuevo Santander, and later Texas. But none of his documents corresponded to anything I had ever been able to find in the historical records of the region.

Like a hierarchy of angelic beings, Lico's genealogies seemed to float sublimely in their own universe of lineages and relations, unencumbered by the burdens of our fallen, sublunary world.

6. Of Spain's remnants among the Tejanos

Spaniards are not known for modesty or self-deprecating humor. A book of Spanish history published in Madrid in the 1850s propounded the belief that "the first male Spaniard was logically Adam . . . the first female Spaniard was named Eve." Later, Miguel de Unamuno would observe, "Me duele España"—Spain pains me, like a wound that never heals.

For Tejanos, to claim to be Spanish might be a cunning dodge from being considered Mexican. Among many of the Mexicanos of South Texas who confessed Spanish ancestry, there was a distinct air of superiority, mixed with a peculiar ennui, accumulated over generations, a wise weariness which comes from having seen it all. For more than two hundred years, a series of empires and states had washed over and inundated them, each one successively, inevitably receding, like so many tides of pale green gulf brine.

And they had finally all come and gone, hadn't they? The plumed vice-roys with their bands of criollo and mestizo soldiers, the feroz Mexican generals and their cruel military governors, and finally the greedy Anglos, latecomers who wanted the lands all for themselves, regardless of whatever had transpired there before. They took the Rio Nueces and still wanted the Rio Grande.

Heritage in Spain was meant to connote a proud family tradition with coats of arms painted in an unknown and distant land, a forgotten cargo of nobility and distinction as seen in old movies and novelas, a rooting in the august tradition of ancient Europe, albeit long ago forgotten by the ancestors. Who wanted to admit to coming out of the broken-down history of Mexico with all of its ruins, its genesis in conquest and plunder, the ensuing somnambulist trudge through time, a great pageant of half-Indios, half *quién-sabe-qué*, who preferred not to remember where they came from?

Other Mexicanos would often defer to those with Hispano origins, and even the gringos acted differently if they thought you were "Spanish."

Rather than powdered gentry, most of those ancestors who first came to the lands of Nuevo Santander and farther north were the renegades aiming to leave civilization behind, border-dwellers staking their claim at the farthest edge of the known world of their day. They did not begin as patricians.

We are descendants of these Spanish sojourners, interlopers between worlds, the old insurrection of any who ever walked away from their dear homelands in Iberia to create a new world out of what they believed to be God-given virgin earth.

Memories of Spain grew dimmer with every day's trek deeper into the formidable landscapes of the north. First it was Cerralvo, 1626, then Monterrey, 1637, towns in the high Mexican desert sierra from which to survey the horizons of terra incognita all around.

And lo, beyond the Sierra Huasteca, beyond the cordillera of the Sierra Madre Oriental they discovered a new Fertile Crescent (so they called it) of rich, arable pastureland, straddling the great river, reaching north along the coast of the Gulf of Mexico for hundreds of miles. That became Nuevo Santander.

For many years, the tierras to the north, storied lands of Aztlán, the birthplace of the Azteca ancestors, were as distant as Mars, postponed for exploitation at least until central Mexico's splendors could be fully conquered, overtaken, and metabolized for the Spanish Crown. The lands of el Norte that would become our homelands were largely an arid, desert expanse, barren of pyramids, Indian cities, thick veins of coveted silver ore. It was to the north that the Españoles remanded their conspirators, the Tlaxcalteca Indios who had joined in their battles against the mighty Mexica of Tenochtitlán. Jews, Gnostic heretics, and others who were targets of the Holy Inquisition also sought out the remote security of the hinterlands of the great Norte.

But two hundred years after La Conquista, the age was beginning when the lures of the north became harder to ignore. By the 1730s, the viceroy of Nuevo Santander, based in Monterrey, gave his support to frontera scribes and bureaucrats in his council who were urging the northward expansion of Nueva España. They sent missives to the king and his Council of the Indies, beseeching blessings and inducements to extend the reach of Spain's divine mission into the vast territories of the unbelievers.

In a 1720 letter from Don Narciso Barquito Monte-Cuesta to the Conde de Montijo, a close advisor to King Charles V of Spain, Monte-Cuesta speaks of his five years of service, inspecting, reducing, and congregating those barbarians of the uncultured lands, *indios infieles en las Fronteras de Santiago de las Valles del Reyno de la Nueva España.*

"So boundless are the pagan lands I have traversed that they will not easily be subdued in the empire's service," wrote Don Narciso, "and we lack the knowledge and the means that would be required to acquire and cultivate this Nuevo Dominio," ending his case with an entreaty for the conde's support in persuading the king of the value of this great new mission that would deliver a host of new souls to the mother church and inestimably increase the opulence of the empire.

Though some short-lived and ill-fated exploratory expeditions had been taking place since the late sixteenth century, the Conde de Montijo endorsed Don Narciso's petition, and sent the letter on to be read to the king.

The settlement of Nueva España's hinterlands would soon be under way.

7. De los Santos y de los Lopez

I grew up in the heart of the Santos and Garcia families, the subject of an earlier tale, an intimate and boisterous tribe of Norteños who held close together in South Texas for nearly a century, escaping the chaos of the Mexican Revolution of 1910. Their bond, a haunted compromiso against the anarchy that had been unleashed around them in Mexico, remained sacred in San Antonio, continuing to gather us together for feasts, masses, weddings, *tamaladas*, dances, and funerals.

Uncles Beto, Richard, and Raul were dashing tricksters who saw practical jokes as integral to their unique code of honor. Our aunts watched over us like tribal mothers, attentive and nurturing as they fried chicken flautas, but able to lay down the law with as little as a passing glance of discontent.

Visiting one of the Santos aunts and uncles' homes was usually an adventure. It might include a trip to Uncle Richard's workshop where a wood lathe was spinning at the speed of light, seeming to hold a chair leg perfectly still as the machine whirred. Hard pears had to be picked, using a long mechanical picking arm of my uncle's devising. Uncle Beto created an entire miniature world in wood and ceramic dioramas built into his backyard garden grotto. With my cousin Eddie, we'd explore the sinkholes and cliffs of the woods on the outskirts of the city, while my dad and Uncle Roger drank beer and talked on Roger's back patio.

Visiting the Lopez was usually a more serious affair. There was an unmistakable world-weariness among the Lopez-Velas of my mother's family, a subtle sense of having lived through it all that seemed less a mood, rather something cured into their very bones, finding eccentric expressions in each of the surviving children of our grandparents, Leonides and Leandra. But this wasn't a universal trait.

There were other Lopez descended from cousins of my grandfather who were entirely different, almost childlike in the way they saw the world, unencumbered by an intuition of the *terribilitá* of life itself. Perhaps the gravitas came from the Vela side. But going back to my grandfather Leonides, many of us carry perpetually darkened bags under our eyes, tending to give the whole lineage detached and melancholic miens.

Yet when these two poles of the Lopez family gathered, the circle seemed to be complete, as if over time the family had found a way to guarantee itself an equilibrium of melancholy and consolation.

Beyond the Lopez, this world-weariness was a South Texas type. You could tell just by looking at them. Not *pobres de tiro*, they were people of a certain quality, *de una distinta calidad*, and it usually turned out that they were mostly descended from old Español families or Mexican *metropolitanos* from cities such as Monterrey, Querétaro, and la Capitál. In the 1940s and the 1950s, it was not a class issue, since everybody was poor or struggling along, but there was an indelible mark of their past detectable in the dignified manner with which they conducted themselves in the world, among their Mexican familiares and among the Anglos.

Los caballeros were always impeccably dressed. Dr. Ramiro Estrada, obstetrician and lawyer, the doctor who had delivered us, the three niños monstruosos Santos, played Chopin and Strauss on his violin, dressed in a black smoking jacket and a burgundy silk ascot. San Antonio's modern Mexican ladies dressed like Lana Turner or Katharine Hepburn, with vaulting coiffures and hair brooches that recalled Goya's majas or the princesas of Velasquez.

Mother and her girlfriends were part of a milieu of young ladies who had formed a network of social clubs with names like *las Golondrinas* and *las Leticias*, and on weekends they would gather at her home for slumber parties that were often interrupted when hopeful lads would appear on the sidewalk outside on Blanco Road to offer occasionally tuneful serenatas. Grandmother would nudge the young women out of the window to survey the singing aspirants in front of the house.

Uncle Lico fancied himself in the ilk of a new urbane Latin noir slick, a modern American imbued with all the elegance and nobility of the Spanish tradition in his old bloodlines. So what if that lofty, heroic heritage had been bleached out of us under the Texas sun and after a couple of centuries in the Mundo Nuevo?

In the last half of the twentieth century, his chivalric manner translated into a persona that was a Norteño amalgam of Hernán Cortés and George Raft. In the mirror, he was the unknown Hispanic member of the Vegas "Rat Pack." Like Frank Sinatra and

Sammy Davis Jr., he called men "cats," and women were always "gals." And as a nightclub owner, his sartorial swagger came with perfect pitch.

Lico would lean back into the leather sofa seat of his big Lincoln Continental, driving slowly, squinting through tinted green tortoiseshell glasses, his aqua-colored porkpie hat cocked to one side, and exclaim as another car rushed past, "That cat must have a roast in the oven!"

Uncle Lico's ultimate exemplar, the subject of a biography he hoped to write, was Gus Garcia, the first Mexican American attorney to argue a case before the Supreme Court. He had amassed his own files of notes and clippings related to "GG," as my uncle called him.

Garcia, he said, looked like a Mexican William Holden, "with goddamned green eyes, and dressed in expensive suits like a Kennedy" he would say. Like any true hero, Garcia had lived a complex life, winning a case before the Supreme Court, and died tragically, allegedly drunk under a bench in San Antonio's downtown mercado.

If he wanted to be derogatory, Uncle Lico would call a man a "bird," as he did once, pointing across the room at another old Mexican man wearing a grey porkpie in a buffet line at a wedding reception we were at.

"That bird was asking around about "GG," *quién sabe por qué.* JP, ninety percent of these inquiries are not worthwhile. A bird always wants this or that, using you, you know. They want a turnkey job, just like that, like I'm gonna give him the GG story just because he's a nosy bird? He insults me, like I'm not capable of telling what's up."

The old man turned and flashed my uncle a kindly smile, raising his plastic wineglass.

"See what I mean? ¡Sin vergüenza!"

The Lopez had long been involved in politics, going back to the time of Cotulla, where my Grandfather Leonides was as much of a city father as a Mexicano could be in those times. Along with his brothers, Leonides was a Mexican Mason, a part of the order of the Woodmen of the World.

He had the only phone in the Mexican part of town, and a large flatbed truck for delivering the grocery and dry goods that Grandfather loaned to other Mexicans for their weddings and funerals. When he died suddenly, even the Anglo politicians and businessmen came to pay Leonides respect at his funeral. The procession was said to have filled the streets of Cotulla.

Mother is a retired education executive, and a lifelong committed Democrat, mainly because it was the only party that had welcomed and championed the causes of Mexicans. She says she first got her interest in politics from her Anglo uncle Frank Ferguson, during the times she stayed with Aunt Fermina and him in San Antonio to attend public school.

Ferguson and Tía Fermina had married when matrimony between a Mexicana and an Anglo was still taboo, though the stigma was lessened by the fact that my tía was an albino and hence an inevident Mexicana, as fluent in studied English as she was in Spanish.

"Over dinner, he'd be talking about political things and he'd always ask me for my opinion," my mother remembers. "He was Anglo, you know, but he always wanted to hear what I wanted to say even though I was a little girl."

As a successful owner of a grocery store, her father, Leonides, never ran for office in Cotulla, but Mother remembers how he proudly showed her around the new red stone courthouse when it was completed, as if it were something he had personally accomplished. They climbed the stairs to the third floor, where the gate opened to reveal a corridor of freshly painted jail cells, waiting for their inaugural inhabitants.

After having been among the earliest founders of settlements in the region, Mexicans didn't much get involved in South Texas politics in those days. That began to change in the 1950s, when Henry B. Gonzalez, the son of a Spanish-language newspaper publisher in San Antonio, was elected to the city council and state legislature there, and was later elected to eighteen consecutive terms in the U.S. Congress.

After a stint editing a Mexican society newspaper in San Antonio, *La Revista Social*, Uncle Lauro ran for city council, my only relative so far to seek elective office. He managed to win the Democratic Party's nomination for his district, but lost in the general election.

"He was very good, he knew lots of people and everybody thought he had a chance," my mother recalls.

"But then, for some reason known only to him, he decided to give his campaign speeches partly in German, maybe to show off to the Anglos that he was trilingual. He learned it when he was in the OSS during the war. Anyway, most of the people who came to his meetings didn't speak German. So it was a disaster."

Were my Spanish ancestors the outliers, border-crossers, Gnostic insurrectionaries, Jewish converts, who could forsake a world to forge a new one? That stays in the blood.

These ancestors conjured a homeland for themselves out of the unknown tierras del Norte de Nueva España. That stays in the blood too.

8. Del misterio de la letra "L" entre los Lopez

In the first place, admittedly, inexplicably, literally, there was always something about the letter L. Maybe it was thus from the beginning, L for Lopez? L-l-l-l-l-l-opez as a way of being in the world, the letter throne, an open hand taking Pythagorean measure, sentinel signature of a rooted and upright lineage in the ageless dominions of old world and new.

L was for Leocadio and Lugarde. Leonardo y Luciano were there also, as the genealogical annals testify, even among some who were Lopez y Lopez, culminating with my grandfather Leonides's family in the explosion of the Lopez affinity for L, universal streams converging, as my abuelo Leonides first married Leandra Vela, and they were to have six children of L:

Leo, Lily (who, *lamentablemente*, died as a child), Lauro, Lydia, Ludovico, and my mother, born Lucille Lopez. On Lincoln Street. In Laredo.

Among Mexicanos de Mexico, one carries the names of all of your lineages, not just that of the father. In Mexico, I am Santos de Lopez or just Santos Lopez. Though it's not immediately evident,

I carry the lurking Lopez insignia nonetheless; in my case it was encrypted from my inception, a secret inscription left embedded in the letters of my secret royal middle name.

"Why do you think I put those Ls right in the middle of your name?" my mother asked me not too long ago, laughing, as I drove us on a road through Texas hill country, the late afternoon wild-flowers all ablaze.

"That double L in the middle of Phillip—they're my initials! L-L—Lucille Lopez!"

Since my childhood, Mother had maintained tireless vigilance over the spelling of my middle name in school documents and report cards, followed later by eagle-eyed scans of anything in print with my signature or otherwise occasioning the spelling out of the two Ls in the middle of Phillip. I don't remember her ever notic-ing when John was spelled without an H, but no Philip missing an L was allowed to pass her scimitar eye.

Yet that only brings us to the doorstep of the ultimate query that haunts our lineage: Why the L, anyway? It is the question, churn-ing like a primeval galaxy, at the center of my name.

We were the inevitable children of an impossible history, indestructi-ble inheritors of an ancient enigma we carried with us in a golden tab-ernacle over the vast grey sea barrens into las tierras nuevas, verdadero mundo nuevo. Crossing the golden sand plains of the land we first dubbed Galiciana, stubbled with purple ceniza, we found rivers that glistened like vias de estrellas. Once the old enigmas took root in the new lands, en Coa-huila, en Tejas, en el valle de San Fernando, the ancestors would never see Madre España again.

That was the age of the Gigantescos, when warrior nomads wandered the boundless terra incognita of primeval Tejas. That was the age of the conde whose coming had been prophesied.

Do not ask for that tale to be told again, do not beseech the singer to fili-gree and strum through all the cascading refrains . . . Que me duele Tejas.

We will prepare now to read the annals of our blood.

Still, whenever I sat at my desk over Central Park, I looked out and saw the Llanos Mesteños of Nuevo Santander, the hilly coastal plains of South Texas. In the first bite of frigid weather, I was writing about the scorching sun endured by my antepasados, the sun that made the highway seem to shimmer like a silver flag that had slipped through time, linking me to a distant age, reminding me of an unfulfilled compromiso.

Nothing would move the tale of the Lopez forward without this old story being told. I felt more and more separated from the life in television journalism I had built in Manhattan; I was quietly suspecting my time there was nearly done.

9. From dreams: an encuentro in a hill country villa

I had left the road that I was on, finding myself in an unknown, yet still familiar countryside. It looked like South Texas, the sun shining brightly on a landscape of burnt grass hills, scattered with thorny mesquite trees, shaded sparsely in pale green foliage. I walked onto a winding, oak-shaded driveway of sandy gravel, marking my way so that I could return later, past the scarlet-flowering cactus, past the ruined stone fountain with a fallen Saint Francis covered in dry moss. The cicadas hummed a sweeter song than I had ever heard them sing, casting their fragile tenor din in all directions.

Hearing each step crunching through the gravel underfoot, I recalled the grounds of an old hill country villa my brothers and cousin and I had discovered by chance near our home in San Antonio's northwest outskirts, when we were growing up and exploring the woods that lay nearby us at the city's edge. Those grounds, which sat on a hilltop looking out over the city, were planted with wisteria and orchards of hard pear trees, spread out among stone ponds and patios left in the shade of small oak arbors.

The abandoned white Mission-style mansion we found there looked as if it had outlasted some forgotten ordeal in an earlier century. The huge front doors had long ago been stolen, windows left broken, and much of the red clay tile roof had fallen in on the house, leaving the empty upstairs rooms exposed to birds, squirrels, insects, and the silvery dome of the iridescent Texas sky.

Following that winding gravel road for a while longer, I finally came around a bend where a large oak tree stood before a beautiful antique villa, this one in good repair, and the front door was slightly ajar. There were no cars about, and no signs of anyone around the grounds. The architecture was in a Spanish colonial style, decorated in colorful Poblano tiles, decked with royal blues, mustard yellow and magenta flowers.

"Hello!" I shouted.

"Hello, buenas tardes," I repeated, walking through the open door into a hallway that led out to a spacious courtyard garden of bougainvillea, honeysuckle, and white oleander encircling a large, tranquil blue pool that looked inviting in the golden heat of a late afternoon.

As I walked through a door that opened onto the courtyard, I entered a room full of people, who, though strangers, seemed familiar to me. There were the Mexican Americans of my parents' and grandparents' generations, distinguished, noble in their posture, the well-dressed men in pressed shirts and suits, the ladies in simple, dignified dresses and elegant shoes.

They were milling about talking among themselves, sipping from tiny cups of chocolate, tea, and coffee that some had perilously perched on their knees. On tables covered in lace manteles, there were trays of pan dulce, leche quemada candies, and tiny marzipan fruits. The room smelled of cinnamon, pomade, and Old Spice men's cologne.

It occurred to me that I had come to a place of my ancestors, a villa located somewhere in eternity. One lady who looked like my great-aunt Pepa welcomed me with a warm smile and an abrazo, and when she announced me to the rest of the gathered folks, they nodded and ahhed and gently applauded. An old man in a slightly tattered brown wool suit stood up and spoke about the nobility of book learning and how we must always remember the ancestors. One of the little old ladies placed a tray before me that was arranged with stuffed chiles, cheeses, and small florecitos of pickled cactus with agarita chile salsa.

And just as I was feeling as if this were a place where I might dwell forever, the lady who looked like my aunt Pepa rang a tiny silver bell and everyone grew quiet. She reminded me of how I must be setting out, and that I should leave before it grew dark.

"Where am I going?" I remember thinking to myself.

"El tiempo está bien corto."

As she spoke these words, "time is short," her voice changed in tone, from her old lady's timbre to another familiar voice. I heard those words repeat, *"El tiempo está bien corto,"* their sonorous machinic hum giving me a start.

10. A voyage to the Gran Archivo de las Indias

Sevilla seems a city perpetually awakening from a slumber of centuries, only to find its celebrated ancient decorated environs in a bit of ruin. Sinewy gargoyles overhanging the sidewalks have withered to weasel skeletons, fractal honeycombs of Moorish arches have gone blurry, their onetime crystalline edges left decayed and worn rough by the sun, wind, and rain in the long count of Andalusian time. Wrestling winged cupids in stone friezes on the Ayuntamiento grasp at phantom limbs, two diminutive hands around a neck, a perfect marble smile left whole from a missing face.

I arrived late one night after numerous delayed flights to find streets teeming, Sevillanos crowded along the barras of numberless taperías, eating from their platillos in the midst of booming, spirited conversation. Along the dark and narrow callejones in mid-February, the trees were full of ripe, spicy oranges, dropping their swollen fruits to the streets at midnight with a thud.

After a fifteen-year spell since my last visit to Spain for the Arrupe documentary, I had come there after a sudden decision on an admittedly unlikely search for distant echoes of my family's history in Nuevo Santander, that place lost in time from the genesis days of Nueva España that would eventually become the Lopez-Vela homelands in north Mexico and South Texas.

I arrived unannounced, unheralded, an inconspicuous and infrequent pilgrim, in search of I knew not what.

I suspected few, if any, records of this hinterland of the far northern tierras fronterizas would have survived or been valued enough to be vouchsafed and preserved for later regard. I was never taught to believe that anything of importance had taken place in the hot river plains of southeast Texas where the Lopez and Velas first walked out of the fog of our remote Iberian past, in such humble colonial settlements as Villa Camargo, Ciudad Mier, and Guerrero.

These were towns that had the *desgraciado* destiny to be born among the last ill-starred campaigns of a doomed colonial empire, only to be left behind when that Imperio collapsed in 1821.

While such places had been among the last outposts of the once magnificently radiant authority and beneficence of the Spanish Crown in infidel territory, the settlers were abruptly abandoned to their lonely watches over the hardscrabble lands and the often unwelcoming *indígenas*. Over the centuries the towns were forgotten, overtaken by ghosts or literally flooded over by the waters of the Rio Grande; only few of the *familias fundadoras* remained behind, as most went south to Monterrey, north to bigger towns in South Texas, or to the already bustling Americano cities of Brownsville, Laredo, Corpus Christi, San Antonio, or Houston.

Ours was a new world history that had taken place outside the glow of the resplendently false imperial sagas that contained the story of how Spain conquered and colonized Mexico. What few records and testimonies that remained were spread out among collections of county governments, small libraries, and churches of South Texas and the state of Tamaulipas, Mexico.

So why return to Sevilla after so long, with the past so well forgotten?

Desde quién sabe cuando, todo el mundo Iberiano pasó por Sevilla.

Everyone passed through Sevilla.

Sevilla had been built in the bend of the river where the Río Guadalquivir became navigable for the broader, deeper-floating ocean-going barques. From its origins under Moorish rule, it had been a crossroads of Mediterranean and African mariners, trading the bounty of all of their destinations in their portolani maps of the ancient oikumene. At the beginning of the sixteenth century, Sevilla became the main port of all that Iberian setting out into the unfathomable New World, the shining, peerless city on the river to the Mundo Nuevo.

That was the home, or perhaps the final embrace of home, for *los pioneros*, the unknown ancestors of so many of us who set out on the Guadalquivir to Cadiz, and then into the open, grey vastness of the Atlántico in search of their fortune in *Nueva España*. Books about that world were initially suppressed, but word of mouth was everywhere.

I had always thought of our Hispano ancestors in Texas being of the most sedentary, conservative, and traditional swath of society. In truth, we were the descendants of adventurers, brigands, and wanderers who would eventually leave behind any tethers to the world that had been their birthright and home. If all else had failed, there was always the New World where there was a chance to start everything anew.

What could have moved them to leave their known world behind? Was it the lure of things imagined, or an escape from an insufferable life? They weren't going to the land of promise and opportunity. They might have feared monsters and godless *salvajes*, but there was also the siren song dream of impossible abundance, as if one could be returned to the splendors of the original garden: limitless land, animals, crops—and slaves.

Did they also imagine the women of the Mundo Nuevo? Did the great mestizaje already begin with fantasies in the hearts of conquistadores and settlers boarding their ships in Sevilla?

All across the modern city, old Sevilla monuments and buildings were being meticulously restored; the cobblestone streets dug up like mosaics and relaid with fresh sand mortar, sooty Mujehdar arch façades being sandblasted until they shone pearlescent in the ochre dusk light. And spread along the walls through the callejones of Sevilla, there is a constellation of ornate painted tile portrait shrines to the host of virgins who are the spiritual patronas of the city, Nuestra Señora de Sol, Nuestra Señora de la Macarena.

From each flowered shrine, these Virgenes, seemingly infinite in their panoply of incarnations, look upon passersby with a jarring, unexpected anxiety and nervousness—a hint of the silent hysteria or muted desperation of old movie goddesses, and unlike the embracing presence of Mexico's Virgen de Guadalupe or the shrill grief of La Llorona. The mood of Sevilla's Virgenes is one of melancholic disbelief in the wake of calamity.

What has it come to? How will we be consoled? How will we be found and redeemed?

In the great life-size "Madretazo" sculpture of La Macarena, her hands are as poised as mudras, outstretching forward uncertainly, but without fear.

Characteristically mortified, yet reassuring.

Yes, we suffer. But we will persevere.

In search of echoes, I had come to Sevilla suddenly, without much planning, during a longer stay in the Northern European climes of Berlin and Copenhagen. But as luck would have it, my sole destination on this trip, the legendary Archivo de Indias, the repository of the documentary legacy of the New World, was under repair. Well after midnight, full of anticipation for digging into the archive's collection the next day, I had decided to walk past the building so I'd know where it was first thing in the morning.

As I approached the grand limestone cenotaph-like structure across the Plaza Triunfo next to the great cathedral, I noticed there was a perimeter fence of corrugated iron, tipped with barbed wire. A shining robot-like backhoe hung improbably from a crane next to a stone plaque engraved with Columbus's signature, commemorating the creation of the library in 1498. Craning to look over the barricade, you could see a row of majestic palm trees ringing the Archivo, but the glass of French doors on one of the second-floor terraces was missing, a rabble of building materials visible inside in stacks against the brick walls.

A large sign listing all of the Sevillean and Andalucian politicos and dignitaries who had made the restoration project possible announced that the work, having just gotten under way, would last thirty months. There had been no notice of the closure on the Archivo's website, which I had perused briefly the day before leaving Copenhagen.

In addition to the inauspicious omen, I would be stranded in Sevilla for a week, a fruitless journey in my always faltering search for the lost ancestors of my family's Iberian past.

But in ample pearly moonlight of the Sevilla night, a small sign, handwritten in ballpoint pen, was taped to one post of the great building project sign.

It said: "For technical inquiries, por favor pregunta en numero 5, Calle Santo Tomas." What could be more technical than searching out and retrieving the lost records of a forgotten world?

IV

El Canto de Cenote Siete
(Con un autor anónimo)

First Legajo

The Arrival of Cenote Siete.

The works and days of the man who called himself Cenote Siete remain a mystery—as he was himself an enigma. His real name was alleged by his confrere to be Macedonio Tomás Mas Aguas de Vela y Lopez, de la casa del Tlacuilo de Tezcatlipoca. But from the time he was discovered, accompanied by his two chihuahuas, Bazúl and Choilita, carrying only a small valise stuffed with papers and writing implements, wandering on foot near the *Sal del Rey* salt flats by the coast, his long face painted with a single black stripe across his nose and cheeks and wearing a rude cloak decked with tiny mirrors, he would answer only to "Cenote Siete."

His taciturn friend and helper, who was known only as Caracól, followed on foot not far behind, pulling a cart stacked with clothing, held down by a shovel, axe, and an old conquistador's helmet.

In a time of great calamities such as ours, the comings and goings of mysterious people are hardly noticed. It is not uncommon that we discover disoriented souls walking about the land, and there were once many more wanderers from the north heading south for warmer climes.

He came to live with the rest of us in the Villa de Revilla, perhaps twenty years after the *Guerra Última*, joining the many who had found their own way to the refuge by the river. He said to the delegation that he was searching for "Teopanzolco," "the place of the old temple," as he translated it. When he was told that those who found him were from the settlement of Revilla, his mood then became greatly agitated, nearly ecstatic, falling to his knees and swaying his arms wildly from one side to the other stirring up the dust into a cloud around him.

"Ancient Revilla!" he shouted. "Revilla Antigua, por fin!"

"Revilla, also known as Revillagigedo in honor of the viceroy, which became Guerrero, and Guerrero Viejo, once it went under the waters for hundreds of years. Does it really live again?" As he was brought to the village in a cart, he kept repeating these words. "Does it really live again?"

To some, he said that he had been born near a spring called La Milagrosa de Freeman in the *balcones* of Tejas, where the land climbs up from river valleys to rocky canyons and gorges. Others he told that he had been born in Aksum, in old Ethiopia, or a place called Mohenjodaro in hoary India, still others he told that he had been born and left behind by his parents in the forest of Tunguska in Siberia. When he was asked where he had been since the time of the conflagration, he laughed.

"I have been not much in this body," he replied, laughing to himself. "I apologize for its sorrowful condition."

I write this now and gather these materials relating to Cenote Siete, as if it meant something to do so, on this day, regarding these cardinal matters. Some are in his own hand, attested to by Caracól—others are of anonymous origin. They were all discovered among his effects.

Your servant, Lucas Guerra, of Revilla Nueva.

By an anonymous author.

It was in the early time of La Zona Perfecta, late in the days of men, that there was a knight who came from the lands north of the ruins of the resurrected Revillagigedo, on the banks of great Arroyo Bravo, at the southern edge of the ochre sands of the great Tejas desert. It was in that time he came to live in that the pueblo once known as Guerrero Viejo, formerly Guerrero, and before that Revillagigedo, and earlier simply Revilla, was named once again as Revilla Nueva—forevermore.

He was of the old Orden de los Cien Recordadores, the Order of the One Hundred Rememberers, *de una famila muy antigua*, descended from a myriad of the aged lineages across many centuries in that part of the world of the Fifth Sun. His true name was Lázaro Nepomuceno Albino Bautista Perez Treviño Chapa y Mireles de López—but most knew him as he called himself, Cenote Siete.

It was said that the Orden de los Cien Recordadores was created during the time of the great Olvidazo, when all memory of anything that had ever transpired, been spoken, written, recorded, imagined, or forgotten was taken up into the skies of La Zona Perfecta, and was then erased forever. The Orden de los Cien Recordadores, if it ever truly existed, was said to be dedicated to the mission of secreting out the lost memories of their onetime homeland, though it must be noted that there was never another known Knight Recordador, save this same Hidalgo Cenote Siete.

In these legajos are collected some of his surviving chronicles and tales, along with fragments of an incomplete biography, all discovered among the materials he left behind in his quarters in Revilla Nueva.

Preludio de Cenote Siete, Un Hidalgo de La Zona Perfecta

Why cherish the memories that have lost all their rememberers?

Que hicimos con las memorias sin recordadores?

We chose not to see the omens of the approaching delugio of memory without a rememberer; the Diasporas of ancestors beyond count, traversing the world again like zombies, their ghostly bodies annealed from tesserae of primeval fog. Who could have recognized the dead when they began to appear among us, as inexplicable and common as bluebonnets in the early spring?

They had been as undetectable as the light of remotest stars, invisible in the nighttime as well as the day. Unknown to us, they had remained suspended in the air, dormant but implicit, inolvidables, able to recur infinitely, the way snow's perfect crystal lattices will emerge unexpectedly out of the chill of the void, always the same, always different. This was the time of the great setting aside of our history, when everything and everyone began to dwell in eternity.

Hidden away in an ancient house hewn from Texas limestone, I said to my own father, "Are we alive or dead?" and he did not reply.

"How much of our memory will linger on," I asked him further, "en posse, in this same ageless stillness, how much left ever unremembered until everything is erased in the gargantuan winds of a dying star, ours or some other?"

And he did not answer.

How does that which remains unremembered continue to touch us?

There were many stories that survived about the people of mis tierras in what was known as Texas of the United States, and north Mexico, lugares mas antiguas del Mundo Nuevo, southwest reaches of the onetime American empire, wild northern hinterlands of short-lived Nuevo Santander, nuestras queridas tierras bárbaras, from beloved Revilla onward, snaking through the dry arroyos of Coahuila and Nuevo León, east to Ciudad Mier on the glistening Alcántara, across the Río Bravo, north to the spring-cooled environs of San Antonio de Valero.

Beginning the story somewhere in Spain and Turtle Island, we walked out of the earliest centuries of América, someone said 1580, 1645, 1736, 1818, or 1914, 2000, or 2012, 2525, and well beyond, into my time, the time of La Zona Perfecta, always carrying our homes with us, always farther on into the great ocean of the now.

The nations that came and went were as fantasmál as aurora borealis.

We were of the Tejanos and the Mexicanos, of those oldest peregrinos of time, Indio como Español, and all their mestizo offspring, the ill-starred children of the Mundo Nuevo.

We were born of centuries of the dispossessing invader—Iberian fellaheen, Sephardic refugees, Gnostics and pirates, frontera scribes, Chichimecas, conquistadores and pobladores. We were born as people of caliche, sand, obsidian, and mesquite. Clear streams of the Sabinas and Nueces, Medina and Guadalupe still refreshed us, in a time when the world was slowly being webbed with shimmering chrome—though we did not notice it happening at first. We were unaware as our veins began to run colder, when the mercury vapors first permeated our skin, gradually filtering into our ancient blood.

That was in the época of impeccable suits, the savage pinstripes in wide-collar pantalones over black silk shirts; the sharply pressed drapes that revealed pointy black wingtips with their transfixing obsidian shine. The coiffures rose like royal crowns among the majas, glowing in their satin dresses and fur shawls. Their great Chevrolets were girded with chrome, glistening in the limpid Béjareño moonlight. Perhaps they had carried their stories so long it seemed possible they were immortal—where we came from, what it was our ancestors were seeking, any news we might have brought out of the abyss of the past.

Gradually, though, we all forgot the precession of the stars and the declensions of the clouds. The algorithms within the engines of creation continued to map their perfect quantum measures onto the very grain of the void's ether, palimpsests of countless hieroglyphs on a grain of sand. That was when all of our compasses turned to ash, the time of the great setting aside, the tarde de luz, an afternoon that augured the beginning of the Zona Perfecta. Our bodies were fabricated anew of galvanized flesh and cobalt-colored light, making our bones conductors of the universal tones of knowledge and forgetting.

If we had an origin, did we also have a destination?

If you want to see the center of the universe, don't orbit anything.

If you want to leave something that could last for eons, then write not in pen and ink, but in planets and stars, and read the sky like a book.

We abandoned our count of days, forgot to calibrate the declining angle of the sun's path in the sky until it came to cast our shadows stretched out in long, thin lines across miles of Nuevo Santander's parched desert floor, into the flat riverine plains of Texas.

We forgot where we were in time, where we'd set out from, where we were going. Our families hid away their sacred histories of this jettisoned past in the molecules of our breath, harboring cryptic messages from the ineffable.

And not a word was spoken of it.

It was in these times that the story seemed it might never come to light again, when the last of the archives would be burned once and for all, our greatest monuments felled, our treasured sanctuaries desecrated, all the gods and sacred relics, maps, and parchments consumed in oldest fire.

Let the coronetas and tambores now sound their doleful racket. Take on the old shimmering armor, girded in silver chain mail, braided with Mylar thread.

How much of our lost story could we reclaim? How much was forever lost in the long spool of oblivion? We could not know what was left to be remembered, salvaged out of the great drift streams of el olvido.

And we began to dream that the long-prophesied playback of our journey would never be complete.

A sus ordenes,
C7
Recordador de la Zona Perfecta, Orden de los Cien,
Planeta Perfecta,
de Revilla Nueva, en un Tiempo Indeterminado

The origins of this lost song (a note from JPS).

As I have reported, I began finding these documents, along with responses from Cenote Siete to writing I left on the screen overnight in my slumbering computers. Other times his unsolicited missives and considerable digressions on a host of matters relating to our shared histories might appear as I spent a morning at the window distractedly watching a red-tailed hawk in hunt, patiently drawing figure eights high over Central Park. Most of these texts purported to have come from Cenote himself. Other agents were apparently involved, as some narratives came from rapporteurs who claimed to know Cenote Siete; and an anonymous author, describing C7's memorial quest, wrote other chronicles. These were not always flattering, and of similarly unknown provenance.

Occasionally, files spontaneously downloaded themselves into my laptop from inserted CDs and DVDs. A treatise on the eighteenth-century birth of "El Niño Monstruoso" in Querétaro, Mexico, mysteriously decrypted when I played a used CD of *The Unutterable* by an English rock band, the Fall, a copy purchased in a Berlin flea market. A commemorative DVD edition of the sci-fi marionette action drama *Supercar* transmitted a catalogue of sunspot activity through the ages. A copy of *La Momia Azteca Contra el Robot Humano*, a Mexican film from 1957, my birth year, contained accounts of C7's viewings of film and video artifacts showing historical events through an apparatus he called his "Chronovisor."

A copy of *Starship Troopers* a friend had loaned me launched a time-coded 3-D animation of the global human diaspora—beginning in the primordial era of Pangaea—millions of years lapsing in an instant, green and ochre continents breaking and churning in massive slipstreams, the small paths of early man branching out first in tentative dendritic tendrils, then exploding inexplicably into an undulating, fluorescing purple and yellow orchid blossom, encompassing the planet.

This is the bounty of our inadvertency.

Afterward, these words kept appearing across the screen, scrolling in grey and fading away into a scarlet blur.

If I left a question, days might pass, but inevitably there would be an answer, a correction, a rejection, a gloss.

One afternoon, a frenetic blue parakeet with a dirty yellow face flew through the open terrace door into my New York apartment and landed on the dining room table. After staring across the room at me for several minutes, he eventually flew to my shoulder and then very slowly walked down and landed on the laptop, imprinting another trove of elaborate codicils into C7's emerging tale.

Could automatic writing happen subliminally, generated through unseen forces and currents, a loquacious Ouija board embedded deep within my computer's hard drive? I had recalled Yeats's "A Vision," Victor Hugo's *Conversations with Eternity*, and the American poet James Merrill's decade-long dialogue with the spirits, *The Changing Light at Sandover*—all important to me through the years, but always straining credulity.

I thought of what had happened to Christopher Smart when he began testifying to hearing voices in the streets of London, dictating the lightning-strike antiphonal poesy that became his Bedlam prayer, *Jubilate Agno.*

That's when I wrote in a laptop journal, "Cenote Siete is my literary creation."

Only to return to the desk early the next morning to find a short question left written on the screen that gave me a shiver:

I first joined you as a child, in a clinic where some of your blood was taken from your body. But what do you make of the long-forsook memory of a car crash, foretold? How is it that a memory can prepare and protect you?

When I was about nine or ten, I was suddenly seized with a hysterical fear that my parents, out for an evening, would be taken in a car crash, never to return again, leaving the three of us orphans, separated and sent off to live with our respective godparents. I would pace nervously to the window to look for them, then back to bed, only to repeat my watch ten minutes later. Nearing midnight, a faint brush of light across the ceiling might be the headlights of their car pulling into the driveway, so I'd rush to the window, only to see an empty driveway, glowing grey in the moonlight.

Eventually, my mother took me to see our trusted Dr. Estrada, and in a private conversation he listened to my account of my paralyzing dread. I remember only that he said death was as natural as waking or sleeping, but that we never know when it will come. In the meantime, we get on with our lives.

I vowed to never again let fear overtake me.

I imparted that premonition to you, so that your fears might be conquered, so that the irksome matter of mortality would not hinder you. Time is always short, but this should not paralyze you.

Three decades later, when my father was killed in an automobile accident, it was as if I had been immunized deep in my childhood past, partly fathoming my loss out of that forgotten time when fear had seemed able to consume me altogether.

I was reminded of a line from a song by the great mad Austin bard Roky Erikson:

"If you have ghosts, then you have everything."

It was then that Cenote Siete's story began to unfold in earnest.

Apologia de Cenote Siete.

Now I will tell how bodies became new bodies, how old lands became new lands.

We were of the inevitable children of an impossible history, indestructible inheritors of an ancient enigma we carried with us in a talavera tabernacle over the vast grey sea barrens into las tierras nuevas, el verdadero mundo nuevo. Crossing the golden sand plains of the land we first dubbed Galiciana, stubbled with purple ceniza, we found rivers that glistened like vias de estrellas. Once our enigmas took root in the new lands, en Coahuila, en Tejas, en el valle del Río Bravo, we would never see Madre España again.

That was the age of the Gigantescos, when warrior nomads wandered the boundless unknown lands of primeval Texas.

Do not ask for that tale to be told again, do not beseech the singer to filigree and strum through all the cascading refrains.

For I am of the seventh strand of the Cenotes, named for the sweet water desert oasis, the hidden jungle spring. For I am of that line that has sought and offered succor, tras los milenios. For it is said this is the dual compromiso of our lineage, to relieve thirst and to offer sacrifice. For the seventh well of ancient Judea was the well of Abraham, the other in Mecca was Zamzam. For at first they were but piles of humble stones, encircling bright blue ojos de agua. For I am a mixture of gravity and waggery. For I am as of the last drops of water from that well. For in the Zep Tepi, the first time, the Sun would rise there on a blessed day to cast one golden beam deep into the cerulean pool that had no bottom, infinite light into infinite void. For it was from there that we all set out in the time of the first great flaring forth. For the light of creation had been secreted away there. For the seventh well was the one set apart for Abraham and his progeny. For so it was said then and ever since, mouth to ear to hand to stone, mud, skin, parchment, paper, light, atom, particle, and fire. For I am as of the last drops of water from that well. For no home was forgotten in our tally in the precession of eons. The scent of loam, the cool shade of Shanidar Cave, the mud dwellings of Jarmo, Hassuna, Umm Dabaghiya, and the first cities of Harappa and Mohenjodaro where the first fitful letters were scratched in soft stone among the people of the Sarasvati. And that was the beginning of forgetting. For time was longer than anyone had expected or could have planned for, so few will remember a scintilla's wisp of these places now. For there is a body and a language for every time. For the blood essence carries a knowing through eons, a path forward, the path to the farthest home. For it was into the cenotes that all that was most treasured was thrown. For it would have been impossible to carry everything forth, our vellum maps, our clay libraries, our diaries of the sky, etched in scrolls of golden foil. For it was into the great Cenote en las selvas de Yucatán that the sacred obsidian-plumed snake was thrown, bringing it to life once again.

For I am of the way of regathering all that we have left behind.

For I am as of the last drops of water from that well.

Of the senderos that interconnect magnetic fields in the domains of La Zona.

It can hardly be surprising that once we learned to employ light to speak and record all of our memories and longing, we would inevitably come to use light to traverse time, discovering how every star affords a perilous caminito into forgotten and yet unimagined epochs of creation. And when we say light, we mean the very quintessence of movement, seen and unseen, all that which is quick, not still, from the chrome flash of bosons at the moment of being reborn, to the great Magellanic cloud of our own galaxy, con sus velas de turquoise, burgundy, and pearl.

You move upward en La Zona Perfecta and increasingly you immerse yourself in the ether of dreams, ideas, and the ceaseless augmentation of particulars.

If you move downward, you move toward the body.

Upward is dream and memory, downward is body.

As the wise ancestors of the Upanishads wrote, "descent attaches itself to the body."

In La Zona Perfecta, it is said everything is done so as not to die, ceaselessly forgetting all antecedents and precursors.

In the meantime, I will remember.

Memory is exalted by death, but memory is resurrection, ceaseless resurrection.

We can speak through every atom of light that ever was, and perhaps find there still all that was ever spoken or writ in this great library universe. All is recorded, all is traceable. No one has seen the boundaries; no one has traversed this ocean to its margins, finding only in every direction the void's storiae and phenomena, all the prolongations of infinity as we surge out to plumb it. Light is beyond the reach of time, carrying the imprint of the quantum world into our familiar, great dominions of history, lit by our incomparable sun.

The glimmering ambient dipole sheaths around the planets are seen vividly at this frequency, as dimpled at the top and bottom as a tomato, tightly girdled at their equators, where the upward arcs of magnetic energy from the poles inexplicably return to the surface. Seen from La Zona, the earth shivers like a hive on its spindle, about to burst open with honey. The web of light that girds the earth is full of animal and plant shapes, monkeys, roses, spiders, dolphins, and more, uncountable zoomorphic splendors of the planet's past.

Only those planets with magnetic fields can be fully connected with us; our streams and pathways are fainter around those, as with Pluto and Neptune, that have lost, or never gathered, the heat of these essential powers of attraction within creation.

The atmosphere around Mars glows pale burnt sienna, its magnetosphere tattered and in ruins, a bundle of dry vines, eroded further by the fierce zephyrs sent out from corona holes across the explosive, unresolving face of the sun. When they pass, you can almost hear dry seeds rattle inside the old husk.

There would seem to be some code regulating these movements, the way fructifying solar winds carry these rich veins of magnetism across the cabal of planets in cycles that pulse in periods of 12 years, 187 years, 3,740 years, 18,139 years, spraying in spirals outward through space, forming those webs of memory that allow us to enter and navigate La Zona Perfecta.

With all of the time that has already passed, the flood of memory has been dispersed, sent out into the void or back through time, every memory that has ever been, returning to its source. So who can now remember where all of the ancestors are buried? Their graveyards, without memorial stones, are everywhere.

Over the millions of years, even the oldest light will be extinguished. Every beacon disappears. Sometimes, seen from an outpost such as Beta Orionis, which can be achieved in one bounding leap, the lights of La Zona hang from the sun across the planets like an old string of tiny Christmas lights, blinking pearly flashes against the blue slate background of the old night.

Magnetism is the medium of memory and the great domains of all of my wanderings, making it harder to traverse that part of the nada where it is thinnest, where the gusts of quasars and novae will give buffetings, where the unbounded chassis of the real still rattles from the echoes of the first blast, and nothing can be still. If there is memory in that void, the empire of fire, the memory of how the nada has evolved, in remorse or ecstasy or unknowing, then we have yet to find a way to touch it, or read its meanings. Nonetheless, we swirl within and amid this oceanic dark energy, keeping our dear, fragile, and unlikely magnetism gathered around us like a bear's pelt to protect us from the winds of an unforgiving winter, the pathways ineluctably opening up before us.

If your eyes could see microwaves, you would perceive this roiling glory of creation in the skies every night, and perhaps be inclined to carve it into stone. Everything is filigreed and full of intent in La Zona, and we can exit and enter all time through any portal, of blood or light, leaving our signatures in hidden places in the world.

Did you ever wonder about those trumpets playing churrigueresco flamenco flourishes in the background of that old radio hit de los años nineteen hundred and sixties, "In the year 2525, if man is still alive . . ."?

That was my idea. But I am a master of nothing. All day, I listen to my cicada heart. Though I drive this caravan of stories, it is my inheritance, a compromiso to traverse las vias infinitas de sangre.

It is not a beat or a pulse, but a fluttering, wings beating in the four hundred colors of blood, air, fire, and time.

How does the ancient continue to permeate the present?

Nature, at the level of the primordial, that is, earth, stone, air, wind, and fire.

In landscapes and ruins, the geogony of how we have dwelt upon the earth.

In maps and writing.

In our paintings and chronicles.

In the oldest realistic human portrait.

In los ancianos.

In Fred Flintstone.

This is a universe of swirl, all of our histories and memory forever churning inwardly together with oblivion, inevitably swallowed into the unfathomable maw of some black hole, as though it was always meant to be that way.

Of the true first discovery of America.

A tale is told of an Iberian mariner named Anselmo who was terrified of going to sea. He had not always been that way; once, he was a master *navigator of sturdy sea-plying ships, able to precisely divine his place on the wide ocean with an astrolabe given to him by an old Moor and a sheaf of portolani maps that showed the coastlines from Iberia to Britannia.*

Then, on a journey to collect saffron and cardamom seeds from the African coast, his ship was carried off in a gust that did not cease for twenty days. Sailors believed the ship had been overtaken by a devilish enchantment and some chose to abandon the ship for fear it was being washed into the river Scylla that courses through Hell's outer precincts from which there was no return. By the time the wind died down, only Anselmo remained aboard, and when he came deckside on the empty boat he was astounded to see land in the distance, a thick verdant line as far as he could see, stretching north to south. But before he could reach the land, he was buffeted by another wind from the opposite direction, blowing again for more than a fortnight. When he came to rest he saw he had returned to Iberia and he found his way home, though no one believed his tale.

Though he vowed never to sail again, he was haunted by the vision he had been given of another world and he was determined to see it again. Anselmo committed the rest of his mortal life to this mission, to once again look upon an impossible world that he swore he had seen with his own eyes.

Afraid to set sail again in the unforgiving seas that had trundled him for so many weeks like a coconut in the great waves, he set out to create a machine that would allow him to glimpse that distant coast once more. The design of his maquina de ojo came to him in a dream. He would bind together a fleet of small but sturdy floating pontoons made of teak, each one tied in a chain to the next, so that they might be unfurled, like a long rosary across the ocean.

The vanguard boat would hoist a sail and a great mirror to reflect all that lay ahead of it. Behind it, a chain of mirrors tethered it to the ship behind, and on and on. Atop each successive craft's mast would sit a helical array of small mirrors, each one cocked at a precise angle of parallax declensions to catch the light of its precursor and send the same onto the next, light passing to light, until the last boat shone forth the image captured by the first. Finally, Anselmo, seated comfortably in a plush leather throne in a viewing pavilion on his homeland coast, the mirror ships' thick tether secured before him, would gaze upon hazy rainbow images of that distant coastline projected through a lens like apparitions against a wall, transmitted from afar by his delicate braid of chained refractions.

Many came to witness, but no one believed what their eyes saw in those many-colored lights dancing on the wall in front of Anselmo, grown old, but always transfixed by the spectacle he had created. There were glimpses of mountaintops, glistening with pearly fire. There were birds with the bodies of lions, coursing the air with silvery wings. Every day, the sun was swallowed into a well of molten gold.

The people returned to their homes and dreamed of a world that lay beyond the world, a home beyond imagining that was awaiting them.

From the ledger of lost treasures.

A brigade of Spanish soldiers in the early seventeenth century was fleeing a band of Apaches who outnumbered them. It was long rumored that, weighed down by settler's freight and a full chest of gold doubloons, they buried their treasure near the white chalk bluffs of the Nueces River, near the ruins of the old town of Uvalde in onetime Texas. We would camp nearby the river, and my cousins and I were always seeking out the telltale mound or some other marker that might point to the untold riches that had been hidden for centuries.

Even in our time, we were still that close to the age of La Conquista.

In the Gran Archivo de la Zona Perfecta, la Colmena, the library of all libraries, the records still corded a time before any dared settle these lands of Nuevo Santander:

> . . . that we are Spaniards and descendant of the first settlers and paci-
> fiers of the barbarous Indian fronteras and that our ancestors and our-
> selves have felt the divine beneficence de Su Majestad, Dios guarde
> a nuestra causa, the transport of ourselves and our families which we
> can not do on our own alas, no, to go forth and populate and extend
> the reach of our nación into las Fronteras in which dwell various hea-
> thenish nations . . . These tierras que habitan las expresadas naciones
> are fertile plains, without forests or mountains, abounding en

pasture lands y aguas correspondientes, with many salt lakes, and there is much silver in el Serro de Tamaulipa . . .

Por Don Juan Antonio Sadro de Guevara, vecino de Monterrey . . .

Anonymous author's note: It is said that Time is shaped like a boundless caracól and it is possible to move back and forth within it as you would in a ship on the ocean. It was possible to enter and exit the spells of history through wide causeways that were left open in the Zona Perfecta when a great number of souls left their bodies all at once, unleashing great bolts of light, whether by acts of nature or acts of man. Cenote Siete spoke of entering past time through a bridge that appeared in the middle 1940s of the Gregorian calendar when there began a series of explosions of the void, like none other before them.

Cenote Siete sees a film of Hiroshima through his Chronovisor.

The film stock is middle twentieth century, an early emulsification still heavy with silver, I assure you.

It glows.

Te lo juro, hijo—del verdadero día de Hiroshima.

It is silent; of course, black-and-white, grainy, at times indistinct to blurred, but at its beginning clear enough to make out. You see a large, open enclosure with walls that resemble ruined rusty brick ramparts of an abandoned medieval castle. It is the light of the late 1940s, without a doubt. It seems to be morning, glints of sunlight, antique sepia tints cracking in the film. The camera is fixed. From above, it pans slowly to reveal an unevenly scattered group of people, standing in a wide dirt plaza, but dressed for a special occasion in formal attire. The sky is visible, a grey slate dome. At one edge of the picture, a steeple with a cross wavers in and out of the frame, a man in a crisp white alb moves past and jostles the camera's lens. Is something about to be inaugurated, consecrated? Perhaps it is a wedding or a graduation? Suddenly, a spectacular flash of light comes that makes everything look transparent, and every head turns, necks chafing against their stiff suits. The camera studiously follows. Tenderly then, puffs of debris break over the walls, thick plumes of brown smoke shooting through the broken stone windows, like ghost arms reaching into the courtyard. The camera remains unmoved. Three more fierce puffs follow, presumably echoing a blast some distance away. A tremor, and then, as the camera pans back to find the people hunched over, covering their heads, several reaching to protect another, the film blurs, some ruins visible, then it breaks, ends . . .

And thus I entered your time through a tear in the seams of creation that Hiroshima left behind.

Cenote Siete, *in the body.*

I have the body.

There is time en La Zona Perfecta, and there is time in the body, my own, or any body I visit throughout time. This cuerpo is not the one I was born with, but it is perfectly usable, if too seldom and inattentively maintained. From the archive of the body's arcana, some of the weights and measures of human physiognomy were fixed in most distant antiquity. It has been known since the days of Osiris and Isis that the weight of a person's heart should be equal to a falcon's tail feathers. Any hidalgón knight might wish for priceless lineaments, a body as resplendent as those of the heroes of ancient Hellas or Teotihuacán. Desgraciadamente, my parts were scavenged and hoarded, a rasquache assemblage of disjecta membra poetae left behind in the early ages of La Zona.

My bones are made of a rare adamantine cerulean glass, galvanized long ago from Yucateca sand in a weightless ossific forge that orbited Europa. Along with the flesh, it is all iterated matter, every cell and capillary inscribed in universal Quechua script into the ether's indistinct quanta, all the hieroglyphy of creation embedded in the skin. My eyes, set deep, are hundreds of years old, passed on body to body, the aqua vitae of the retina retaining all that has been seen, in clarity or haze, through the ages since their generation.

In La Zona I am without anatomy, solamente vestido en la Merkaba, a body of light.

To enter any body in time, or to return to my humble earthly frame anew, I have only to utter the words,

"I have the body."

I feel it first as a doleful rush, crouching backward and leaning in a tuck as the Tibetans have long instructed for use at the moment of dying, and instantaneously I am within it again, back to front, unfurling knees from chin, slowing down until all the senses are synchronized and transmitted inside once more in the warming blood.

Thus am I inspired again within my old dear carapace that dwells outside La Zona, in the elements-old Sixth World of air, earth, water, and fire.

I cannot cipher the whole physik of it—it is as mystic as first breath itself—only that the same confession never fails to draw me back, always fixing the body in time under one of the sun's numberless ages, configuring and manifesting itself around the very same spindles and braids of magnetism that bind La Zona together. And what I carry and protect in La Zona, I receive and harbor in that body, all of my talismans, all memory and longing radiating out from the spear points of the liquid crystal ganglia. Likewise, whatever I may gather in the body is mirrored into the receding horizons of La Zona, every syllable and vibration of my bodily reckonings awaiting me there when I return.

V

En Tierras Bárbaras

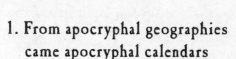

1. From apocryphal geographies came apocryphal calendars

There were rumors of an unremembered ancient earth past of which there was only inconclusive evidence, inexplicable artifacts like gold necklaces embedded in coal, human footprints next to dinosaur prints, buried deep in fossils under the ground; vast craters that had filled up with salt, stone, and earth or been inundated by the seas and oceans over the millennia. When I looked at the moon through a telescope, it was startling to see its battered, lifeless bone-colored face.

Had the earth also taken so many fearsome impacts? Would it ever again? The ancestors kept their secrets of living through shattering trials descending from the heavens.

In this way, they had eventually been forgotten.

For those who had lived through such a cataclysm, they probably chose not to recollect it, to revisit the great terror and loss of such a debacle. Twenty generations passed, each one struggling to gather their lives together again, and gradually the memory of disaster was lost forever.

In one of the old bookstores of downtown San Antonio, I discovered the books of Immanuel Velikovsky and found there a story of how Venus originally entered the solar system as a comet, its great sulfurous tail blighting the oceans of Mars before grazing the earth and taking its place as the second planet from the sun. Esoteric paleomythographer Zechariah Sitchin claimed that the ancient Sumerians had preserved a different version of the story. In their records, they had spoken of a wandering planet called Nibiru that had collided with Venus and would return again someday to shake our skies once more.

When the Iberians first arrived in Mexico, they did so as the progeny of a peninsula that, over the previous two thousand years, had seen numerous civilizations rise and fall, some leaving no record at all. References in ancient scripture, including the prophet Ezekiel, named the people of Tarshish, a place thought to have been on the southern coast of the Iberian Peninsula, as possessing a noble culture which mined and refined precious metals and stones. Later, its location and lore were forgotten entirely.

Tarshish was a place of excesses and atrocities, resplendent in jewelry of gold and precious stones, and it vanished without a trace; the prophet Obadiah spoke of Israelites journeying to a place called Sepharad, the land of rabbits, that came to be known as Hispania.

In deepest antiquity, sixty-five million years ago, the northern tip of the Yucatán Peninsula had been the impact site of the vast Chicxulub asteroid, among the candidates for the event that resulted in the extinction of the dinosaurs, marking the landscape with a crater that was the first of a series of cataclysms that would befall the land, echoing continuously, faintly, through the millennia that followed.

Though most of the Spaniards did not know it, ancient Mexico had been the home of a myriad of civilizations that appeared, fluoresced, and then disappeared, often abandoning the grand pyramid cities they had constructed. The earliest had been the Olmeca civilization on the southern Caribbean coast, followed by the Teotihuacán culture and the classic Maya, all of which vanished, only to be rediscovered hundreds of years later. Most of the indigenous people believed that our present age was the Fifth World that began with the lighting of the first fire at the great city of Teotihuacán near Mexico City, preceded by four others that had each ended in catastrophe, each one remembered as another in the series of world "suns."

The Aztecs prophesied that our world would end in a great shaking of the earth. The earlier classic Maya shared the belief that the world had been destroyed four times before, but they were precise in their measurement of the time left under our fifth sun. Unlike ours, their calendars had beginnings and ends, each with their appointed times. Our present age had begun in the year 3114 BCE. The end of this so-called "long count" of the Maya calendar was not simply the last day in a distant future that they had gazed forward through time to count.

It was presumed among them to be the end of the age, anticipated for December of the year 2012 in our Gregorian calendar.

In *El Libro de los Libros de Chilam Balam*, these were the words of the noble priests, the Ah Kines:

> You will know that day because the heavens will move and the earth will walk.

So it was that the peoples that met in Mexico had deep legacies in common that they might build a new civilization upon: forgotten ancestors lost in unremembered cataclysms, and expectations of still more cataclysms to come.

2. Hidden past gradually returns to light.

I wish I weren't such an inadvertentist.

Instead of watching for the signs of some new discovery slowly taking shape over many years, I might find my way through these family stories and investigations much more quickly. In truth, I was mostly resigned to the fact my family's history in early Mexico and Spain was hopelessly lost.

Many Mexicano families can refer vaguely to their Spanish ancestry; others have the documents that demonstrate it. In San Antonio

and throughout South Texas, there is an extensive subculture of organizations and individuals committed to keeping the legacy of Spain
alive in our families. Some are focused specifically on the geneaol-
ogy of families that originated in the Canary Islands. Others, like
the Bejareños, are solely interested in the first families of San Antonio. Members of the Hispanic Genealogical Society have the broadest
scope of interests, tracing the lineages of Hispano families from across
South Texas. My friends Guadalupe and Aida travel around the region
in a van that contains boxes of birth, baptism, marriage, and death
certificates from the villages of the Villas del Norte, a documentary
record they once brought into my family home's kitchen in San Antonio, and within two hours we had traced four generations of Velas in
the villages of Revilla and Mier reaching into the eighteenth century.

Each trip home to South Texas harbored another small revelation, a remembered story, or an artifact, like Grandmother's red
leather address book, that might reappear suddenly out of oblivion.

I began spending more and more time in my ancestral homelands, closing up or subletting my New York apartment and making
journeys into las tierras Tejanas. On the eve of one of those trips,
I was joined by Tom, one of my oldest friends, visiting me as he
passed through New York on his way to a long research sojourn in
Berlin. By then we were veterans of packing for the travels required
by our respective investigations, and we could spend whole evenings
talking, drinking wine, and doing a series of triages on the books,
papers, media, and other gear that would be needed for our trips,
concluding with Herculean presses to latch the still-overstuffed
suitcases that had been packed.

Any trip begins with the critical decision of which cumbersome
books I should lug out onto the road, if only to expose them to the
light and weather of other latitudes. Slim volumes were of little concern, but traveling with *Don Quixote* was a burden. Curiously, it
seems books about Spain's history in the New World average about
four pounds each. To make matters worse, I'm obsessive about traveling with a small crate of drafts, notes, and clippings, usually making my peregrinations hopelessly heavy-laden.

So I was trying to reduce my burden, perusing the books I was planning to take with me to see if they were essential. Anything tangential would be left behind. Even inadvertency has its rigors.

I wanted to send Uncle Lico a message, but he had been dead for ten years.

"The Lopez ancestors were the founders of Camargo—Los Velas were descended from the founders of Revilla and Mier."

That's what I hurriedly wrote amid my preparations, after reading an article in a book I'd had tucked away on a shelf for years, titled *Explorers and Settlers of Spanish Texas*, a book I'd perused long ago but never bothered to explore deeply for any history relevant to my family. This time, I discovered an article there on the life and audacious career of one Colonel José de Escandón y Helguera, the so-called "Father of South Texas." Audacity, of course, was the pre-eminent character trait of the old school of conquistadores.

Escandón was born a child of privilege in 1700 in Soto La Marina, Santander, the province in northern Spain, and came to Nueva España when he was only fifteen. He joined a mounted military unit in the Yucatán, acquiring the equestrian martial skills that would prove invaluable to him in the decades to come. He soon established a reputation as an effective soldier against the Maya, combining prowess in battle with a talent for negotiation with the indigenous peoples.

Eventually he moved to Querétaro, where he excelled in the ongoing war against the Indios Chichimecas, and his ardor in these military pursuits quickly gained him royal notice in Mexico City, as well as back in Spain with the governing Consejo de las Indias, the Council of the Indies, which oversaw the administration of Spain's colonies in the New World.

Beginning in the 1740s, setting out from central Mexico, Escandón financed and led four expeditions into the forbidding mountain recesses of the Sierra Gorda, northeast of Querétaro, where he reconnoitered the landscapes and violently suppressed the Indians well enough to establish permanent settlements for the Spaniards in what had recently been regarded as an incorrigible wilderness of hostile natives, resisting all attempts at pacification.

Uncle Lico had only spoken of Escandón as a *gran persona* of the territorio's history, "un varón chingón" as he once called him, laughing, never mentioning any direct link between our ancestors and the conquistador. But as far as Lico knew, our antepasados never directly encountered Escandón.

Along with the host of families accompanying him, Escandón was to found twenty-three new towns in the remote territories he newly christened Nuevo Santander, including the towns of Mier, Camargo, and Revilla—all of which had been homes to my ancestors from the Lopez and Vela lineages.

Prior to Escandón's campaigns, a special junta that had been formed years before in Mexico City to grapple with the problem and the promise of the Costa del Seno Mexicano was languishing. The Costa del Seno, as the region was widely known, was the still uncharted and menacing region in the distant northeastern lands of the new empire, stretching from the Gulf Coast to the Sierra Oriental. It had been briefly surveyed in a number of expeditions toward the end of the seventeenth century, from which a few inconclusive portolanis and relatively useless territorial maps were prepared. There were already silver mines in the north, and it was said more abundant deposits of precious metals waited to be discovered in the mountains to the north beyond Monterrey. Farther north still, sparsely forested rolling scrubby grasslands beckoned for traditional Iberian livestock agriculture that had already found a foothold in Coahuila.

The Indios of those badlands were said to be of two kinds, Malhuecos or Comecrudos. The latter were said to be a docile lot who ate raw meat and were friendly to the Spanish. The former, however, were the most extreme form of savage ever encountered by the Españoles anywhere in the world, irredeemable infidels who allegedly had no idea of God whatsoever and lived only by their bloody and murderous cunning. There was great wealth to be extracted from these wild lands, but there was also the prospect of a harvest of souls for Christ that motivated many.

After being chosen in 1747 to lead an expedition into this region, José Escandón organized seven divisions that were to set off from different approaches, to broaden the Spanish reconnaissance of these territories.

In the elaborate map that documents this ambitious undertaking, the various routes appear: Camino que llevó la Tropa de la Provincia de Coaguila, Camino de la Tropa de la Bahia del Espiritu Santo, Camino que llevó la Tropa de Cerralvo, Camino que llevó el Sargento Mayor Guevara, Viaje de la Tropa de la Huasteca, Viaje de la Tropa de Tampico, and Camino que llevó de la Tropa de el General Don Joseph de Escandón.

The lands were given the name of Nuevo Santander in honor of Escandón's homeland in the northern Iberian Peninsula, and Escandón was given the honorific title *el Conde de la Sierra Gorda.*

Upon returning to Querétaro with all of his men, Escandón drafted a plan of settlement that would see fourteen towns and missions created across those lands. Settlers were recruited by offering cash inducements, relief from taxes for ten years, and a royal land grant. The delegation that left Querétaro in 1748 was a historic march of Spanish imperial expansion, the last of its kind in Mexico, leaving behind settlers in newly founded pueblos in the dust of its trail—among them Santa María de Llera, Mission Peña del Castillo, San Fernando de Güemes, San Antonio de Padilla.

Over the next twenty years, Escandón gathered settlers from older settlements such as Cadereyta and Cerralvo, and farther west from the towns of Coahuila. He mounted the series of expeditions that founded the historic towns along the Río Bravo, including Revilla, Camargo, and Ciudad Mier.

These were names that had always appeared in the fanciful atlas of Uncle Lico's family research. Suddenly, their true story in our ancestral past was beginning to come into focus.

Like most explorers and conquistadores in the earlier history of Mexico and the New World, Escandón was eventually brought up on charges, accused of aggrandizing himself from royal funds, not properly attending to the evangelization of the Indios, and failing to make the mandated land grants to the settlers who had joined his expeditions in expectation of their receiving titles to lands of their own.

In the 1760s, having founded more than twenty Villas del Norte, and after a lengthy investigation, Escandón was indicted by the viceroy in Querétaro for the cited failures. The conde had long opposed the distribution of lands to individual settlers, believing this would only foment discord in the young settlements.

Escandón presented a passionate defense of his actions during his trial in Querétaro, arguing that the allotted royal funds had been properly accounted for, that three thousand Indios had been converted to the Holy Church, and that he had refrained from making individual land grants in the considered belief that they would only fragment these frontera settlements, with the sturdy pobladores choosing to retire to their private lands rather than building and fortifying the communal pastures and town environs that could be better defended against Indian attacks.

Fatefully, the Conde de Sierra Gorda was to die under indictment in Querétaro, only to be acquitted posthumously. However, in 1766, in the course of these legal proceedings, the presiding judge of the viceregal court sent a delegation to the remote region to preemptively make the promised land grants to the patient, long-suffering settlers. The essay named the officials who led this delegación, officially known as the Autovisita General de 1767, which resulted in many of the historic land grants still held by old families of the territory. Juan Fernando Palacio was the principal inspector, assisted by José de Osorio y Llamas. The first name almost leapt out from the page.

I went back to one of Uncle Lico's holographs of the familia genealogy, the one that began with an account of the families' original land grant, and there was the name—Don Fernando Palacio.

Fernando de Palacio.

That name was from one of Uncle Lico's quirky genealogical documents, containing facts related to Royal Land Grant #28 del municipio de Ciudad Camargo, granted to my grandmother Leandra's family.

This was the first time there had ever been a traceable historical reference among my uncle's quixotic family annals:

> On the twelfth day of the month of August, in the year 1767.
>
> On behalf of the Virrey de la Nueva España, Don Fernando de Palacio granted to Don Pedro Jose Gomez Vela a porción of land near the place known as "el Paso del Teo Adame."

With dates and names attached to specific places in specific years, Lico's archive of the Lopez and Velas began to unfold, like a puzzle that had been waiting for a secret code to be solved.

Each of the lineages began to be revealed—out of Guerrero, Camargo, Mier, Cerralvo, and Querétaro.

Ancestors' names, as Lico had recorded them, were to appear in the official histories of all of these places. Once these threads were revealed, very soon our bloodlines were spooling back into the sixteenth century, the clocks running backward, the forgotten trails of our ancestral diaspora, reckoning out in reverse across the maps of old Mexico and Texas, and eventually Spain too.

At his death in the Columbian quincentenary year, Uncle Lico hadn't known how close he had come to finding our true Iberian ancestors.

Before long, much more of our story was to fall into place.

3. The death of Leonides

There are few surviving photographs of my abuelo Leonides Lopez, none of him from his childhood or youth. In one studio portrait from 1908, sepia-tinted, full of shadows and glowing orbs, he's a vital young man, seated with one strong arm leaning on an ornately carved desk, a pen and notebook alongside an oil lamp. Broad-shouldered, he wears a white shirt with suspenders and black pants. His long muscular hands rest calmly on his knees as he gazes with a distant, pensive expression into the camera. With his dark features, wavy black hair, handlebar moustache, and penetrating eyes, he almost looks like a Tejano Emiliano Zapata.

He has the serious expression of an isolated soul, touched by fear but steeled with determination. After his parents died while still a child, he and his two brothers had been sent to live with the family of a Lopez uncle working at the La Mota ranch, near Cotulla in Texas's La Salle County. Unlike many of his uncles and cousins he did not choose to become a vaquero and remain with the ranch life.

Instead, uncommonly for Mexicanos, he became a businessman,

opening a dry goods and general store emporium in the Mexican neighborhood of Cotulla, a town seventy miles from the Mexican border at Laredo. He may've been able to start his store with the assistance of William and Amanda Burks, owners of La Mota ranch. Lily Amanda, Leonides and Leandra's second child, who died as a baby of diphtheria, was given her middle name after Mrs. Burks.

In another photograph taken nearly thirty years later, and just before his death, my grandfather sits at his roll-top desk busily piled with papers inside the store, his hair nearly gone, his burnt olive color faded to beige, his large frame looking burdened now, leaning back in his chair, a calm expression reflecting accomplishment and resignation.

Death would come suddenly for Leonides, the orphan.

It was July 19, 1935, the hottest time of the year in Cotulla, one of the hottest towns in deep South Texas. In one of its few claims to fame, national weather forecasts often report Cotulla as the hottest place in the country.

"Today in Cotulla, a hundred and five!"

My grandfather's Lopez had found their way to Cotulla after the Treaty of Guadalupe Hidalgo, making Texas a part of the United States. The Lopez had left behind royal land grants in the Villa de Camargo, choosing instead to seek their fortune in Texas, newly a part of the American republic. The border had been contested for fifty years since the war of Texas independence, the Texans claiming it was the Rio Grande while the Mexicans insisted it was the Nueces River, farther to the north. The Nueces was just south of Cotulla, so the Lopez remained border people, accustomed to dwelling at the farthest edge of any contested dominion.

That day had begun for the Lopez family in the most ordinary way, with the tinkling bells of the burro-drawn cart of the egg man arriving before dawn in the dusty street in front of the long porch of the grocery store. Uncle Lico said the sound of that donkey's loud braying and chewing on his bit used to wake him up every day. That morning, the children were all awakened early and called out to help when the Southwest Pacific train bound for Laredo made its *madrugada* delivery stop in Cotulla, at the station platform just across the road from the Lopez store.

By the time young Lico got dressed and made it outside, his father Leonides was already there, lit cigar and pencil in one hand, the other with a clipboard of orders, well into inventorying the arrival of a monthly lode of provisions; sacks of flour and sugar, tins of tobacco, bolts of cloth, large spools of baling wire, and, much to the excitement of my aunt Lydia, many boxes of candies—caramel lollipops, orange and lemon hard sour suckers, bundled nests of bright red licorice strings.

Uncle Lico remembered a haunting omen from that morning.

Señor Carranza, exclusive undertaker to Cotulla's Mexican dead, was receiving a number of coffins from the offloaded cargo of the same train delivery.

"His *chamacos* were there helping him load those pine boxes on their old broken-down carreta," Uncle Lico recalled.

"Daddy would always loan his fancy carriage for the proper funerals, you know for the fancy Mexicans. Everybody else was happy with the carreta."

Señor Carranza had let Lico observe several embalmings, and my uncle would periodically delve into the mortuary and cemetery business throughout his multifarious career.

"'Hey, Señor Carranza,' I shouted to him, 'you expecting a lotta business or something?' I was laughing real hard, but he just looked at me, bien curioso you know, he just stared down at me from up in that open train car, he had this big moustache and a fedora, and he just looked at me, como real serious, sabes? A look on his face like a Greek statue. And I swear I remember thinking to myself, 'Uh-oh.' And that was the day my daddy died. The day everything changed for us. Weird. Cats like Carranza could just feel that sort of thing, like he knew, or something. And it turned out we ended up getting the first pick. Ain't that a damned shame?"

After such a big shipment at the Lopez Grocery Store, the next hours would be all drudgery. Daily business had to proceed, a dozen orders to be taken and filled for customers, even as Abuelo Leonides, unaware that he was dwindling away his last morning on earth, managed the unpacking, counting, and shelving of the new *abarrotes* and ranch supplies. By late morning, Leo, Lauro, and Lico were still hauling the sacks from the wagon onto the store's loading dock at the end of the porch.

My aunt Lydia was behind the counter meticulously arranging the candies into their labeled jars. Grandmother was at the great roll-top desk in the office, entering the new inventory into the store's ledgers, checking for omissions or overcharges in the shipment orders and invoices. By then, my mother, Lucille, the youngest of the Lopez brood, was playing at a cousin's house down the street.

Leonides, a tall husky Mexicano, was walking the creaking wooden aisles of the store, checking a list and putting an order together for a customer who was due at noon. With no warning, Aunt Lydia saw him lean over and catch himself with one hand against a shelf, gradually crouching down onto his knees.

"I asked him, 'What's wrong, Papá?' but he was already going down, and when I got to him he looked up at me real dizzy, and his nose was bleeding, like it always did."

Leonides suffered from spells of heavy nosebleeding that my mother remembers could fill washtubs with his blood before they would cease. This was to be his last.

Aunt Lydia screamed for her mother, and her three brothers came in running.

Leo, Lauro, and Lico quickly helped their father to his feet. His face bloody, Leonides pressed his hands to his temples and complained of a very bad headache. Grandmother quietly wiped his face with her own plain white handkerchief and instructed her sons to take their father to his bed.

Though it was not widely known, Leonides was a year younger than Leandra, and they had met when she first arrived in Cotulla in 1908 to teach at the Mexican elementary school. A year later they were married. Despite whatever *chisme* was spoken of how Grandmother had stolen the cradle by marrying him, the orphan Leonides had married very well.

Leandra may have grown incredulous about any romance that ever existed between them, but she had always possessed a confidence and knowledge about what needed to be done that he had somehow never mustered for himself. In fact, she was the businesswoman and entrepreneur; he was the store's promoter and resident personality, regularly receiving visitors such as the Texas folklorist J. Frank Dobie. People would arrive seeking to use the phone, the only one in the Mexican neighborhood, and he'd warmly greet them. In the evenings, he'd sit on the porch with compadres, smoking cigars, talking and laughing well into the night.

The details of the store were less interesting to him. Leonides brought the business, and Leandra managed it. He was barely making a go of the store before marrying her.

Yes, Grandmother wasn't just another Mexicana. Leandra was a proper metropolitana, university-educated, as she would remind you, from an old and distinguished Hispano family in the old town of Laredo, which, she would say, was like Paris back in the day. Her family was said to have descended from the founders of Mier and Revilla, two of the Villas del Norte established by Colonel José Escandón during those fateful, final conquistadorial campaigns in the mid-eighteenth century.

Leonides had only been schooled to the sixth grade in a La Mota ranch schoolroom, where all the Mexican workers' children were educated. Supposedly, his family had also once been bien importante in the old town of Camargo, another of Escandón's villas; but if so, they had lost quite everything over time, and eventually it wasn't even worth thinking about anymore.

Así fue la cosa.

Leandra loathed Cotulla, where Leonides's few remaining relations in the world had settled and found refuge from the world of treachery, killing, and thievery that had chased them north and west out of Mexico. She had never meant to stay there, and he had always promised they would eventually leave.

Yes, she was perpetually hectoring him, wanting to sell everything they owned and move north to San Antonio, where she had already sent their children to study in alternating years so they wouldn't grow up being taken for simple Mexican country folk. And he had finally agreed they would do so, in another year or so, following other Lopez who had ended up in the old mission city to the north.

But instead, though he couldn't have known it, Leonides was

preparing to die on an afternoon in sweltering Cotulla, Texas, the last of his Lopez lineage who would be buried in the dear, parched, and godforsaken borderlands our ancestors had begun settling almost three hundred years before.

Uncle Lico sought out my mother playing jacks with some cousins a few streets away, and told her that their father had just died.

4. Down the border: a journey to Guerrero Viejo

Walking through the present-day ruins of Guerrero Viejo, the one-time Escandón villa of Revilla, you would never know it had been the most important town of the colonial world of northern Nueva España. Founded in 1751 by ninety families, among them Velas and Lopez, it must've once seemed as if the town would last forever, especially after surviving the depredations of Indian attacks and scarcity of food and shelter in the earliest years of its settlement.

The town sat on a promontory overlooking the Río Bravo at the bend where the tributary Río Salado met the great river, forming a deep, still lake that proved to be the farthest point upstream that was navigable for commercial riverboats, making Revilla the largest steamboat river port for nearly two centuries. Eventually, Revilla became known as Revillagigedo, and then later as Guerrero, to honor a Mexican military hero. The colonial town was built in the classic style of a frontier Spanish settlement, with the church and municipal buildings constructed around a central square, presided over by an octagonal gazebo decorated with ornamented wrought iron railings.

The streets and alleys of Guerrero radiated out from there, down to the river on one side, reaching all the way to a flank of hills to the south.

I went there to see one of the forgotten, nearly erased birthplaces from the Lopez-Vela patrimony. In 1954, after all of the remaining inhabitants of the old town were moved to a new town called Guerrero Nuevo twenty kilometers downriver, the old town went under the waters of the Río Grande, dammed up to create the vast Falcon irrigation reservoir.

Hundreds of residents from some of the oldest families of the town had kept a vigil from the nearby hills over several weeks as they watched the river streams first encroach, and then gradually engulf Old Guerrero. Roads that had once led into town and across the border ended in the lapping waters of the Río Grande. For weeks afterward, amid the strong new currents, some said you could hear the church bells ringing from deep underwater.

Then, toward the end of the twentieth century, with the onset of a historic drought that has not yet abated, the waters began to recede, and Guerrero Viejo, as it has come to be known, was returned to the daylight, a fossil of another time, astonishingly well preserved under the currents of the Río Grande for fifty years. Today, you reach the ruined city by turning off the frontera highway in Tamaulipas, across the border from Zapata, Texas.

The sign says, "Guerrero Viejo, 16 km," but the arduous drive in takes an hour and a half, so washed out is the meandering dirt and gravel road from its half-century sojourn under the river.

Then, after an hour making my way in, I was mortified to find a locked gate barring access to the road for the last stretch to reach the town. I stopped the truck and got out to investigate, when I heard a voice call to me.

"Ay-tale, joven! Ay-tale!"

I looked off to where the voice had come from, beneath a mesquite tree that had been strung with a tarp, with plastic gallon water bottles inexplicably hanging from the limbs of the trees, filled with colored water.

"Pásale, por acá, joven."

An old man was sitting in the shade of a hot day on a small bench beneath the tree, gesturing for me to come over and holding out a key to me on a long piece of rope. He was tiny, dressed in sandals, Mexican campesino whites, and he introduced himself as José Maria Vidaurri. White-haired, with a little goatee, almost tooth-less but grinning, he proudly announced himself as ninety-four years old.

"My family lived here on that hill back there, so we never had to leave, *y aquí estoy todavia*. I'm still here."

Somehow, it had fallen to Don José to become the sentry at Guerrero Viejo's resurrection, and he gladly passed me the key to unlock the gate.

"It was very sad, you know," as he remembered the "drowning of Guerrero," indulging one of the infrequent visitors to pass that way.

"It happened all at once and turned everything upside down. For a little while, the pueblo lived in tents. For some who had nothing— they got new houses in Guerrero Nuevo. But *para los que tenían*, the ones who had nice houses, well it was like they lost everything."

José Maria's family house nearby was saved, though for some years they had lived on what had become a small island in the river, but they lost all of their pasturelands and eventually were forced to get rid of all of their cattle.

"And back in those days, each cow was just a few pesos a head. I let people just pick one, and I would shoot it right there. They just took the meat with them, off to the new Guerrero."

Finally, driving on through the dry brush and thickets, I entered the cobblestone streets of the deserted town and found it largely grown over, but with all of the buildings startlingly intact, with some of the original red, blue, and green paint still showing. Looking down the streets, the brushland had taken over the sidewalks and alleyways, and doors and windows were missing from most of the structures. Walking through one house into what must've been the salon, a small pile of shoes lay in a corner where they'd been placed in 1954. In the courtyard of another house, a large busy beehive was humming from the eaves of a veranda.

In the little plaza, the gazebo had lost its roof, the pedestal where a statue of Vicente Guerrero, an early viceroy, once stood was bare, the granite posts of a colonnade were lying willy-nilly on their sides. Across a small street, the walls of the church had streaks of mud on them, but the bell tower remained intact. Gazing through the chained gates into the sanctuary, a cross with a gorily crucified Christ was laid against the stone platform where the altar had once been. There was an effigy of the Virgen de San Juan de los Lagos, the *patrona* of Guerrero's church, set in front of the stone. The floors were bare, but a lonely long-legged blue heron lazily ambled around the large empty space, letting out a shriek every now and then.

Getting up to leave before the fall of darkness, I looked down at the stone bench I had been sitting on in the plaza and saw that it was inscribed with a name:

Augustín López (1782–1848)

5. How it was that Leonides's earthly sojourn in Cotulla grew longer

For Grandmother, it was always, "next year, we'll move him to Laredo."

When he died in July 1935, Abuelo Leonides's expeditious summer burial in Tío Jose's family plot in Cotulla was meant to be only a brief earthen sojourn. In the Cotulla summer heat, it was important to get the *difunto* into the ground quickly, after lying in state overnight in the family home.

His funeral was one of the grandest for a Mexican that anyone had ever seen. And despite the fact that he was a Mason, from the chapter of the Woodmen of the World, and as such would ordinarily have been excluded from a funeral mass, Grandmother exerted her considerable powers of persuasion upon the priest to allow Leonides to receive a full religious funeral, which was attended by Mexicanos and Anglos alike.

Grandmother's plan had been to transfer his body soon afterward to the grander Vela family plot in the oldest cemetery in Laredo. Grandmother had never loved Cotulla and she would not abide Leonides spending eternity there, even if it had been his home for most of his fifty-two years. This would happen as soon as possible after dispatching the business of closing the grocery store, securing leases for the other properties in the town, and moving her children to San Antonio.

Even into the afterlife, Abuelo Leonides carried his orphan's destiny with him. It would be 1954 before the plans were finally realized to disinter his bones from the Cotulla earth and transport them an hour to the south, to Leonides's last repose on the border with Mexico, just a few miles north of the Río Bravo.

Life in San Antonio had been very demanding for the widowed mother of five, with children ranging in ages from nine to twenty.

Grandmother would not allow the children who were still in school be sent to San Antonio's segregated Mexican schools. My mother walked out of one such school on the city's Southside. The two oldest boys, Leo and Lauro, were already teenagers. For them, the city's always festive, brassy Mexican nightlife with its boundless pageant of feminine beauty was an invigorating change from Cotulla's sleepy twilights and early bedtime.

Uncle Leo showed a predilection and a talent for card games. Uncle Lauro, tall, dark, suave, and already carrying an elegant, lonely air of being from far elsewhere, was more inclined to adoring *las chicas Béjareñas*. Grandmother watched her two eldest sons particularly closely, passing judgment on any alliances she deemed unsavory, whether among conspirators or romantic *aspirantes*.

But Grandmother's lengthy delay in arranging Abuelo Leonides's encore funeral may also have been occasioned by something that took place just after his death in Cotulla. A month after his funeral there, there was a knock at the door in the early evening.

"Buenas noches, Doña Leandra."

Grandmother received a lady visitor into the salon amid stacked boxes that were already being packed for the move to San Antonio before the beginning of the new school year.

My mother, always curious, told me how she overheard their conversation from a room next door.

"You do not know me, Señora Leandra, my name is Gertrudis Ramos. Forgive me for coming *sin aviso*."

The woman was younger, perhaps in her late thirties, and Grandmother's patience was already straining under the burdens of all of the tasks of moving. She turned another lamp light on to have a closer look at the woman.

"What may I do for you, madama?"

"Forgive me, but I was very close to Don Leonides, señora."

Grandmother then stared icily at Gertrudis Ramos, who had started to weep.

"What?"

"We were very close, Señora Leandra."

"What do you mean by that, madame? My husband was a friend of everyone here."

"Señora, he is the father of my daughter, Segunda."

Grandmother let out a shriek, standing up.

"What did you say? ¿Que me dijiste? Sin vergüenza! How dare you?"

"He loved Segunda very much, she's three years old now."

"Segunda? How many do you have?"

"Tengo solamente ella. Pobrecita. She is named after Leonides's mamá—por eso, Segunda."

The room went quiet for a while. Eventually, Grandmother moved toward the front door.

"I don't care why you came here, and I don't care what *cuentos* you tell about your daughter. He made no mention of these *mentiras*, if you're coming to see if he put you in his will. I never want to see you again."

The woman left without protest.

Mother always kept track of Señora Ramos and Segunda, the child who was her alleged half sister. Eventually, they too moved to San Antonio, and Segunda went to the same high school as my mother, eventually marrying a pharmacist friend of hers.

Did she think the story of Abuelo Leonides's second family was true?

Mother remembered the many nights Abuelo would set out in the evenings after dinner, dressed in a suit and a freshly ironed shirt, to sleep out on their little ranch, he said, coming back in the morning. That's just the way things were.

And Segunda?

"Well, she really looked a lot like us," Mother observed, grinning. "But we never mentioned it to each other. And she died a few years ago."

This revelation may well have taken some of the urgency out of Grandmother's desire to move Leonides's bones to the Vela pantheon in Laredo. Let him pass a little bit of eternity there in the dry knotty earth under infernal Cotulla. For a while, he was forgotten amid the new life in San Antonio.

Nearly twenty years later, it was "the boys"—Lico, and Lauro—back from the war and out of the army, who pushed for their father to be taken on his last journey to Laredo. Grandmother went along with it, but my uncles found the Mexican gravediggers in Cotulla who would retrieve Abuelo from his sleep in the Cotulla tierra and then take him to Laredo, where they would dig his new *tumba* in the cemetery where Grandmother's parents rested, and where Grandmother would find her last repose.

A priest would await them all in Laredo, to readminister the sacred rite of extreme unction, which is ordinarily performed before death. Instead, by order of Leandra, it would now precede Abuelo's second burial. Grandmother had insisted on this in light of what she had learned after Leonides's death, and she wanted it done regardless of the theological objections or sacramental casuistry.

He had received final blessings once before, back in 1935, but she didn't want to risk that he hadn't repented himself of his shameful secret child before dying. So the *despedida* blessing of penance was reprised.

She would do Leonides that one last kindness.

6. In which Leonides makes his last journey in the old tierras bárbaras

Near the end of the century, I was in Laredo with my mother and visiting Lopez cousins from Maryland.

Robert Lopez was the younger son of my uncle Leo, a longtime morning radio news DJ in Baltimore using the on-air name "Lopez," doing morning news and hosting a weekend program aptly called *The Spanish Inquisition*. I had always told him he was our walking cultural experiment, a Mexican raised in captivity, away from the environs of ancient Tejas. Uncle Leo and Aunt Lola had moved to Maryland in the 1950s, partly to escape the disapproval of both of their families at what was then a controversial mixed marriage between a Mexican man and an Anglo woman. Never mind that both were Texas-born Americans.

In the years before, Bob had begun to make trips to San Antonio, as I put it to him, "in search of his awakening inner Mexican."

"I'm half-Mexican," Bob reminded me. "My mom's a Cherokee German."

Of all of my brothers and seventeen Lopez cousins, Bob was the first to begin wondering with me about the origins of the Lopez-Vela family story, even though he had grown up so far from the homelands. On this trip he was with his wife, Jean, and their ten-year-old daughter, Leandra, who was making her first trip to the ancestral homelands. Though Jean was very fair, and Bob light-complexioned, Leandra had been born with the dark-eyed *morena* Lopez look, and she delighted immediately in the curious Mexican world of San Antonio. She was the second child in the family to be named after Grandmother. The day before our trip to Laredo, we went to Karotkin's, an old western wear emporium in the city's downtown, and bought Leandra her first pair of cowboy boots, brown and pointy-toed, with curlicued pink thread piping decorating the shaft.

In Nuevo Laredo, on the Mexican side of the border across from Laredo, Texas, Leandra accompanied me to one of the noisy, parti-colored wooden shoeshine stands with bright red awnings in the plaza.

With Norteño tunes blaring from a battered red transistor radio, two *chamacos* began the elaborate choreography of a proper frontera shine, starting with a vigorous terrycloth wipe, rubbing in the shine paste, proceeding to first buffing, complete with back-and-forth samba dance steps, then twirls, before unleashing a battery of air guitar flourishes to daub the boots with cream, rubbing that in, then another buff, culminating in the signature technique of passing a flaming torch over the shoe of the boots, "para que se brillan bien," one of the kids says, smiling up at us with two gold front teeth.

Leandra watched it all with an elegant bemusement. "Puro Lopez."

Having a late lunch at the Rincón del Viejo, Nuevo Laredo's famous capital of roasted cabrito, the regional delicacy of charcoal-broiled young goat kid, we ate outside on the restaurant's patio on a temperate afternoon in the spring. A shopping cart rattled out of the kitchen, heading across the courtyard toward the rustic grill shack. It was piled perilously high with an unwieldy heap of cleaned and skinned cabritos, still dripping from their overnight basting in spiced milk, preparing for the coming evening's legion of diners. In an instant, Leandra grabbed the family video camera from the table and ran out in front of the cart of carcasses, so that she could shoot its approach. She held out her hand, and the grinning kitchen porter stopped and let her get close-ups of some of the skulls, containing my mother's favorite part of the cabrito, the brains.

She finished, the man continued to the grill with his cargo, and she came back to the table laughing, gurning her face in mock disgust.

Very, very Lopez, we all agreed.

It was a very Lopez journey that day.

Earlier in the morning, we had stopped in Cotulla and found the badly aged and chipped stone bench in the town plaza where Leonides's and Leandra's names were still inscribed. On the seat, someone had scrawled "La EME Siempre!," the graffiti tag for the Mexican Mafia, a violent gang that has spread widely through the border region and cities with big Mexican populations.

Mother showed us the Welhausen Mexican school where LBJ had taught for a year, making all of his students memorize Walt Whitman's "O Captain, My Captain." When we came to the place near the railroad tracks where the Lopez Grocery Store and home once stood, we found a vacant, overgrown lot.

In one spot, we thought we could still detect the lines of a broad foundation of a building, weathered over, but still marking out a shape in the sand.

Mother pointed to a small hill where she said the porch of the house had once stood. She remembered once when she had been given a dollar coin by her father and told she was not to lose it. Immediately, she tossed it into the air, laughing as it flipped and twinkled high above her, only to miss catching it; it landed instead

somewhere in that fine straw-colored sand—and it was never seen
again.

"It just disappeared into the sand," Mother recalled, "like it had
never been here in the first place."

After his death, Columbus's bones were briefly buried in Val-
ladolid, until they could be taken to the island of La Española,
according to his wishes. After three years under the ground, he
was moved to a crypt in a monastery in Sevilla. Eventually he was
moved again, to Santo Domingo, but his remains were later sent to
Cuba when the French took over the island in 1795. The explorer
was evicted once more, from Cuba, in 1898 when the Spaniards
were expelled, and then lost altogether, until recently when DNA
testing confirmed their true whereabouts in a sepulcher within an
ornate silver-encrusted chapel in Sevilla.

Hernán Cortés, "El Gran Conquistador," died miserably of an
intestinal infection and was buried in Sevilla. Nineteen years later,
his bones were moved with great ceremony to Coyoacán in Mexico
City, then they were lost for centuries, to be only recently rediscovered. Maybe this was some part of the destiny of Spanish pioneers
in the New World, after a lifetime of wandering and displacement,
to spend eternity looking for a final resting place.

It was in the Christmastime of 1954 when, after being dead sixteen years, Abuelo Leonides finally took his last drive down the highway from Cotulla to Laredo in the back of a battered pickup truck.

7. How my grandfather was resurrected, then buried again

Grandmother only got out of the Hudson in Laredo once the newly
dug grave was again covered over with fresh dirt. She quickly posed
for a photograph between Leonides's grand new gravestone and the
more modest, aging memorial to her parents, Emeterio Vela and
Toribia Gonzalez de Vela.

Doña Leandra was wearing a blousy royal blue silk dress that
sparkled grimly with burnished pewter polka-dots. Her December

funeral ensemble included a large moon-shaped brooch of old pearls that was pinned to her bodice; a wilting corsage of small white roses was off to one side. A starburst brooch shone from her pushed back black hat's brim, a large white hatpin crowning her head like a ceremonial feather.

Earlier that morning, she hadn't gotten out of the car at the cemetery in Cotulla, choosing instead to catch up on her sleep. Mother had picked her up at 5 a.m. in San Antonio, so that they'd be in Cotulla by 7:30 to meet uncles Lico and Lauro and the gravediggers.

Near the town of Dilley at dawn, Grandmother had insisted on picking up a hitching GI in army greens, chatting with him the next twenty miles, and later stopping to buy him breakfast at a Mexican diner in D'hanis, where they left him. Grandmother always picked up hitching GIs, but he was a Mexicano from the region, and Leandra wanted to know where his home was, from which family he was descended, and where his ancestors had come from. By the time they got there, the sun had already risen over the old Mexican *camposanto* in Cotulla—and there was no sign of my mother's brothers.

Grandmother impatiently directed the way to the Lopez plot, pointing forward and asking Mother to stop the car when they were still twenty yards from the grave.

"It's right up there under that mesquite, Lucille, with the broken-down little black fence. It's a Woodmen of the World gravestone that looks like two logs in the shape of a cross. I'll wait here."

Once they were parked, the three gravediggers appeared, yawning and stretching outside a nearby shed on the cemetery grounds. They had spent the day before digging down past the sand into the harder clay, until they nearly reached Leonides's body, waiting for the family to arrive to witness the exhumation. Lico and Lauro had promised to oversee the whole procedure, but they never showed up; instead it fell to Mother to watch as the three *sepultureros* delicately hoisted up her father's remains with a cradle of hemp ropes into the brilliant morning Cotulla light.

"I guess they just got cold feet, my brothers," my mother recalls now.

There was hardly a coffin left at all, only a dark, velvety sheath of hardened earth that collapsed into shreds when it met the air. His black suit and big leather boots had largely disintegrated, leaving only scraps that crumbled as they were moved.

Leonides's white bones were visible amid the long splinters, as shoulders, arms and hands, pelvis, one foot, then trunk and legs were lifted out—but Mother looked away when they retrieved her father's skull to place it first into the new polished mahogany coffin, resting in the cab of a Chevy pickup.

"Está muy bien preservado, Señora Santos," one of the diggers told my mother, admiring how well preserved my grandfather's bones were.

"Tenía huesos muy buenos, tu papá."

There was no need for commentary, no need to regard the old bones any longer than necessary. Mother wanted to get the whole thing over as quickly as possible and get on the road to Laredo. Grandmother made the *sepultureros* drive the truck 40 miles an hour, with headlights on, all the way to the border, with she and Mother following in the Hudson. Once they reached the city limits, they were to drive 20 miles an hour, and, nearing the cemetery, slowing to 10, as would befit a proper funeral. The people of Laredo were accustomed to paying homage to the dead in long funeral processions, but a slow cortege of two vehicles, one of which was a pickup with a coffin hanging out its back end, was a strange spectacle that drew onlookers' quizzical stares.

Two more gravediggers were waiting at the Vela plot when Leonides arrived. Grandmother asked Mother to park well off from the tomb, which had already been dug. When Mother walked toward the grave, the *sepultureros* were talking among themselves, the ones from Cotulla shaking their heads and staring down into the hole in disbelief.

"Señora Santos, disculpe, but the men are saying that there is already someone down there."

"What do you mean?"

"*La tumba ya tiene cadáver.* Somebody else is already buried down there."

Mother looked down into the musty earth and saw the form of

another *muertito*, the same angular silhouette of bones she had seen with her father in Cotulla.

"Who is it?"

"*Pues quién sabe, señora.* There's no way of knowing. It looks maybe like a man. The men say there are no papers saying anybody's here. It's an old cemetery, so who knows?"

The plot was the exclusive Vela family resting place in Laredo, with Grandmother's parents, sister Fermina, and her husband all alongside.

Were all of the borderlands scattered with bones?

Why were they all suddenly coming to light again?

Was it Abuelo Emeterio, Grandmother's father?

Was it a stranger whose stone had been discarded and his plot sold again?

There wasn't time to seek answers. The priest had arrived to perform the last rites, and Grandmother was staring from the car, wondering what all the conversation was about. This, my mother knew, would send Leandra into hysterics and likely lead to a full inventory of ancestral remains, and perhaps evicting that soul's bones from its resting place in the Vela plot.

"Just put him in there," my mother told the gravediggers in exasperation. "And don't say a word to my mother."

In the photograph, taken by my mother about two hours later over the freshly covered grave, Leandra wears an expression poised forever indeterminately between a scowl and a smile.

Then she paused a moment in front of the marble *lápida*, dedicated to "PADRE" and decorated with engravings of a crucifix flanked by two roosters, haloed by braids of grapevines hanging with ripe fruit. The priest was there finishing his prayers, and Grandmother dug through her purse to find an envelope she had prepared for him, stuffed with twenty one-dollar bills. He was still praying as Doña Leandra handed it to him, and he nodded hastily through one last sign of the cross and turned to walk away.

"The padre smelled like tequila," Grandmother told my mother as they walked back to the car, never mentioning Leonides.

Nearly fifty years later, we are back at that grave with my mother, cousin Bob and his wife, Jean, and their daughter, the latest Leandra Lopez, her new, just-polished boots gleaming in the hay-colored late afternoon light of Laredo, Texas.

In 1974, Grandmother had taken her place next to Leonides—and whoever else had been in everlasting repose down there with the rest of the old Velas. The great stone was inscribed with her memorial on the opposite side of Leonides's epitaph.

I had brought an old pair of elephant-skin Tony Lama boots that were ready for retirement. Over the years, I had left favorite pairs of my spent boots in strategic places around the world. We had bought two large sprays of orange zempazuchitl flowers, long known among Mexicanos to be the preferred blossoms of the dead, so bright that they could be seen from the afterlife. Leandra helped me arrange the flowers inside the boots, and we placed them in front of our abuelos' gravestone.

The Lopez were never much for sentimental goodbyes.

We got into Mother's silver Lincoln Town Car and headed out to find the highway north back to San Antonio.

VI

El Canto de Cenote Siete
(Con un autor anónimo)

Second Legajo

At the emergence of La Zona Perfecta.

All of the satraps and hegemons, the caliphs and caciques of yore, are gone.

The ruins of the onetime sultanates of America and Mexico, their cities and roadways, are strewn about the still uncharted landscape of our Santander Eterno. Those who have crossed the parched chalk desert to the north of the río, a fifteen-day walk few have attempted, have told of seeing the rubble of cities frozen in massive rolling glaciers of glassy trinitite that still bear the forms of dust clouds blowing across the land at the instant of the great light.

To the northeast there is a region of perpetual tornados.

The skies of the fifth sun were almost infinitely more resplendent than they appear today. Our skies, the skies over Revilla Nueva, are virtually black, only the faint orbs of the planets visible, grey motes twinkling in the void. Taking up a large part of the southern sky, there is one constellation of three stars in the shape of a vast spinnaker, the constellation Vela.

Mid-sky, the faint blur of the Milky Way is broken.

And the north is only obsidian emptiness.

By then, the Gulf's shore had moved out beyond where the eye could see, exposing cliffs and canyons that seemed bottomless.

Cities were revealed that had lain underwater for eons, and some said that they were made dry again so that the spirits of those who had once dwelled there could return and reoccupy the rude dwellings they had left behind. This unsettled the people, intuiting that there was nothing left of history but to welcome back the dead and to reconcile themselves fully to the conclusion that there would be no triumph, no apotheosis, no epiphany. Only the reawakening of the diurnal lives of the ancestors lighting up their inundated cities once again.

At least here in Revilla Nueva, so it was. All of the ancestors had returned.

The ancestors are like a fog that covers the foothills of the sierra. You can see them from far off, floating, running their hands through the treetops; but by the time you make your way to them, they have disappeared.

The signs had been appearing for some time, but it seemed improper, or premature, to acknowledge them. It was as if extraordinary events were just a part of everyday life, the list of augurs, the gob-smacking discoveries, the serendipities long heralded but still unexpected.

A truckload of rosaries bursts into flames, melting the metal beads, spilling out to cover the highway in a brilliant molten sheen that reflected the sky. That was the day we noticed that the properties of gravity had changed. More than that, it was not just that the calibrations of all weights had each been adjusted in one new universal measure; rather, the measure of gravity became as ephemeral as the weather. One day we could barely keep our feet on the ground. The next morning, feathers would fall like anvils, capable of causing you grievous harm.

All of this came to pass after the installation of La Zona Perfecta, that day of the afternoon of light, the bright tarde de luz when I swung out on the arm of that great tower and let go, only to be carried into the light.

And when I fell from that tower, it was a fall into an unfamiliar sleep, a caesura in memory that lasted I know not how long.

When I awoke again, I found myself seated alone in a small hot room where I could see light streaming in from in between the planks of the walls. There was a slow, steady humming sound, pulsing and undulating in waves that echoed back and forth, radiating and reversing—a sound so low and soothing I felt it in the marrow of my bones before I heard it. And then lo, I heard my own voice, speaking slowly, deliberately, the ghost of myself, saying,

"Tengo el cuerpo."
Whereupon it gave me such a start I rose up and shouted,
"Como?"
Only silence followed.
How could this be? I had been with my friends in the open plains of the
Llano River. We were climbing the tower and playing the old game, the
"juego triste."
"What did you say?"
I asked again, and only silence.
But when I sat back onto the old chair with a woven straw seat, I heard
a voice inside of me again, I know not whose, over the din of the constant,
throbbing hum.
"I have the body."
I focused on the room around me, de repente, I realized the cuartito was
full of bees, thousands and thousands of bees.
I looked down at my body, which appeared to have aged fifty years.

By an anonymous author.

The makeshift "psychomanteum" was built in a room in the ruins of the old Revilla library, a small stone building with arches a few blocks away from the plaza, near the banks of the río. It was there that Cenote Siete lived.

After most of the rest of the building fell, this room was left standing alone in the courtyard. Gradually, it became overgrown with yellow bougainvillea vines around which the bees of the land gathered and swarmed in great heaving clumps that dripped from the roof to the ground, giving the impression that the stone structure was alive, almost as if it were breathing.

Hidalgo Cenote would retreat to this place, closing the old wooden door behind him, and spend many hours there with his own thoughts. On these occasions, his friend Caracól would linger outside with the old man's two chihuahuas, sleeping in the shade of a nearby thatch veranda. Sometimes the old man remained inside for days on end, emerging only to walk to the riverbank and wash his face, ignoring anyone he passed on his way.

The interior was dark and cool, like a cave, illuminated only faintly by a few small beeswax candles on the floor, spaced out around the room's perimeter. The air had the scent of burning wax and stale honey. In one corner, there was a small shrine to Don Pedrito Jaramillo, a healer said to have come from these lands in the days of Nuevo Santander. To one side was the ancient conquistador's helmet he was carrying when he was found.

In the middle of the room was a large old wooden chair with armrests and green leather cushions, flat and shiny from prodigious wear. The oak legs and arms of the chair were carved in an elaborate corkscrew pattern, with bases that looked like taloned feet.

Just in front of the chair, positioned at the level of a sitter's knees, was a broad stone cistern filled with what looked like viscous black oil. This was the famed instrument of divination Caracól said that after sitting comfortably to the front of the chair, the hidalgo would close his eyes and gingerly lean forward on his arms, extending his neck so that when he opened his eyes, he was gazing into the murky reflection of his face in the oil. And there he would remain, unblinking, staring at his reflection until he would sit back and write his paginas of notes on a small board he kept on his lap.

After a long spell, Caracól would hear the door slowly open and Hidalgo Cenote would emerge, stiff and limping on his bad leg. He carried his paginas as if they were precious ore.

"Enough travels for today, Caracól," he would always say, walking to refresh himself at the river.

"Sí, mi Generál," Caracól would say, following along with the little dogs, "enough traveling for today."

I have the body.

Sitting alone in my casita beside the psychomanteum, when I can smell the fires of the cocinitas de Revilla Nueva, smelling chiles tostadas, hearing tortillas being patted and turned, then I can see all around me webs of blood-colored light filaments, reaching out in every direction, and each thread is the pathway of one ancestral lineage, radiating out from my ombligo, my navel, a single golden thread that quickly splits, quadruples,

becomes eight, then sixteen, multiplying in wavering bands that pulse out-
ward like a tide in every direction, to each farther body and home of the
ancestors, and then older, and older still.

By these threads I may travel out into every body ever connected to this
web, whether centuries, millennia, or eons into the past, divining my way
in a free fall, maintaining the attentive posture of a warrior, until I open
my eyes to take in a new sky, the wisdom of La Zona Perfecta allowing me
to know that I have come to the year 1747, 1894, or 1957.

I have your body, John Phillip, and it is 1976. We are reading the dia-
ries of Meriwether Lewis, namer of worlds. I have the body of Rafael Vela
and it is 1753 and I am with Colonel Escandón and we are walking along
the river at twilight. I have the body of Francisco, cacique of the Comecru-
dos, washing the hands of José Escandón upon our first meeting.

Because humans are creatures of forgetting, each body adapted to become
a vessel of memory, not just of the sovereign occupant of that cuerpo, but
all memories of all ancestors of all times, no matter how insignificant,
inscribed in infinitesimally small ciphers in every cell of our flesh. The blood
is a radio whose airwaves are time—the memory blood harbors broadcasts
through all time, into the future and into the past.

This is the Codex Humano upon which I conduct my researches.

I may see anything my ancestors ever saw. And when I leave them, I
do so as imperceptibly as a tide returning to sea. I may leave behind with
them images, words, thoughts, strains of songs they might never know were
anything other than their own imaginación fructuoso.

From a codex of the *Immaterial Empires*.

A wise man said, "The North is like a sea." It is the place of peregrination
and diaspora, the place of lost maps. To the northeast there is a region of
perpetual tornados.

This is how bodies became new bodies, how old lands became new lands.
Everything that was has been left behind, and a new story begins, the time
of the sixth sun. I will read the Codex Humano. I will recite the histories of
the lands of Nuevo Santander, long before the age of the Zona Perfecta.

In my many journeys, I have traveled far and wide into the time before, navigating in the channels of ancestral bloodlines in the manner described in the Upanishads, using the neglected capacity of our essence to sail through time in the way birds fly through the heavens seeking north, south, east, or west. I have flown through the skies of the past, descending into the bodies of my ancestral precursors spread out through the ages of creation, but most of all, those who lived in the early days of Nuevo Santander. I have peered out of ancestral eyes, I have received their stories like a blessing.

This is a part of the Codex Humano *titled* Immaterial Empires, *the record of that first time so that the tale shall never be lost again. Memory is no guarantee against forgetting. There were* mares enormes de memoria, *great seas of memory crystallized deep within the machines, and yet the archives were gutted, their legacies voided, drifting out into oblivion—there is no assurance that our dearest stories will not be forgotten altogether.*

In fact, there was so much memory, so much posterity embedded inside our machines, it gradually cast a shadow across our world, it overtook the mundo de historia *we had accustomed ourselves to dwelling in for untold ages.*

So I will tell one part of the story lost in that shadow, remembered by my own means, my glorious ancestral ethnogonies, my woeful recapitulations of the songs of the antepasados.

The Tejano Hesiod.

En La Zona Perfecta, all ancestors are beloved. This is a bond that echoes outside of time, out of the past, into the past, and into the future. What is the bond? The common knowledge, carried in the lineage, of the poignant mystery of our incarnation. Every lineage carries that mystery like a family secret, and spoken or not, every generation receives it and passes it on.

Where the dead are, and where the living, splinters blown across a vast desert, the last, small fragments of a building that stood for ages but cannot be pieced together again. All of them are here at once, always hidden, except when bathed in the light of cometary radiance or, better, the coronal glow of a solar eclipse. Their ghosts can be seen as shimmering bodies then.

So many are forgotten altogether, yet they too are present, even if no evident records of them exist, as if they had been abandoned forever in the abyss of the past.

Many were denizens of the three great empires that came before La Zona, each one reaching farther into the unfathomable Before of the New World; the Empire of Blood, the Empire of Memory, and the Empire of Fire. Every citizen of these Imperia bore the indelible scar on their hearts: The sign of radiant entwined snakes, the hermetic emblem of La Conquista in the Gran Archivo de La Zona.

Gods and men both sprang from the same primordial dust, "how the gods and mortal men are born from the same source," as the Greek poet Hésiodo once sang it, and they lived like "gods without any care in their hearts, free and apart from labor and misery . . . and they died as if going to sleep." It is said those first ones, the warrior sojourners of that first age all became "divinities, powers of good on earth, guardians of mortal men . . . being hidden in air and going all over the earth. They were the golden race, the first to be hidden under the earth. The silver race betrayed the gods and abandoned all homage to them." Then came the bronze race, the one born from the mesquite trees and the sandy earth, "devoted to doing war's wretched works and acts of hubris." These were misshapen beings of great strength with invincible arms, "bronze weapons, stone hearts, bronze houses, stone eyes, bronze tools."

These fell as victims to each other's slaughtering.

Then came the heroes, the demigods, the conquistadores who brought their brigantinas across the vast desolation.

> Would that I now were no longer alive in the fifth age of men,
> But had died earlier or had been born at a later time.
> For we live in the age of the iron race, when men shall never
> Cease from labor and woe by day, and never be free from
> Anguish at night, for hard are the cares that the gods will be
>   giving.

Those were the years new winds began to blow.

They said the fireball was three miles across. Seen from the moon, it was a damsin orchid blooming against a matte ochre wall. A cascade of perfect circles radiated out as the flowering fire spread out across the planet,

*rippling around and around the globe until the whole mass appeared to
shiver, as if teetering on the edge of disappearance.*

El Requerimiento.

In the age of the setting out of the naos, for them, there was no America.

Never America, but Nueva España, Nuevo Santander, Nueva Galicia,
Nueva Extremadura, Nuevo León, even Nuevo Mexico, as if a lifelong
diaspora to a distant land was simply a matter of recasting and reorienting
your home geography upon virgin earth, fixing alignments with the same
cardinal directions, the same sky and terrain, mutatis mutandis, inscribing all into the worldly order of things as it must have been laid down by
the creator, that mankind's triumph would be made manifest in Iberia, y
toda su progenie.

What a strangely wonderful explorer's ambition, to remake your home
wherever you find yourself in the unimagined world, as if that home were
the one dominion of your birthright and as such must be replicated everywhere, at any cost and to the greater glory of God. We find and make our
home anywhere.

Granted, los Iberios knew such geomancy was not to be undertaken
lightly.

The unknown world was first claimed under the divinely appointed hege-
mony of the pontiff and the king—with the recitation of the Requerimiento.

From the beginning of the age of reconnaissance, there were faint-
hearted postulations of the rights of conquest. But scripted by theologians
and jurists of the Court, the words of the Requerimiento operated beyond
the reach of mortal argument. It was instead a litany of the sublime order
of the universe, demonstrating how all lands were subject to the same cosmic rule, on behalf of King Ferdinand and his daughter Doña Juana,
"subduers of the barbarous nations."

We are all descended from the same two parents, expelled from the
paradisal garden that was their first troth with God, and was very likely
located in Iberia. The children of Adam and Eve have dispersed across the
planet.

Conveniently, there was no commandment: Thou shalt not conquer.
There was no commandment: Thou shalt not enslave.

As the anuncio reads,

> . . . on account of the multitude which has sprung from his man and
> woman in the five thousand years since the world was created, it was
> necessary that some men should go one way and some another, and
> that they should be divided into many kingdoms and provinces, for in
> one alone they could not be sustained.

*Thus did God eventually come to place all nations under the charge of
one man, called Saint Peter, "that all should obey him, and that he should
be the head of the whole human race, wherever men should live, and under
whatever law, sect, or belief they should be; and he gave him the world
for his kingdom and jurisdiction." Peter's absolute authority passed to the
popes, and through them to the king and queen of España.*

*Tributes and donations would be required and in exchange the caciques
with their people could continue to receive gifts and privileges from their
vassals, retaining dominion over their former lands.*

*The message of the Catholic faith would be preached and promulgated
in the new lands, though their leaders would not be forced to convert,
though the Requerimiento noted that "almost all the inhabitants of the rest
of the islands have done."*

And if the leaders did not agree to these conditions,

> we shall forcefully enter into your country and shall make war against
> you in all ways and manners that we can, and shall subject you to the
> yoke and obedience of the church and of their highnesses; we shall
> take you and your wives and your children and shall make slaves of
> them, and as such shall sell and dispose of them as their highnesses
> may command . . . and we protest that the deaths and losses which
> shall accrue from this are your fault, and not of their highnesses, or
> ours, or of these soldiers who come with us.

And they spoke all of this with a wanton purity.
The royal notary would step forward to sign his witness that the

Requerimiento had been duly read, establishing Spanish dominion over the lands.

The ledger of lost treasures.

According to Juan Bautista Chapa, the once anonymous co-chronicler of the earliest expeditions de Don Alonso de León into nuestras tierras Mesteñas, based on the records of Governor Don Martín de Zavala, these were the names of the Indian nations that were encountered in the 1620s, just in the vicinity of the villa de Cerralvo, Nuevo Santander:

Aguijagua, Alazapa, Amacueryo, Amapoala, Amito, Amituagua, Amoana, Amoguama, Caculpaluniame, Caguayoguame, Caguchuasca, Caguilipan, Cajaquepa, Calipocate, Camacuro, Camalucano, Camuchinibara, Canacabala, Canaine, Canameo, Canapeo, Capae, Capujaquin, Caraña, Caraara, Catuajano, Cayaguaguin, Cayague, Canapuro, Coalimoje, Comite, Congue, Conicoricho, Coote, Cuepano, Escabel, Guagui, Gualolote, Gualegua, Guamipeje, Guampexte, Guanapujamo, Guanpe, Guelamoye, Guinaima, Iliguigue, Imimule, Imipecte, Janapase, Jimiopa, Lespoama, Maciguara, Macomala, Matascuco, Moquiaguine, Noreo, Palaguine, Panuia Quetapone, Quiguascguama, Quinegaayo, Quinemeguete, Sayulime, Sologuegue, Tacuanama, Tancacoama, Tatoama, Tatocuene, Teguampaxte, Yechimicuale.

None of these nations survived the wars waged against them, and none of their names have been spoken for hundreds of years. Their languages were lost, along with the names of their gods. When they perished, others appeared to replace them, legions, and they too succumbed to disease and war. The soldier chronicler Chapa observed,

> We must attribute this depopulation to the many sins that the Indians commit and that their ancestors committed. Although these nations have not taken part in idolatries, they had (and still have) many superstitions and abuses. Therefore, His Divine Majesty punishes them and is annihilating them, so that in the course of time all the Indians of New Spain and Peru will be exterminated, as those who may live at that time will see.

The historian in the ruins.

Though a few adamantine Spanish and French souls had ventured there to stake claims since the discovery of the New World, the lands of the Seno Mexicano in the remote northern hinterlands of Nueva España were rugged and unyielding. There were tales of how the peaks of the Sierra Huasteca cut the sky to ribbons there, and that the clouds then rained blood, giving succor to forests of ghastly fauna full of monstrous beasts and marauding bands of heathen, hirsute godless folk whose faces were set in the middle of their chests.

In one of the first accounts of the Indios del Seno, Alonso de León explained how of all the pagans ever encountered anywhere in the world, only the Indios of these lands had been found to be utterly without any belief in a supreme being. Other heathens had bowed to their heathen gods, but these savages under the dominion of Nueva España presented an even more egregious insult to the creator.

They were not false believers. Worse, they were true unbelievers, infieles salvajes verdaderos, the truest savage infidels of all time.

Beyond the mountains of the northern cordillera, there were rumors of vast, stony deserts full of predators—crazed gatos de monte, razor-fanged serpientes, gigantic scorpions, and anthropophagous harpies with wings that shimmered like black velvet and eyes that glowed like coals. And still the settlers, among them my ancestors, set out for those lands.

Why would they go there in the first place? What was it that drew them to the very end of the earth? And they didn't make their journey just to have a look around, but to settle forever, to build a new home upon unknown earth, the tierra from which they would send forth their progeny into the unmapped desert of the future.

Why would a Spaniard born in Spain at the time of Columbus's journey across the ocean, for such was the provenance of the first generation of conquistadores, leave the known world behind to mingle with all of these monstrosities of nature?

"Because we were Jews," said the Historian, as we sat in the ruins of the gazebo in the ancient plaza of Revillagigedo.

"They were conversos, Jews that had converted to Catholicism at the

time of the expulsion of 1492. Because they wanted to get as far away from the Inquisition as possible. And even then, the Inquisition came looking for them. Even in the New World."

But if you were ready to abandon Spain and go to such a distant, unknown place, why not remain a Jew? Did they come to these torrid lands to build new hidden, secret sanctuaries for devotions they had publicly renounced?

The Historian pulled a worn scroll of old yellowed photographs from his pocket and began thumbing through them, each one as supple as paper-thin leather. He carefully pulled one out and held it up to see.

"Look at this," he said. "My Jewish grandfathers."

The color photograph, blurry from age and handling, showed three men dressed in magenta robes with golden sashes tied to one side. Two were tall and guero, the one in the middle was shorter and darker, almost prieto. He was holding a goblet aloft, his dark eyes fixed on the golden cup. To his left, in one hand, the man held a candle, decorated with elaborate wax flowers, in the other he held a sword. The man on the right held a large book out from his chest. Their faces were all rapt, expressionless, as if captured inside the sudden flash of a transcendent moment.

"This appears to be some sort of ceremony, no? They are People of the Book, and this is some kind of ceremony."

Such tales took their place alongside the insistent but unproven rumors of a lost world civilization, Atlantis, Mu, Lemuria, reminding us how everything we know is apocrypha, testimonies regathered in the aftermath of a cataclysmic and forgotten diaspora.

Everything was apocrypha on the planet of perfect mystery.

And then we found our blood was teeming with the mysteries of our antepasados.

VII

El Real Archivo de Indias

1. De la tarjeta provisional #00213477

Though the four-hundred-year-old main building of the Archivo General de Indias was to be shuttered some years for renovation, the reading room with access to the archive's vast collection was still open, relocated to a stone building across the street lined with orange trees, in the shadow of the great Catedrál de Santa Maria de la Sede.

I had only a few short study days to spend in Sevilla for searching through the Archivo's records for documents pertaining to the Vela-Lopez family story.

"What is the nature of your proposed study?"

"Perdón?"

"What is the research you propose to undertake in the Archivo? If you are granted a *permiso*, I mean."

Directora Ruiz, as she introduced herself, of the Archivo General de Indias, was an elegant, urbane Sevillana, dressed in a beige silk pantsuit and a purple chiffon scarf, with a perfunctory, businesslike air. She sat confidently behind a large, ornately carved teak desk, in a vaulted-ceilinged room within the limestone building that was the temporary home of the Archivo. She was already impatient, even a little perturbed, with me for arriving at the library without the proper papers of identification and references from esteemed academics or politicians to petition for access to the collections on my behalf. Ordinarily, she informed me, permission to use the archive had to be requested by correspondence at least six weeks in advance of a proposed study visit.

I had come that morning only with my passport and the suggestion that they do a Google search on my name to prove I was an author with research interests likely to be served by documents and other materials in the Archivo's holdings.

"*Googlear?* Tsk, tsk, tsk," Directora Ruiz had replied quickly, shaking her head. "We do not do our research on the Internet here, Señor Santos."

But she was preparing to take her morning break, so she asked me to return an hour later and said she would see what she could do regarding my request then.

Installed in an old building that had once been a grand market, the Real Archivo de Indias, as it was first known, had been designated in 1785 by King Carlos III to house and catalogue all of the documents of the Consejo de las Indias, the governing body of royal councilors who oversaw all of the policy and administration of Spanish America—las Indias. Though Spain's rule in las Américas was by then nearing its end, the Archivo in Sevilla, and others like it in Simanca and Cádiz, became the repositories of the mountains of policy, correspondence, reports, maps, censuses, inventories, anything written, inscribed, or signed that pertained to Spanish imperial governance in the Mundo Nuevo.

If there were any documents relating to the establishment of the Villas del Norte, perhaps even mentioning my ancestors, they would be there. After a nervous lunch of fideos with piñon nut pesto and other tapas at a taberna nearby, I returned to Señora Ruiz's office to find her in a slightly more buoyant mood.

Suddenly, she was asking me questions to complete the form for permission to use the Archivo.

"Are you a historian, Señor Santos? This is a historical archive."

"I'm looking for some of the documents relating to my Spanish ancestors in the far north of Nueva España. I'm Chicano, Mexican American, from Texas."

"Chi-ca-no?" She asked warily, writing on a notepad.

"Some spell it with an X."

"C-h-i-x-a-n-o?"

"X-i-c-a-n-o," I replied.

"Que curioso."

"I'm looking for the story of how my ancestors came out of Spain, and how they went to the tierras mas norteñas de Nueva España."

"Is this for a historical work?"

"Yes, and cultural . . . y quizas un poco de ciencia-ficcíon, como en Don Quixote," I said, grinning.

Directora Ruiz looked up at me over her eyeglasses, apparently only mildly amused. "This has nothing to do with your last book, then?" she said, adding with a smile, "which I saw on Amazon. That one was about suicide, no?" She looked down at the form again, surveying it up and down.

"Well . . . ," I replied, "not entirely."

"And that one had nothing to do with Spain, puro Mexico, no?"

"It dealt more with my father's family. My mother's family was Español."

"Well, regardless, you know this is not a public library, per se. We operate under royal authority, not the offices of the state. People don't just walk through the door and receive a *permiso* just like that. We are an international institution of research. You see that, don't you?"

"I am very sorry for the short notice," I offered, and then added, "and very grateful if you can help me in this instance," just trying to keep my foot in the door. Could the whole journey have still been for naught?

She queried me with a forced inquisitorial tone. "You don't intend to write any nonsense about España, do you? You know . . . *la leyenda negra*?" She was only half-joking.

"Directora Ruiz, I'm only trying to unearth the story about where we came from, the Mexicanos of what became Texas—the

story of los Iberios who journeyed to that part of Nueva España that
was called Nuevo Santander."

"*Nuevo* Santander?" She sighed, wrote that name down on the
form, and then told me I would be granted a *tarjeta provisional*, a
temporary permit that would be good for my stay in Sevilla. For
future visits, I would have to present the proper credentials to gain
admission.

"But frankly," she said, rising to shake my hand and dismiss me,
"I regret to tell you I don't believe you're going to find anything relevant to that subject here, señor. I'm afraid this Nuevo Santander
was a very remote place in our history, and you may find our librarians haven't even heard of it. I have not. *Pero, buena suerte!*"

And with that, like the entrance to Oz, a pair of large glass doors
at the other end of her office opened with a whoosh and she gestured for me to take the steps at the end of a long stone corridor, one
flight up, to find the reading room.

There, one of the librarians of the Archivo would be waiting to
help me in my futile quest.

2. A catalogue of lost libraries

Herodotus tells a story of how his predecessor, the Greek historian
Hecataeus, on a visit to ancient Thebes, had proudly recited to the
priests of Zeus sixteen generations of his own lineage of descent
from a god, only to have them present him with their own lineages
of kings stretching back three hundred and forty-one generations,
which Herodotus reckoned to encompass a total of 11,340 years into
the past. And no man had ever descended from a god, they added.

In San Antonio, we tore down those buildings that reminded
us of earlier times. Our lineages virtually forgotten, we have paved
over our oldest stories to build the suburbs. These were only the latest in our long efforts to extinguish and relinquish the past.

When it comes to our earliest origins, *everything* is apocrypha.
We spin tales of the unremembered based upon evidence we find
buried in the ground, embedded deep in hoary ice, in rumors of

secrets kept among the storied Illuminati, said to be keepers of a tale the rest of us have abandoned.

Provence and Iberia hid away their secrets in caves and distant mountain chapels, in remote villages along the Mediterranean coast. They hid away their virgin cults in lands rumored to be the last refuge of Mary, the mother of Jesus, and Mary Magdalene, who were brought to those lands in a boat piloted by Lazarus, whom Christ had risen from the dead. They hid away statues dedicated to ebony virgins, relics of the apostles, of James, the brother of Jesus who was said to have first brought Christianity to the Iberian Peninsula; some stories even spoke of a lost sanctuary that harbored the head of Jesus, the true grail.

The geography of southern France and northern Spain was a craggy mountainous region, bounded by the Cantabrian range to the south, crisscrossed by the peaks of the Pyrenees. For many, it was a geography of heresy, a part of Christendom where the heretical personal Pentecost of the Gnostics, deniers of Vatican authority, still burned in the secret recesses of human hearts. Is there a still more remote story hidden within this geography? Does that story remain alive within the descendants of those lands, unknown even to themselves?

The lands of northern Iberia were the final, fleeting refuge of the Neanderthal. They likely were the lands where early humans became extinct humans, where the Neanderthals encountered *Homo sapiens*, perhaps even mingling with them. Early humans painted terse poetic visions of their lives on the walls of caves throughout the region. And many years later, for seven centuries, the same lands would become home to all three Abrahamic faiths, before their progeny would set out to conquer and re-create their world in the Mundo Nuevo. There, once again, ancient peoples would encounter each other for the first time, establishing borders between civilization and barbarism, and then slowly transgressing and erasing them.

How many came across great distances, through the millennia, to arrive there?

How many were there before the parting of Pangaea, the great earth island of earliest times?

How do their stories pertain to us? Don't you wonder this too?

Where are the sentries that can gather the echoes of the distant past, can sense the feedback from the future, from the colmena of La Zona Perfecta?

Even that which has been long lost can suddenly return to the light.

Using remote sensing satellite photography, archaeologists have discovered ancient roads crisscrossing Syria, ancient canals in the high Peruvian desert, perhaps even evidence in the Atlantic Ocean of concentric platforms that supported the buildings and towers of legendary Atlantis, as described in Plato.

Recently, reports surfaced of the discovery of a site in upper Egypt that may prove to be the grand lost library of Alexandria, with lecture halls that accommodated as many as five thousand students, built around stone stages where their scholarly teachers would hold forth with all of their lore of the ancient world, much of it forgotten after the library's mysterious destruction and disappearance.

Libraries had been a part of my world from as far back as I could remember, beginning with the Westfall branch of the San Antonio Library in our neighborhood, where I first read books about astronomy and space travel, the makeup of the solar system, the Milky Way and the surrounding galaxies. There were also hidden treasures waiting there, like William Goyen's sadly forgotten *House of Breath*, a tale of another secret Texas.

There have been many other libraries for me since then.

The main library in San Antonio was built alongside the river that had nurtured the city from its birth and had remained a presence in my family's life through centuries, including the scene of my grandfather Santos's death. Gazing out the big picture windows, leaving whatever I was reading, I would remember that was the same river where my grandfather's body had been discovered back in the late '30s, a secret legacy never touched on as I heard the tourist barges float by, their captains regaling the visitors with colorful tales of historic San Antonio.

There were many unseen forces that brought all of us to San Antonio's downtown library, from the students cramming or cribbing for exams, to the homeless man with his plastic bags full of clothing, lazily paging through Heidegger's *Being and Time*, to old ladies sitting at the microfiche display kiosks, perusing archived city newspapers from the 1920s.

In the Radcliffe Camera of the Bodleian Library in Oxford, I listened every hour for the sluicing of the urinals in the basement of the stone building, a great cascading tumult that sounded as if a thousand springs had been unloosed, running down the stone steps of the circular building, while all the scholars remain fixed on the tomes spread out across the desk before them. Everyone there was consumed in some hermetic pursuit, as if time was wasting before the fever to answer some esoteric question would consume them.

One don walked around the main reading room of the Bodleian in an academic gown that was tattered to ribbons at the hem, climbing up and down tall ladders to high stacks and then perching there, paging through some tome, while he kept one leg hanging through the steps of the ladder. Unshaven, hair unkempt, and a bit gamey of scent, he was said to be the son of a famous Oxford philosopher and a mad musicologist mother. At his desk, ungainly piles of notes scribbled on torn scrap paper stood alongside makeshift newspaper placemats with half-eaten figs and plums, but the head librarian let him be, explaining to me once that he was completing the major work of his lifetime, which would reestablish, once and for all, the veracity of the music of the spheres.

Looking around the reading room of the Archivo, it seemed as if all of the people of the world had convened there in search of lost common threads that improbably linked everyone to the saga of the Mundo Nuevo. All of us were delvers into the chronicles of that lost world.

There was a distinguished elder *catedrático* who looked like one of the señores anónimos from the portraits by El Greco, thumbing through a bound set of prints. At another desk, a small man who looked to be a Peruvian Indian gazed at a massive computer monitor displaying a series of quipus, knotted strings that were used by the Incas to record the stories and everyday accounts of their world. One Asian woman was the most daringly appointed scholar, dressed in a tight leopard-print skirt as she lifted maps onto an illuminated table for closer inspection. In another corner of the large stone room, a black scholar in a three-piece suit was barely visible over piles of documents pertaining to the Caribs that had been laid at his workstation.

At the Archivo, there was no reticence about sharing the bounty of documentary evidence that had been amassed over nearly five centuries regarding Spain's destiny in the New World. Originally established by Christopher Columbus, the library was first mandated by a royal cédula of Emperor Carlos V in 1544, ordering that all papers referring to the Indias, whatever the dominion, should be gathered and preserved in a single trove.

At the Bodleian or the British Museum, you might be brought a single-page document, sealed inside a laminated sleeve, and then be watched by a guard while you studied it. At the Archivo, librarians brought out the documents in great bales of files stacked in wheelbarrows, each set of papers wrapped in canvas sheaths that were tied loosely with cloth bindings stamped with the royal seal of the Archivo showing two pillars and a caravela setting out to sea.

Lopez and Velas appear in the manifests of some of the first ships to the New World—and in one of the first accounts of La Provincia de los Tejas. Rather than the predicted lacuna in the colección that Directora Ruiz had warned me of, I quickly discovered a vast chronicle of the lost world that encompassed the patrimony of my lineages of Lopez and Velas in the remote region of Nueva España known as Nuevo Santander.

Though these records had not been requested by other readers for many years, there were five large legajos (folios) in the Archivo's collection that relate to the story of the expeditions of exploration, founding, and settlement of the towns of Nuevo Santander, all under the heading *Expediente sobre la Población y Pacificación de la Costa del Seno Mexicano*, dossiers of proposals, reports, and assessments of the campaigns of colonization between the years 1736 and 1775.

In the very same times that the villas were being founded, new discoveries were being made about the antiquity and origins of Castilian Spanish. In 1786, William Jones discovered similarities between Sanskrit and

*Latin that led to a new science of linguistics that illuminated the prove-
nance of Spanish among other ancient languages that came from India.*

These documents are all meticulously inscribed and sewn
together into folios that each reported on the state of affairs in
each of the Villas del Norte. All of the towns my ancestors had
helped to found as members of the expeditions of José de Escandón
appear there, including Revilla, Mier, and Camargo. As I already
suspected, my family's story was inextricable from the story of the
last conquistadorial adventure of Nueva España. The story of our
onetime Spanish, then Mexican, then American family was hidden
away there, deep within the old archive in Sevilla, and we had never
even been taught to think of ourselves as Españoles.

These codicils testify to the elaborate apparatus the Spanish
Crown's rapporteurs must've traveled with, portable desks, ink-
wells, and writing instruments of wood, bone, and feathers, damp-
ing vellum covers to dry the freshly written pages.

*Consider the libraries they carried with them, scriptures, the great works in
Latín y Griego, all carried on the backs of burros in large leather saddlebags.*

The earliest legajos contain accounts of the first journeys into the
forbidding lands of the "bárbaros," quickly followed by the initial
petitions to the Crown and the Council of the Indies to support missions of settlement and evangelization in the infidel territories. The
greatest challenge, according to these optimistic colonizers, would
be the hostilities Spaniards encountered from the many communities of indigenous peoples scattered throughout the lands. In one letter from Antonio Ladrón de Guevara in 1748, well after Escandón's
campaign had begun, Guevara refers to the "Barbaridád y Aposta-
sía" of the "Yndios," from el "Ansiano," the eldest, to the youngest,
"la criatura mas ygnocente." According to Guevara, all were treated
fairly and brought into church when possible, but the Christianity
of the Españoles guided their conduct. Though he denounces some
Yndios Christianos as apostates—he complains that during peace
they have been allowed to come and go among the Españoles "sin
la menor diligencia de reducirlos ala Ley de Dios." This criticism
of laxity in pursuit of evangelization of the Indians was particularly
blamed on Escandón.

Even more confusing, Guevara reports, is the problem of who the Españoles' real foes are, for "when there are hostilities, it is hard to know who is fighting due to the great diversity of [Indian] nations."

These legajos also compile mounting evidence and pertinent details of a world being discovered.

There were hand-drawn portolani maps of the Costa Seno Mexicano, the Gulf Coast, showing the original place names given by the Spaniards, including one, Matamoros en Bagdad, near the mouth of the Rio Grande, shortened later to Matamoros—meaning killers of Muslims, echoing old enmities from Iberia.

There were the earliest maps of the region, more abstract, even poetic, than practical, one showing overlays of thick, wavy watercolor lines capturing the dense and seemingly endless series of hills and mountains of the Sierra Huasteca. Other maps, painted in the round, evidenced the hands of indio artists, incorporating styles of drawing from the indigenous world in their mandate to create a new Spanish cartography of the unknown tierras.

Beyond the Valley of Mexico, Nueva España emerged as a series of cartographic hallucinations over two hundred years. The earliest maps showed the wild stretches of the north, like an almost boundless sea. This was the age of the "northern mystery." In the mapa de Enrico Martines, 1758, you can see the domes and steeples of the seven great cities of Cibola arranged in a zigzag, each one with chevron flags flying, defended by wall and parapets. The tales of Fray Marcos de Niza sent many hidalgos into the vast desolation of the north in search of their fortunes in the splendid legendary cities of Marata, Tontoneac, Quivira, Avis, Petatlán, Tiguex, and Cívola. Might there be another Tenochtitlán?

In the 1587 map of Richard Hakluyt, Quivira appears on the Pacific coast, Tiguex is on a large inland lake and noted as the home of the noble Teguayos. Perhaps they had been Zuni villages. Perhaps Marata was a cluster of abandoned pueblos on the Gila River. Perhaps Avis was Acoma. Tontonteac was Tusuyan, the land of the Hopi. Francisco Coronado was said to have drawn a map of his journey to Tiguex, but it was lost in his letter to the viceroy in August of 1540.

A 1796 map showed the Rio Grande flowing into the Hudson Bay. And a map from 1797 showed the legendary cities of Cibola near the western edge of the continent. Both of the originals of these maps were lost in Mexico City when the National Archive was plundered after the Mexican-American War.

As for the location of the Villas del Norte, the La Paz map of 1783 shows Mier and Revilla, as well as San Antonio de Valero, situated in a great shaded zone labeled *Apachería*. The 1768 map by Jose Antonio de Alzate y Ramirez marks Camargo as well. Several maps from this period point to places from where the Aztecas were believed to have come before settling in the Valle de Mexico. Alzate's map shows a certain "Laguna de Teguayo," far to the northwest of Camargo, with the legend of "the Indians destined for Mexico." An earlier map, by Francisco Alvarez y Barreiro from 1728, includes the Laguna de Teguaio, "de donde salieron los Indios Mexicanos con su principe a Poblar a Mexico." And in 1701, a German cartographer's map showing the Rio Grande notes, "The People about this river are continually in wars with the Spanyards."

For the forty years covered by the five legajos pertaining to Nuevo Santander, frontera scribes roamed these hinterlands with their writing gear, assembling their elaborately calligraphic and bound accounts of each new settlement, ironically attesting to the formation of new domains in what was already a dying empire.

Perhaps it's not surprising then that some of their stories are full of an unmistakable foreboding.

Through the study of a host of learned sources from many centuries, Beatus of Liébana, a monk from Asturias, in his **Commentary on the Apocalypse** had discerned that his times, toward the end of the eighth century, were already under way with the story of the seventh and last millennial week, auguring the last days of earthly time.

> These are the twelve Disciples of Christ, preachers of the faith, mentors of the people. Although all carry out the same work, each one of them received a specific region to preach in: Peter Rome, Andrew Acaia, Thomas India, James Spain, John Asia, Matthew Macedonia,

Phillip Gaul, Bartholomew Licaonia, Simon Zelotes Egypt, James the brother of the Lord Jerusalem . . . This is the church reaching through the world. This is the sacred and select seed, the royal priesthood disseminated throughout the world.

Mexican writer Carlos Fuentes described Mexico's relationship to Spain "as if the Atlantic were more of a chasm than a bridge." Perhaps Mexicans preferred seeing themselves still at the ends of the earth—and many Españoles act as if all that had happened in the time of New Spain has been forgotten and fully absolved. Mexico had been the place where the dreams of Spain and the prophecies of the lineage of Abraham might come true. Mexico, as the latter-day offspring of ancient Iberia, represented the fitful unfolding of the final prophecy—which would ultimately bring the triumphal end of time.

There were stories of miraculous events in those lands from as early as 1710, when an earthquake was said to have been halted when an artist displayed his portrait of San Francisco to the heavens. Another painting depicting this event showed the artist passed out in front of his canvas, an angel taking up his brush instead to complete the miraculous portrait.

By the time of Escandón's campaign to found the towns of Nuevo Santander, the age of Nueva España was already beginning to wane. Already two hundred and fifty years old, Mexico was outgrowing its colonial trappings. The signs and wonders of an earlier age that had affirmed Spain's exalted destiny in the New World, and human history itself, had passed.

Instead, there were new, more ominous presagios.

And then, in another account from the year 1789, multiple documents reported the birth in Querétaro of a niño monstruoso, taken by the host of doctors and scholars who had interpreted her birth to be an augur of the most serious reckonings in store for Mexico. The many drawings of the niña in this folio depict a newborn girl, anatomically displayed, drawn with a taxonomist's dispassion—with another fetus being born from the baby's womb, its legs already visibly emerging.

Somehow, nature had been overturned in Querétaro.

According to one attending doctor's report, it was a prophetic synecdoche, and a sign of the chastisements to come for the great hubris of Spain's adventure in Mexico: a child giving birth to a child. It was said this poor creature was God's accusation of Nueva España's height of hubris, a human conceit that was surely destined to fail.

Perhaps the news of this birth eventually arrived even in remote Nuevo Santander.

By the time of Escandón's death in 1770, Nueva España would only last another fifty years. The Conde de la Sierra Gorda was tormented by his own depredations, but he was spared the fate of seeing Spain's sacred mission of colonizing Mexico come to an end.

3. In the month of August, on the twelfth day, in the year of 1767

That was the year the bedraggled settlers of the Villas del Norte of Nuevo Santander received their long-promised royal land grants, delayed for twenty years by their onetime leader, the Colonel José de Escandón. It was the year of the historic "Autovisita" or "Visita Generál," the viceregal delegation sent from Querétaro that visited each of the twenty-four Villas del Norte to apportion the mandated royal land grants.

In every villa, settlers were gathered in the central plaza as the grants were announced, and in the succeeding days the viceroy's representative would visit each of the families to perform the ritual of land dispensation where a deed would be read, prayers offered, and then cut pasture grass would be tossed to the four directions. From that point on, ownership of the land was considered a *compromiso* with the king, a royally vouchsafed property.

In the centuries that followed, the progeny of those settlers struggled to maintain their claims to these lands as a succession of different regimes assumed power over what became Mexico and then Texas, dispossessing many of their tierras by myriad bureaucratic calumnies, and for others, managing complex legal negotiations as the original grants were carved into smaller and smaller parcels of land bequeathed to the rapidly multiplying scions of each successive generation.

When human memory has failed to maintain the story of our ancestors, property deeds have often filled in much of what has been forgotten. In this case, Grandmother's ancestors were granted lands to the north of the Rio Grande, in what was to become Starr County, on the border with Mexico in South Texas. There were no grand deeds or parchments to guarantee these titles. Instead, written faintly in her aged zigzag script, inside the cover of Grandmother's final little red leather address book, were the facts pertaining to this remaining Spanish legacy that she had inherited with her sister:

Fermina Vela Ferguson, Porción 69, share 299, Starr County,
Leandra Vela Lopez, Porción 69, share 197, Starr County.

The "porción" was the standard unit for the royal land grants that were given to the settlers of Nuevo Santander. Most porciones were rectangular tracts of land usually with a half mile of river frontage, extending inland anywhere from eleven to sixteen miles. To this day, throughout the Rio Grande river valley of southeast Texas, many families have maintained ownership, often with great difficulty, of these two-hundred-and-fifty-year-old landholdings, and many in the region know the historic porción numbers associated with the oldest surnames of the territory—the Llanos Mesteños, as they had been known in the early years of Spanish colonization.

These grants were made on both sides of the river, and Grandmother's and Tía Fermina's were on the north side in Starr County, a notoriously corrupt Texas satrapy, legendary for the dead men's votes that delivered the election of LBJ in his first Texas senatorial election in 1948.

"Porción 69, share 299, in Starr County?" my friend Homero Vera, a noted historian of the region, asked during one of my visits to the valley. "That was a part of the Guerra family grants, out of old Revilla, on the Mexican side, that became Guerrero."

Grandmother had never mentioned the Vela land grants to me, but she had spoken proudly of Guerra ancestors, though little more than that we were related to some of the many Guerras who live in San Antonio and in the valley, where the Guerras retain extensive ranches and properties and are distinguished citizens and success-ful professionals from Brownsville to Hebronville.

In the Archivo documents relating to Revilla, I found the name of Vicente Guerra Cañamar listed in the first census as one of the orig-inal founders of the settlement in 1750, during one of Colonel Escan-dón's campaigns. No extraneous papers or materials can be taken into the Archivo, so when I returned to my room that evening I scram-bled to find a genealogical research publication I had brought with me that contained the same name, Vicente Guerra Cañamar, as the patriarch of the Guerra family, already residing in Revilla in 1750.

Uncle Lico's genealogical family disk had established how Grandmother's grandfather Jose Maria Vela had married Dorotea Guerra de Ruiz Guadiano, the daughter of José Ignacio Policar-pio Guerra and his second wife, Maria Francisca Ruiz Guadiano. Their only son, Emeterio Vela, was my great-grandfather. But it was through that great-great-grandmother Dorotea that Grandmother had inherited her share of the onetime vast Guerra porción.

Uncle Lico discovered another document that detailed the origi-nal grant to grandfather Leonides's family, citing the circumstances of the original acquisition by Don Antonio Lopez, followed by a litany of the generations of offspring among whom the first, large piece of land was divided. My lineage of Lopez were descended from the union of Cecilio Lopez de la Garza, grandson of Don Antonio, and Josefa Olivarez, which produced four children, among them my great-grandfather Viviano. Dying young, along with his wife, Segunda, Viviano would leave their children, Blas, José, and my grandfather Leonides, early in their lives as orphans.

Their claim to the great history of Spain, which had been pur-chased rather than granted from the Spanish Crown—those rem-nants of Porción 28 that my uncle Lico had been so proud of, near the old Villa de Camargo, were left behind when the Lopez left for Texas, and they were gradually forgotten.

And as for Grandmother's and Tía Fermina's remaining shares of the old Guerra porción, Leandra and her sister dutifully maintained all tax payments on the small parcels of land in Starr County, and it was ten years after Grandmother's death in 1974 that Mother and her siblings finally decided to sell the land, though the family maintains mineral rights to this day. Mother says oil companies and other landowners are sucking all the oil out with a "crooked straw" from miles away so that they'll never have to write a check to the family.

But once the Archivo records allowed me to connect Grandmother's Vela lineage to the Guerra family, the question that had long puzzled Uncle Lico until his death was finally answered: Who were our true Spanish ancestors, and where did they come from?

At least one of our ancestral lines, the Vela-Guerras, passing through Revilla in the age of Escandón, originated in the northernmost territories of Spain, on the coast beyond the Cantabrian mountain range, in the old village of Llanes, in the storied province of Asturias that had always remained unconquered.

Our ancestor, Antonio Guerra Cañamar, had left Llanes sometime in the 1580s, heading for Mexico City, which had been conquered only sixty years before.

4. From dreams: the unexpected gift

It had happened days before I left Sevilla, but I hadn't remembered the shell from the dream until I saw a little crescent-shaped grotto, the one alongside a little cool covered patio, in the ornate courtyard of the great cathedral, built around a onetime mosque. The pool inside was hardly bigger than an oil drum on its side, and the surface of the water it contained was completely covered by a web of tiny cloverlike leaves, mottled with dozens of red tube-shaped blossoms that had fallen from a bush just above, coming to rest on this carpet of floating green shoots.

Beneath the surface, goldfish were swimming lazily around the beams of sunlight. I was awed, taken by surprise, by its beauty, its carefully tended randomness—its quiet spiritual presence. The stonework was meticulously finished in chips of black volcanic rock that gave the grotto an almost ancient feeling. Nearby, a great New World caiman, stuffed and tinted green, was hanging from the rafters of a great corridor.

The stones of the grotto's crescent wall had been applied like a mosaic, and every two feet or so there was a miniature shell, pearly white in color, breaking up the grim shade of the rock.

When I saw those shells, late in the afternoon Sevillano light, I remembered another shell I had seen before.

Was it the night before? Was it the week before? When had I had that dream? Or did I even have it at all? Could I remember a dream that I never had?

An elderly woman dressed poorly and walking barefoot in the cobblestone street walked up smiling and handed me a great shell she was carrying, the size of a large watermelon, and then she quickly walked past, disappearing into one of the narrow alleys. Holding the shell, I suddenly couldn't remember where I was: Mexico? Brazil? Spain? I knew only that I was on the road, traveling, and in a hurry to get to some other destination where I was expected.

I held it in both hands, feeling its considerable weight, turning it over to see the opalescent glows of its pearly interior, transfixed by the ghostly luminescence it exuded. And then, when I turned it over to look inside the *caracól*, I saw what looked like an animated map of the heavens, all the stars and planets slowly wheeling by, shot through by comets, illuminated by tiny novae.

I worried to myself: how would I pack it to take it home, considering that I was traveling uncharacteristically light, with only one bag? It wouldn't possibly fit, but I could not leave it behind now that it was in my hand.

VIII

El Canto de Cenote Siete
(Con un autor anónimo)

Third Legajo

By an anonymous author.

From the old Palacio Municipal across the Plaza de Vicente Guerra, to the crumbling sillar granaries at the edge of town, from the Río Grande across the small horn of land to the Río Salado, sounds carried and echoed through the ruins of the Villa de Señor San Ignacio de Loyola de Revilla as if every note struck, every slightest disturbance of the air by voice, wing, blink, or step or was imprinted onto the void and then suspended on the faintest breeze, sometimes for days and weeks, and some remained even longer, coursing through the avenues and callejones like ageless wraiths.

The piercing "Here! Here! Here!" call of an egret seemed to come from the norte, sur, este, poniente. Somewhere, a child's voice was reciting the Chichimeca alphabet. Sandals against the dusty cobblestones, from every direction, could sound like whispered banter, ricocheting susurrations. And the crazy blind rooster that was said to have lived for two hundred and seventy years crowed for the dawn at any hour of day or night.

Mixing with the flowing water of the little cascada of El Salto on the Salado, the sonorous hum of millions of bees swarming around the Templo de los Años, the onetime library of our ancestors in the center of town, perpetually filled La Nueva Revilla like the murmuring whir of a great machine. From inside the honey-laden templo, inside the black-walled psychomanteum, someone was whispering the old droning prayers used to open the sky.

That was usually Cenote Siete, recognizable from his raspy voice.

I have the body.

Everywhere the caxtopines went they left a fire in their trail. They carried the fire with them inside of their heart and set it loose like a hungry gato de monte. There was a path of fire even across the desert, so they would know how to return to their first homes. They brought fire over the great sea and brought fire to the river. Only the sky was left untouched, only the ancestor stars are beyond their reach. Any of our relations who were touched by them were set on fire, an invisible fire that burned inside of them. The ones who went to live with them forever disappeared inside of new bodies. Molcahualtiloya. They were made to forget who they had been before. Molcahualtiloya. All of our beloved ihuanyolque, all the tlaca who had been our relations.

They disappeared inside of new bodies and planted seeds we had never seen before. And after this, nothing happened. But they will remember. Conmatizque ihuanyolque. The relations will remember.

Near where the Cactzopines had camped, the Comecrudo cacique asked his attendant to kneel in the middle of a flat area of the rocky ground, while another attendant swept the bigger stones away with a mesquite branch. He gestured to the first, shouting commands as he pointed to spots on the ground, drawing lines with a long stick across the dirt and directing his minion further as he made hatch marks and waves.

El Conde Escandón and his men were puzzled at first; some worried the indio might be inscribing some oath to bring their devil god.

Pebbles were piled up here, hills.

Irregular balls of paistle moss were laid out in a line, a chain of mountains.

Stands of twigs, thickets and forests.

The cacique dribbled water out of his gourd where the webs of streams and rivers ran, one thick line at one end.

That was the Río del Norte.

Look here, he was saying, staring at the conde, extending his hands over the scene.

He was the cacique of that world, only he knew it in its entirety, because he already dwelled in eternity, from whence landscapes are visible in their totality. The dominions of the Comecrudos wanderings resided entirely within him.

But once Escandón saw all these perimeters and horizons laid out like a topographical map, he began calculating any distances he remembered from his journeys.

This was no Sierra Gorda. These were the hunting and sleeping places, the hills inhabited by lion gods, these were the entrances to the heavens and underworlds of the Comecrudos.

Showing the Cactzopines the panorama of his heart's domain was the gift of an ominous knowing that would surely awe them and send them away forever. After all, that had worked before.

As best I could, I traced the outlines and shapes onto several hojas of parchment that were folded in the pocket of my deerskin vest.

The cacique looked over my shoulder at this drawing and began to laugh.

The journey before Nuevo Santander.

These were the numerous distant paths that led the ancestors to this world.

You saw that great ceiba en Villa Antigua, on the banks of the Rio Tabasco where Cortés and his men tied up the brigantinas to begin our story. For our tale only truly begins when two worlds previously unknown to each other, Español and Mexica, began their fateful collision, que no?

And so Cortés found his role in this predestined cosmic conspiracy among the Mexica's foes and tributary Indian nations his army encountered on their march from the landing near Vera Cruz in the Gulf region to the westward slopes of the Sierra Oriental. The most powerful among them were the Tlaxcaltecas, those who would later be sent to the north, themselves *once an imperial power, eager to overthrow the Mexica empire that had dominated them for generations before the arrival of the Spaniards. With the Spanish conquest of the Mexica, the seat of their nascent empire was installed in the ruins of the Azteca capital, Tenochtitlan, Mexico City, and remained there for the centuries that followed.*

Gradually, the colony of Nueva España would extend farther to the north and west with the establishment of Guanajuato and Querétaro, but the farther expanses to the north remained a forbidding expanse of desolation, las tierras de salvajes. The awesome and horrible, undiscovered and irreducible savage antiquity of the north was dismaying even to imagine. Early rumors, promulgated by the Indios, spoke of the fabulously rich seven cities of Cibola or the golden precincts of a legendary city of gold, El Dorado, that would dwarf even noble Tenochtitlán. Meant mainly to distract their conquerors, these alluring tales came to nothing as various seekers, plunderers, adventurers, and wanderers returned from their exploratory expeditions, haggard, hollow-eyed, barely surviving, their ranks dwindled by illness, starvation, and ambushes from the Chichimeca.

These stories were not preserved in any epics or family tales handed down in families generation to generation. They barely merit mention in books and historical accounts of the era.

If Mexico City was not a destination far enough for a Spaniard to escape and forget his once-dear known world of the Iberian past, then the desolate north still beckoned, especially if their burdens and armaments could be ferried by accompanying bands of Tlaxcaltecas, dispatched by the colonial administration to the farthest hinterlands to take them out of harm's way as the feverish spiral of vengeance of the vanquished Mexica began to gather force.

Soon after the Conquest, many of them followed the Sierra Occidental path to Santa Fe, and on to Taos.

Or, traveling northward out of old Monterrey, which came to be the viceroy's seat of power and home of the Inquisition, there were two entradas into Tejas, carefully avoiding the Chichimeca territories along the Río Bravo in between. One lay to the north through a ford in the river that would come to be known as Piedras Negras for the smooth black stones of the riverbed there.

That was the passage to San Antonio de Béjar, first mapped and traveled

*to late in the 1600s. The other entrada veered farther east from Monter-
rey to the still older outposts of Cerralvo and Cadereyta, and then on to
Revillagigedo, Camargo, and Ciudad Mier, which your Lopez and Velas
would remember as their home of origin. In fact, they were never more
than pueblitos, but ciudad sounded so much more august and permanent,
perhaps a necessary gloss for extending the reach of the Imperio into the
savage lands of the north.*

And so it began.

*Over the centuries, the family advanced its way slowly over a small
stretch of the earth, from Ciudades Camargo and Mier to Laredo, then to
Cotulla, and eventually to San Antonio.*

*The journey continued, the prophecies and missions continued, the dis-
coveries mistaken for conquest, succumbing to la reconquista and all the
counterrevolutions that followed, only ever the same story, believe what you
may, until the great setting aside, the last encogimiento de hombros, the
beginning of the time of La Zona Perfecta.*

No world, no time, no body, no mind—but always the same story.

What was the right story to tell?

*There was a story written fleetingly and tempered in the heated air of
primordial Texas, a story that could never be erased or dispersed.*

Great upheavals were visited upon us, but still the story continued.

Ledger of Lost Treasures.

*A great old hidalgo I once knew remembered how, as a child, he had been
taken to a panadería by his grandmother and she told him to order whatever he wanted. When the baker asked him for his preferences, she stopped
him when he raised his hand to point to his greatest delights.*

"You can only have the ones you can name," she quickly insisted.

*"What will happen when we have forgotten all the names of our beloved
panes?"*

*Pastries and confections wrapped in beautiful papers. Conchas y
campechanas. Monos y marranitos. Polvorones y piedras. In Iberia, it had
been also bocaditos de lomo y montaditos de atun. Savory chorizitos with a
thin slice of jamon serrano, served on a thin baguette. Documents wrapped
in canvas bales, tied in white muslin ribbons in a fourfold knot.*

These lands emerged over time, an island gradually born out of a dream sea.

Each historic journey, though forgotten now, left its indelible imprint in the salt of the sea air, forever present and always visible in La Zona Perfecta, appearing as luminous filaments that were once a brilliant crimson, now faded to a burnt pink. By the extent of fading in these luminescent threads, gently undulating in the magnetic currents, you may discern the antiquity of the path that left them.

In 1519, sent by his excellency Francisco Garay, governor of Jamaica, it was Alonso Álvarez de Piñeda who began his journey in la Pascua Florida following la Costa del Golfo in four caravelas, with nearly three hundred men, tracing portolani maps of the entire expedition, feeling his way through the bays and around the shallow inlets, arriving finally in the domain of the Seno Mexicano, then continuing to Veracrúz, leaving no doubt that this was not an island chain but another true continent.

In Veracrúz, he shared a meal with his countryman Hernan Cortés, who was beginning his own expedition to the interior of Mexico. Though he allowed Cortés to view his new map, he would not allow him to copy it, and when Cortés sought to arrest him, Piñeda fled north to return to La Florida.

It was on this trip that he came upon our Río del Norte, the mouth of which he encountered decked with palmas, in the land he proclaimed as Amichel in the name of Spain—populated by pygmies and giants he reported seeing living in cities of dwellings made from mud and reeds. Although Piñeda believed these lands to be perfectly suited for settlement, it would be almost two hundred years before Spaniards would return to live there.

Governor Garay of Jamaica sent another expedition forth from Jamaica, led by one Diego de Camargo, who took his boats up the Río de las Palmas, as Piñeda had named it, until he was rebuffed by Coahuiltecas, who killed eighteen of his men and chased him with their canoas back into the deep waters of the Gulf. The surviving stragglers of the Camargo expedition reached Veracrúz, only barely, where the last boat sank and Diego de Camargo died. When two delegations arrived to find Camargo in the succeeding years, they realized his mission had failed and the land was to remain beyond reach for centuries.

This was how our lands were anointed in the sweat of undying war.

Lucas Vásquez de Ayllón was made the first adelantado of the territories north of Pascua Florida of la América Septentrionale, though he knew neither their nature, breadth, nor extent.

His emissary Esteban Gómez, a thalassophobe who preferred skirting coastlines, marked the way from La Florida north to the shorelines of Labrador, and for this reason to this day we still refer to the lands of the north and east as la Tierra de Gómez.

Vásquez de Ayllón founded the first settlement of the Old World in the New, called San Miguel de Guadalupe. He sent Pánfilo de Narváez on a journey to seek the mythical kingdom of Appalachia and to explore the western lands of the great vastness all the way to the Río de las Palmas, which we call the Río del Norte. Only four of their number survived that mission, Alvar Nuñez Cabeza de Vaca and Estevanico, who became healers in the course of their trek, and the two soldiers Alonso Castillo and Andrés Hurtado. Their desperate delegación marched just west of here, where Revilla would be built, following the river to the north, then heading south in search of Iberian compatriotas.

In 1540, Francisco Vásquez de Coronado was the first to sketch the plains of the river valleys that flow into the Golfo de Mexico, though those maps had to be abandoned in the flight from an ataque de Apaches. And then it was perhaps another one hundred years before another Spanish soul would venture into these tierras bárbaras.

It was then that mis antepasados first came into these lands.

So that none of this will be forgotten.

El cuento de los Borrados.

It is difficult to fix the time in which we began to dwell en La Zona Perfecta.

Many of us had heard stories of los Borrados, of those who were said to have submitted themselves to have their memories wiped clean, their genetic hoards blanched out, to become vessels of the flood of memory that the great difference engines had unleashed upon the former world, a new universe of memory that lacked rememberers sufficient to accommodate its bounty.

Los Borrados got their name from the electromagnetic neural wash that cleansed their memories away. They were the erased, the ones who had been divested of memory, made clean. The human brain remained the most prized storage medium for the overflow of knowledge being generated by corporations, governments, and ever-resilient criminal organizations. The Borrados had a sullen but untroubled look about them, as if something distressing had occurred to them, but just as quickly they had forgotten it.

They were everywhere in La Zona Perfecta, medio-zombified, once they had been transduced.

They would forget everything that had been their own: sunlight at breakfast on one velvety morning, their own mother's voice, the great works of Cervantes and Spenser, the deep ledgers of memory hidden in their blood. In their place, they were transfused with the encoded and compressed recordings of vast volumes of binary knowledge.

Everything was serialized, parsed, and correlated, but no chip array, self-evolving crystals, or factoring gene could encompass the gathering minutiae that would soon eclipse the Quinto Sol, dawning our age of the Sixth Sun. There was more memory, especially concerning money or catastrophes, than the machines themselves could fathom.

The flows, cascades, eddies, and sprays of lucre from many nations straddling the planet were used to decorate buildings. The beating of butterfly wings, those that were allowed to continue flying freely, were indexed and extrapolated upon, anticipating gusts, squalls, and hurricanoes for centuries to come. Nary a single exhalation from a sparrow's beak would exeunt unnoticed, for fear it might someday cause the collapse of the noble, aged monuments of Giza.

In exchange for their prized flesh memory, los Borrados were nurtured and treated as one would the highest order of courtesan or priest, giving audience only to a select few who would approach them as oracles. How would the price of gold fluctuate within a designated interval of moments? Why had a teacup, centuries old, teetered in a muslin tablecloth's fold and fallen from the table, shattering, the night before? Where would gold be discovered next? How much was left? What would be the color of my great-great-grandchild's eyes?

Some of them were kept in quarters that were generously proportioned and sumptuously adorned. Others wandered the northern Coahuila deserts like the prophets of ancient times. Then we began to hear that one by one, after years of service as the sacred carriers of memory, the Borrados began to vanish. Not all at once, either, but that their bodies were slowly ebbing, as if fading into transparency, as if the mysterious flesh was being gradually rendered from within into multinomial equations, logarithms, and equations as light as air, and then they became the air.

The changes upon us within La Zona Perfecta were still under way.

The Darshan of Niobe.

I would not have believed it if I had not witnessed it for myself.

It was in the pale ruins of Revilla Nueva, which you know in your time as Guerrero Viejo, along the path of the old Río del Norte, where the remnants of an old church were perched at the edge of a onetime river cliff. In the early years of the age of the Sixth Sun my liege companion, Caracól, had learned of a certain Niobe, yes, a Borrada, who was being attended in the courtyard of an old sanctuary near the plaza, so we set out to find her and see if the rumors of their confounding fate were true.

I had expected a crone, a hag, a wizened old dame barely holding on to her breath. Instead, Niobe was a girl child of eleven or twelve years only, with green eyes and skin as purple black as the peoples of distant Ethiopic lands. She wore a simple turquoise dress of tattered cotton, with a silvery veil that cast a shadow over the smooth skin of her tranquil face.

Dozens of others were already gathered in the pecan-shaded arbor when we arrived early that morning, all of them standing in a line to see her, beseech her, to pose their litanies of questions.

As I drew closer, her small hands reached out and took mine to pull me closer. Her palms felt as dry and wrinkled as someone a hundred years old, and her arms were emaciated and weak, as light as a bird's wings. My eyes averted her face when, suddenly overcome with a sadness I had not sensed mounting in me before, I went to bend down on one knee, lowering my head before her, fumbling to say,

"Hermana Maestra, bienvenida."

But she laughed and pulled me back up toward her.

"This is your house as it is mine."

Gazing directly at her, I could see that parts of her face were disappearing into what looked like currents of a bluish static glow. Small currents and swirls of the electricity were detectable, in flashes.

She pulled down the veil to cover her cheek and spoke to me in a voice that was part child's song, partly the hum of a machine.

"Hidalgo Cenote, how far have you traveled?"

I stood there dumbfounded that she would address me by name.

"We came originally from Medina, from the plain of the Llano River."

"And you came to see me, Knight?"

"That is our great honor," I replied, gesturing to Hermano Caracól.

"I am a little girl!" she said, giggling.

"Where is your home, Maestra?"

"I am from Tokar, near the port ruins of Suakin, on the Red Sea."

"How did you come to the Mundo Nuevo?"

"I don't know, it's very long ago now."

"What do you remember of your home?"

"All of our memories have been tucked away for good keeping."

"Do you remember a single thing?" I asked again.

"Everything has been protected."

"Where?" I beseeched the child. "How, Maestra?"

"Like a river running backward, Hidalgo Cenote, we have returned our memories to the past, where they are awaiting us."

Niobe reached toward me and touched the back of my hand.

Suddenly, I remembered the face of she who I had not thought upon for an entire age, my companion before the beginning of La Zona Perfecta, one of the Hundred Rememberers, the Knight and Protector, Marena.

Her olive skin was glowing in the seaside twilight radiance, her exquisite face full of the resignation of a final farewell. I had not known that she had become a Borrada.

We were on a beach. Her lithe, strong body was strung as taut as the sails of a catamaran, effortlessly tacking on a coursing wind. Flower petals of every color were blowing by us in great nebulae. There was a rain of light, a river of light, oceans of light, every sweet bell, every chime that ever was, a universe of light. Her body became as transparent as clearest glass, all of the light passing through, undiminished.

Would she leave me? She was done with her ancestors, she had professed to me. She was done with the mystery of their lost destinies. She would seek them no more.

I saw the windblown cedars by the shore, their roots gripping the earth in the eternal gusts. If I could only count the waves, if only I could name them, then perhaps the world would stay as it was, forevermore.

I remembered how Marena had disappeared before me in one lingering beatific smile that seemed to promise some distant return, some hope of another embrace, but before I could really discern this, she had disappeared.

I cherish the memory.

I was alone at the ocean's edge, clear, dulcet tones coursing through the fluted waves as they rolled onto the beach, lapping at my feet.

Recalling that day, at that very moment, the face of Niobe la Borrada lit up in one shimmering shiver of electrostatic light, making her seem transparent for a spell, and then she too was gone.

I watched her disinhabited clothes fall slowly into a small wrinkled heap on the sandy ground before me.

IX

Old Mexican City Twilight

1. On the last of the duendes in Texas

Mother's cousin Sonny remembers growing up on a ranch between Cotulla and Laredo along with his brothers and sisters and their grandmother Abuela Tomasa, who lived with them in a little room that had previously been an attic on the third floor of the Lopez ranch house.

"Her room had a little window that let her look out onto the field where my daddy had sorghum planted. And she would just spend all day sitting there fanning herself, rolling smokes, and looking out that window. She always talked to me when I came home from school about things she saw out there in that field. Once she said she saw an eagle flying around the field, looking for mice, and at the hottest time of the day it came and landed on the windowsill," Sonny remembered, laughing. "And it ignored her, until she got up and shushed it away.

"But the day before she died, when my mother found her in that chair, *ya muertita*, but with her cigarette still lit—well, the day before, when I came home and knocked on her door, she told me to sit down there right in front of her by the window and she was pretty shook up pointing out into the field. There's a duende out there, Sonny, and it's been looking up at me all day.

"And she was all shaky, but I looked out there and all I saw was the sorghum and a couple of birds.

"You know she always said she saw duendes, sabes, little people como old Spanish ghost leprechauns, but she'd say they were helping with the crops, pulling weeds or picking up stones. But this time she was spooked, man.

" 'Me ha estado mirando todo el día,' she said. 'I've seen it before with its little friends out there, but this time he's here for me.'

"And the next day she died, verdad. The old girl was right."

Sonny looked at me. "What do you think of all that, primo?"

"All what?"

"All that talk about, you know, cosas extrañas, mysterious things, el mundo de espíritus."

Sonny looked serious, almost conspiratorial, as if he was accustomed to being scolded for that kind of talk.

"You don't see that much anymore. You don't hear those stories. I think the duendes are all gone now."

His eyes widened, suddenly looking urgent and sad.

"Primo, maybe even the duendes die."

2. How Grandmother kept her ghosts with her

By the time Leandra moved into her last San Antonio house on West Russell Street in the late 1950s, she needed a large duplex just to accommodate the ghosts that moved everywhere with her.

Her parents, buried in the much-vaunted Vela crypt in Laredo, were so long dead they seemed to belong to the time of the Bible. Leonides, her husband, was nearly thirty years dead; her firstborn daughter Lily died as a child of whooping cough, buried alone in Cotulla; Leandra's confidantes, her beloved sister Fermina and her brother-in-law, Frank Ferguson, buried in Laredo; her eldest son, Leo, her favorite, who had left Texas for Baltimore, where he died; all of them long dead, and though she could seem as if she were unaware, Grandmother knew, begrudgingly, all of these ghosts would remain with her.

There were photographs of all of them spread out through the house, along with several of LBJ, one signed and dedicated fondly to Leandra, showing the former president and Cotulla school teacher sitting on a wooden fence, holding his favorite beagle.

This is the compromiso of our lineage: You may pretend that you are on your own, but the ghosts are always with you. No invocations or conjurings are required. We are here so that the ghosts can continue to roam the world.

Emblematically, Grandmother's final home was in the Beacon Hill neighborhood near downtown and the place called Five Corners, where the old city roads from the south converged with the roads to the north. It was also a natural catchment area for the many creeks feeding into the San Antonio River, so whenever it rained the waters would go cascading down West Russell, turning right onto Blanco Road, then down to Fredericksburg Road and farther down to Five Points, sluicing streams of memory eventually into the river that would make its way south into the Rio Grande Valley and the Gulf.

Grandmother never especially acted as if she wanted me to know her, perhaps because she believed that by remaining unknown to her grandchildren, her centuries-long cargo of ghosts could be left behind. She had brought her family to the new American city so that her Lopez de Velas would forevermore be divested of ghosts. They would find their way in a new American society, built over the ruins of New Spain, her family's onetime great cause.

Grandmother was no clairvoyant and she had little interest in spiritual matters, but she knew they were there, watching aimlessly out the windows of her front room in the hour just past dawn, crowded around the kitchen table at her every meal, shuffling resolutely down the long hall to her bedroom at the end of every day.

Did they never go outside?

Did they never become nostalgic for the sunlight or a fresh breeze?

Some years later, her maid Maria Moya thought the whole situation had become *demasiado*, the occupation of ghosts had become *una infestación*, particularly for the familia that lived in the other apartment in the duplex. Grandmother could ignore them, but the woman who had two young children next door complained of hearing footsteps and long sighs in the middle of the night, a sudden inexplicable scent of flowery talcum powder, a cold gust on the back of her neck that would make her hair stand up while she was praying.

Maria Moya could not convince Grandmother to let her do a cleansing of her home, but she was allowed to do a limpia of the apartment next door; for three days she was burning copal, mopping the floors with Pine-Sol and rosewater, replacing all the light bulbs with *globos de cién*, basting every corner of each room with 100 watts of ghost-banishing incandescent light.

"Los espíritus no lo aguantan," she would explain, through her characteristic squint.

Was it the copal, the Pine-Sol and rosewater wash, or the light bulbs that repelled them?

"Ni uno, ni el otro, todos toditos," she replied conclusively, spirits hated them all.

And how would she prevent the ghosts from just adding to the overcrowding in Grandmother's home?

"Pues, con la zempazuchitl," she said, presenting a Piggly Wiggly brown paper grocery bag full of orange chrysanthemum petals, which she proceeded to drizzle from the front door, across the porch, down the steps and along the sidewalk, over the curb, and into the street.

"Y de aquí, buscan su camino de nuevo."

Once led to the street, the ghosts would find their own way.

But weren't we abandoning our ancestral ghosts, sending them out to live rough on the streets of eternity hidden throughout San Antonio's geography? They need to rest now, Maria Moya answered, and anyway these are just friends and acquaintances of our ancestors.

"No te apures, mijito. Allí se quedarán siempre."

They would always remain.

Grandmother's antepasados of the Lopez and Vela families would still be standing there shoulder to shoulder along the walls of her home, perhaps a little wary that they too would someday be expelled.

3. How the world slowly found its way to San Antonio

During the war, Uncle Lauro was a spy; at least he said he was. He was a Mexican American spy in the Old World, the European theater, WW2, Germany, OSS, wartime and after. And he spoke English, Spanish, and German.

"I saw horrible things," he once told me, already well into his cups. "Don't ask what."

I tried not to listen.

He had taken a fall in his castle-like stone house on West King's Highway late one night and cut his head on the edge of a coffee table hard enough to open a gash that would not stop bleeding. One hand was shaking on the armrest of the car; the other held a towel bundled into a turban against his head.

"You see, back then we infiltrated the bad guys—or they infiltrated us, that happened too, Germans who wanted to work with the Yanks, a few of them who said they couldn't stand the evil anymore."

Then he stopped.

"Sometimes we did horrible things," my uncle pleaded, his uncertain eyes looking straight into mine, as if he were waiting for some ablution or admonition from me. "One time, we were trying to get this guy to talk, just to scare him you know because we thought he was a fake, but he was a tough son of a bitch, and they could be like that, the Krauts. Tough. But then the gun just went off, like a firecracker. An accident, a head shot, but an accident, I just don't know. We left him there, but it seemed . . . a damn pity."

I asked no questions.

Does not change always come upon us and flourisheth most among us in the times of revolution and chaos?

European social categories didn't really apply in the context of New World lineages. It hardly seems right to say the Vela and Lopez lineages were bourgeois. By dispossession and migration, my ancestors gradually set themselves loose from the land they had settled under such duress.

Long before my ancestors were overtaken by history, transformed from Españoles into Mexicanos, then into Tejanos, and then into an American *minority*, they were the inheritors of an already ages-old legacy that had imbued in them a belief that they were charges in a prophetic mission, that their efforts to build towns on the scorching frontier of Nueva España was a part of the completion of prophetic labors, the prophecy of the coming of Christ's eternal kingdom on earth.

We have lineages of families and lineages of stories. They were Spanish, but the story of themselves they carried into the New World really began in the distant lands of Mesopotamia, Galilee, and Jerusalem—lands they would never see. When their Iberian world was left behind for good, the struggles began to understand who we had become and what we were going to make of our new American selves. We are still evolving.

As the climactic fulfillment of prophecy never ensued, no angelic trumpets' stentorian blasts over South Texas landscapes, no Christ wafting down on thunderclouds of judgment over the Rio Grande, apocalypse was supplanted by a series of calamities and dislocations, and at some point the Velas and Lopez took what they could and set out to find their place in Texas, in America.

The great sage Emerson, on the prospect of the annexation of Texas with the United States in 1844, said: The annexation of Texas looks like one of those events which retard or retrograde the civilization of ages . . .

When had the lineages ebbed and flowed?

After emerging from a history of war in the borderlands, between Españoles e Indios, Anglos and Mexicanos, Americans and Tejanos, joining in the wars of the United States became one way of becoming Americano.

Stories like Uncle Lauro's were few, intrusions from a European past that seemed distant, if not wholly irrelevant. Uncle Leo had served in World War II in Burma, Uncle Lico had joined the Army but never left Texas. My cousin Bob had said Leo, his dad, was an "adjutant," a paper pusher.

"But he would've been into light profiteering as well, scams, card games, quick deals, that kind of stuff."

The Lopez lost no one to the modern wars, and only a couple of my cousins served in the military corps. I knew our life in San Antonio was connected to that outside world too, but it wasn't clear how. It always seemed as if everything of national importance was taking place elsewhere—rock and roll, the civil rights movement, the war in Vietnam. Beyond what I could learn of these goings-on through television, I sought out dispatches from the distant world in national and international newspapers that my father would drive me to find in coin-box vending machines near back entrances of shopping malls.

In San Antonio then, that's where you found the news of the world.

Radio and television also harbored the trove of the parts for a future language, a place beyond the direct circumstances and cultures of my childhood and adolescent years from which I could dream of a lingua franca that might connect our lives together with those of others around the world, united by familiar tropes and tales. There was another tribe that bonded across borders and nations: The displaced, dispossessed and wandering, the exiled, the benighted, the excised, and the forgotten. It was only the media, books, newspapers, TV, and pop music radio that brought us together, illuminating our secret commonalities.

My dad was driving me down Vance Jackson, past the car wash, the Arco Iris taquería, and the Jack-in-the-Box, on another trip to find newspapers.

"Why does all that stuff matter to you?" my dad asked as we headed for the Wonderland shopping mall to find a copy of a newspaper published back then called *The World*.

On other journeys, he had taken me to bookstores where I had bought paperback copies of *The Communist Manifesto* and J. Edgar Hoover's book of ravings on Communism, just because I wanted both sides of the story.

"We've got everything you need right here. Just take care of yourself. Get an education. Make some *moh-nyay*."

"I want to make waves. We're a part of the world too."

He laughed. "You want to make waves? How're you gonna make

waves? You need a big boat to do that, and you don't even have a boat."

4. Mexicans enter the airwaves to find their story

We lived by the radio. That was in the days when a radio announcer woke us with the greeting, "Thank the Lord, he's given us another day!" The same San Antonio easy-listening AM station ran a promotion to give away a new mink coat, which you could win by answering your phone, "Think Mink." It rarely was cold enough in San Antonio to justify donning a mink stole, but that didn't matter. If the DJ happened to be calling and you answered appropriately, it was your lucky day. For weeks, Mother strictly enforced an all "Think Mink" phone answering policy. If the Slimline phone rang, you answered with a simple "Hello" at your own peril.

In San Antonio, WOAI had one of the most powerful AM signals in the country. By day, the world might be bounded by stories of politics and mayhem, crime and punishment, the weather, and the time. But once night fell, mysteries ensued. One of the most popular programs of the day was the Allen Dale show, an early showcase on the airwaves exploring the worlds of the paranormal and high strangeness, by that time a long-established theme of meetings between worlds in South Texas.

San Antonio had been the scene of many reported UFO sightings, legends of a creature that was half woman, half donkey, and ghost stories abounded. With the persona of a crotchety but curious skeptic, Dale would do news interviews with witnesses and authorities, and field calls from ordinary listeners. Project Blue Book, a UFO-debunking military report of the time, dismissed tales of anomalous aerial phenomena as so much swamp gas, meteoric illusions, or merely sightings of newfangled satellites crisscrossing the sky. Disgruntled listeners called in, incredulous of the Air Force's dismissal, convinced the truth was being hidden.

Hence, from its inception, paranormal radio became conspiracy radio. When there was a wave of cattle mutilations out in West

Texas, Dale did a spellbinding interview with a sheriff from the county where the beasts had been discovered in a pasture, their eyes, tongues, ears, and anuses surgically removed, and their bodies emptied of blood, though there was no evidence of bleeding at the site. After much speculation regarding satanic rituals, government experiments, or the possible involvement of UFOs and their occupants, one peeved caller checked in with the authoritative explanation.

"I don't know what everybody's so confused about. It's an election year, and once again, the Republicans are looking for any ol' asshole to run for governor."

Our Jurassic media of that time offered a deeper insight into the mysterious world.

When my uncle Roger bought a new television set in the mid-'60s, my dad bought their old model, an RCA behemoth with a broad, curving green glass screen mounted in a polished mahogany case. With golden switches and a bronze frame for the screen, its speakers shrouded in a cabinet with pleated brown fabric behind an ornate grille, it looked like it had been manufactured in the time of Ferdinand and Isabella.

To turn the set on, you'd pull on its little stamen of a power switch, thereupon producing a great echoing bass boom. As the tubes inside began to heat up and fluoresce, glowing clouds of electrons gradually took recognizable shape on the screen before us.

"*Project Terror!* Where the scientific and the terrifying—emerge!"

Running your hand over the glass, you could make small, crackling static trails over the picture. It was Bela Lugosi as Dracula, our long-forgotten Vela ancestor. It was an army of resurrected skeletons making battle in *Jason and the Argonauts*. It was Klaatu in his elegant silver spacesuit, the colossal robot Gort at his side.

And when the set was turned off after *Project Terror* had ended, the last image would linger and fade very slowly, eventually dwindling down to one phosphorescent dot that could glow for a long time, shrinking gradually to an infinitesimal dot before disappearing.

Television was a consolation for me, a reassuring beacon that signaled to me that the outside world carried on, that history continued uninterrupted by the anticipated apocalypse, a nuclear holocaust, or even the Second Coming.

When I began making television programs, it became an instrument for me to take out into the world, a window through which I could witness the lives of other people in their struggles to remake their societies. Television became my testimonio.

In a series of documentaries from that time, I traveled through Latin America with a mentor, Virgilio Elizondo, to report on the awakening of poor communities to new understandings of the Gospels as a call to social justice in the movement that was broadly known as liberation theology. I had always regarded that label as a hilarious contradiction in terms; what I knew as theology was anything but liberating.

The movement had some of its inspiration in the ideas of Father Arrupe, the visionary leader of the Jesuits whose story I had told in that earlier documentary. In rural Nicaragua, in the pueblos jovenes occupied by poor squatters outside Lima, in the streets of São Paulo with the homeless, I saw a very different kind of church, a radical rethinking of Christian theology that grounded the spiritual life of communities in the struggles for literacy, health, equity, and justice. These sorts of stories were not primetime ratings grabbers in American broadcasting, but I was behind the camera witnessing these events as the latest chapters of cultural upheavals in the New World, carrying on the story that had begun with the arrival of the first Spanish and Portuguese explorers and conquistadores with their vaunted evangelical mission. All those centuries of oppression and exclusion of the poor and indigenous world were suddenly being questioned and slowly, haltingly reversed.

But the legacy of conflict continued too.

For at the very moment of this movement's stirring all across Hispanic America, the Vatican, led by Cardinal Joseph Ratzinger, the man who would become Pope Benedict XVI, unleashed an unstinting onslaught against the leaders of the movement, from Mexico through Central America, all the way to Brazil.

And by the end of the 1980s, the movement was effectively squelched. This most extraordinary expression of the highest aspirations of the church—as a world community of justice—was cut off at its first flower.

My only other Lopez cousin to use the media as a way of connecting to the world was my cousin Bob, the primo who had been raised in Baltimore and became a widely known and respected newsman on the morning program of one of the big FM rock radio stations. On air, "Lopez" was famous for his sharp-tongued, left-wing atheist wit and for not suffering fools lightly. And his martial bent went well beyond the broadcasting arena.

On one visit to Baltimore, he picked me up at the train station with daughter Leandra, age eight, and took me directly to a farm in the Maryland countryside where the owner, a radio fan, allowed him to use a large remote pasture for target shooting. He opened the trunk of his sedan to reveal an impressive arsenal of beautifully maintained firearms, from a Glock 9 pistol to a pair of shotguns, high-caliber rifles, and two automatics, including an Uzi.

For several hours, as Leandra dutifully reloaded magazines for us, we shook the stillness of the Maryland afternoon, blasting clay pigeons out of the sky, shattering watermelons on a table fifty yards away, trying to hold steady as the gyroscopic kick of the Uzi pushed back against you. It took me a while to settle into the rhythms of the fusillades after a long hiatus from shooting, but Lopez was all business, taking a bead on his distant targets and proceeding to send a series of cans flying off their posts. Though he was a committed pacifist, a lifetime in suburban Maryland had clearly not taken much of the conquistador out of him.

In another version of this story, I would've spent a lot of this life with my cousin Bob. In another version, he might not have been the original Chicano control experiment, a mestizo soul raised in captivity among the gringos of Maryland, but would've been another complicated, displaced Mexicano on the northern side of the borderlands, perhaps still believing, as he did, that the British were the greatest cultural achievement of humanity, that God mattered not a whit, even less the farrago farce of UFOs; but nonetheless he was spiritually, historically, culturalmente "puro Mexicano."

The next morning, the two of us got up before dawn to do his two-hour-long Sunday morning radio program, *The Spanish Inquisition*. As we ate doughnuts from his favorite emporium and emptied a carafe of brutal coffee, I told stories about our Lopez-Vela ancestors in South Texas and old Nuevo Santander, while Bob reminded his listeners that our ancestors were already busy building the New World when theirs were still making a scarce living as chimney sweeps in dirty old London.

"This morning is just a history lesson for all you folks who think the gringos are the be-all and end-all of American society. Cousin John Phillip's here to say it ain't so."

When he plunked down the button to take the first listener call, a gruff voice sounded out:

"I can't believe I've got to get up on a beautiful Sunday morning, turn on the radio, to listen to you two spics talk about the good old days. Why don't you just go back to Mexico and give us all a break, eh?"

To which Bob smiled and replied, "Isn't America beautiful?" and moved us on to the next caller.

The question of the morning was whether we were Mexicans, Texans, Indians, or Spaniards. That wasn't an easy query to answer, I said. On his mother's side, Bob claimed to be part Cherokee. And he confessed to being ashamed that twenty years before, he had adamantly insisted in a newspaper interview that the family was pure Spanish.

We continued, laughing through much of the show, talking about the Alamo as an example of how badly the matter of undocumented immigration can be handled, about how LBJ had been a teacher to our parents in Cotulla, and still we had remained mostly poor; and every now and then he'd break and throw in a song from his personal catalogue, which he referred to as "More Mutagenic Music for Modern Metropolitan Living." As the Specials eerie Ghost Town" ended, caller after caller continued to attack me or Bob with taunts of "Remember the Alamo!" or "Ay-yay-yay-yay . . ." and Bob seemed to know them all by name, "Spider" or "Huck" or "Mona Ramona," but immediately after the show, he grew very serious.

I wondered if all the jest and joust wasn't really weighing heavily on him after decades on the air. I certainly felt weary, just after two hours. But as we set off in his car through the foggy downtown Baltimore streets, Bob told me that he had been diagnosed with advanced-stage lung cancer, and the prognosis was not good. He wasn't yet fifty years old, and he told me his father, my uncle Leo, had died at age fifty-two. I didn't mention that our grandfather had died at the same age.

For the rest of the ride home in the late Baltimore morning, the road was full of silence and sadness.

5. Retracing the path by which I returned

There is a green notebook from April of 1983, just after I left behind a scholarship for doctoral studies at Yale and returned to Oxford to spend the summer with Nancy.

The notebook is a mix of critiques and prognostications, readings from the papers of the day, collages of clippings and pictures, drafts of poems, sketches in prose, and notes from a spell of undirected browsings in the Bodleian: Edward Said's *Beginnings*, Jacques Derrida's *Dissemination*, the Marquis de Sade's *Venus in Furs*, Adolfo Gilly's *La Nueva Nicaragua*, Paolo Freire's *Cultural Action for Freedom*, Armand Mattelart's *Multinational Corporations and the Control of Culture*, Lenin's *Imperialism, the Highest Stage of Capitalism*, and Antonin Artaud's *Collected Works*, from which I copied,

"There are some fools who think of themselves as beings, as innately being . . . I am he who, in order to be, must whip his innateness."

In a life that had always been without much of a scheme or plan, there had never been a time when I felt more adrift. I had left the well-endowed path of becoming an academic that had always been my only, admittedly vague program for making a living out of what interested me—literature, culture, and the creative life. Nancy was still studying for her degree in international relations at Oxford, and she took me in, giving me shelter and consolation in her loving embrace. We believed our immersion in theory could bring upheavals in our disciplines, and ultimately in the world itself.

In that green notebook, there is a dialogue about the crossroads I believed I had come to in my life, for better or worse:

Q: What reasons could you possibly have for giving up your situation of complete comfort and ease? Why abandon all the promise of an extraordinary career?

A: Who chose it? Under what circumstances? You wake up one morning to find you're in a ghastly Japanese rotating hen coop. The rules of conduct are unacceptable. They are a part of a machine of false identifications. Some act of self-elaboration and escape becomes necessary because conflict, which had been a kind of sustenance, has given way to control. New terms of action must be manufactured, at any cost.

At the bottom of the page, there is a quote from Nietzsche that offers only cold comfort: "All knowledge originates because of separation, delimitation, restriction: there is no absolute knowledge of a whole."

After nearly ten years away from Texas and Mexico, I was as far from feeling connected to my homeland as I have ever been. Oxonians had little understanding or interest, for that matter, in the world I came from, the tierras fronterizas of South Texas, the storied birthplace of Tejanos and Chicanos. For all they knew, I was Persian, Greek, or some other flavor of Mediterranean, and they pronounced my name accordingly, as *Sahn-tahss*.

But Oxford was also a *cuna espiritual*, a nationless sanctuary for scholars and curious readers of humanity's knowledge traditions from every corner of the planet, a place where I found common interests and shared passions with a host of other displaced people, Irish, Armenians, Jews, Cypriots, Palestinians, among others. Accustomed to being outsiders, we all found our home in Oxford.

All of us believed there was a deception at the heart of the great canon.

Every text was a palimpsest of error, misprision, hidden insight.

We imagined that we were a part of a revolution in human thought, a revolution from within words themselves that could change soci-ety and history. Whether we were studying politics or literature, history or anthropology, new versions of old canons were emerging in a host of previously unheard new voices. Out of our diverse histo-ries, fraught with legacies of exploitation and deception, programs of power and subjugation, everything could be decolonized; every practice of knowledge could be set free.

I might've stayed there and renewed the journey toward a life in the university world, where many of my dearest friends pursued that shared vision.

Instead, by the end of that year, I had returned to San Antonio.

I returned to the story of my ancestors.

6. In which the old family drifts farther apart

There is an etching from the late nineteenth century of the great oak double doors of Mission San José, built in 1718, showing them wracked and crumbling, falling off their hinges against each other. Much of the elaborate stone carvings surrounding the doors are chipped, the saints in their nichos missing limbs or pieces of their garments. At the turn of the twentieth century, San Antonio had been an Ameri-can city already nearly sixty years, and the Spanish legacy left behind from the settlement's earlier age was fully in ruins.

It shouldn't surprise us then that the families descended from that history experienced a similar fate.

The American descendants of the Lopez and Vela clans formed a loosening galaxy of increasingly estranged cousins gradually spread-ing out widely across the globe from our homelands of South Texas. Among my first cousins, though we were fond of each other, always finding raucous fun when together, we didn't grow up close.

Our families kept to themselves. In the generations born between the 1940s and the 1960s, there were lawyers and doctors, politicians and priests, cops, secret agents, and criminals, scientists, engineers, preachers, poets, actors, and musicians. A few died very young, a prematurely widening wreath of Lopez death.

Beautiful Lydia, my flower child cousin, died at twenty, already a mother, in a bathtub, a death as mysterious as Jim Morrison's; perhaps due to some mayhem, it was rumored, perhaps drowning in a diabetic coma, as my aunt explained. Her brother Leo died at thirty-two, succumbing to an angry cancer of the brain that may have been induced by chemicals used in his strenuous work maintaining railroad beds in the woods of North Texas.

After a long, somewhat colorful career as a car salesman and real estate broker in San Antonio, Uncle Lico's son Freddy, the oldest of my Lopez cousins, became an evangelist. Baptized anew by a Chicano preacher from Laredo, he eventually converted his sisters too. When Lico died of a heart attack in 1992, Freddy tried to forbid the traditional rosary that Mexicans pray over the body at the *velorio* on the eve of a funeral. This gesture of new religious zeal drew a withering response from my mother, his aunt Lucille.

"Dad secretly accepted Jesus Christ as his personal savior, Aunt Lucille. He doesn't need any rosary because he's already in heaven."

Mother fixed Freddy in her withering motionless stare.

There had already been a quarrel about all of the visitors who were leaving prayer cards of San Judás, the patron saint of lost causes, who had been Uncle Lico's favorite. Mother had insisted that they be left with her brother, but the children insisted they be removed. But on the matter of the rosary, there would be no acquiescence. Mother spoke to her nephew just outside the door of the funeral home chapel.

"You can wait outside the chapel if you like. There will most definitely be a rosary."

Meanwhile, the preacher from Laredo was beginning to work up a sweat and distress his perfectly combed-back black hair, playing gospel music out of a beat box, asking all of the old Mexicanos to stand up, raise a hand, and accept Jesus Christ as their personal savior.

"Now, there's no need to wait like Lico here did. A few weeks ago, he sat with me privately and accepted Christ into his life, just in time. He didn't know he was about to die, most of us don't, but he was just in time, that's what counts, he was just in time to get right with Christ, that's why he's looking down from heaven now, saying, 'I'm sure glad I made my peace'—so who of you all will come to Christ tonight? You don't know when your time's a-coming, so stand up now and raise a hand and accept Jesucristo as your personal savior, because he's waiting. Stand up now and raise your hand! Stand up!"

Rocky, an old real estate buddy of Uncle Lico's and my dad's, must've been dozing, because he woke up after the preacher's last exhortation to stand up, and so he did. He stood up and all the old Mexicanos looked at him aghast, as the preacher began to come over to him. Rocky was dazed for a moment, looking around to see why no one else had stood up, until his wife, Esther, a Cotulla girl who had grown up with my mother, pulled him back down into his seat. Freddy came over to the preacher and whispered into his ear, and the two left the chapel so that the recitation of the rosary could begin.

A few years later, my cousin Larry and I went to see Freddy at the University Hospital in San Antonio where he'd just had multiple bypass surgery on the same day he'd gone into the doctor for a routine checkup. Freddy, who was a minister and pastor with his own church by then, had been overweight for decades and didn't eat healthily; his arteries were badly clogged, requiring immediate surgery.

He looked almost beatific in his hospital bed, exuding a peace I hadn't seen in him before. Freddy's round Lopez face had always looked Samoan, and his stocky build had made him appear to be a Pacific Islander. Though he was still a little pale, his spirits were strong and he was happy to see us and eager to tell us something very important that had transpired during his urgent operation.

"It was incredible, guys," he said, beaming a great ear-to-ear Lopez smile. "The Lord spoke to me, he spoke right to me on the operating table."

"You sure it wasn't the anaesthetic?" Larry asked, chuckling.

"Hey, cuz, I know the Lord's voice—that's my business, man— and you know what? The Lord told me exactly what to do. That's never happened before. I've always prayed for direction, but I never got marching orders before."

"What did the Lord say to you, Freddy?" I asked.

"He has given me a mission to start a church."

"Hey, cuz, you've already got a church," Larry replied.

"The Lord told me to start a *new* church. But here's the thing, man. The Lord told me to start a new church *in Oahu*."

Larry and I both started laughing.

"No lie, man. In Oahu. They need the word there and I'm going to take it to them."

Freddy was already wearing a Hawaiian floral print shirt in his hospital bed. And as soon as he was released, he began preparations to set out for Hawaii to build his new church, and ride his beloved Harley-Davidson roadster on the island's highways. He did just that and fulfilled the Lord's charge to him, creating a church in Oahu, which he led for some years before dying suddenly and swiftly of a heart attack.

7. When the Alps came to Béjar

During the late '60s and early '70s, downtown San Antonio fell on bad times, abandoned like many older American cities as citizens headed outward to stake their claims in the new suburbs. While still bustling during the workday, by night people grew scarce, and San Antonio became a ruin once again.

La Vuelta de Houston street, with the onetime grand promenade of the crowds past the Majestic and the Texas theaters, past the Gunter Hotel, Joseph's Men's Shop, and Woolworth's to Alamo Plaza, was now empty. Old hotels became flophouses. Borachitos and gringo drunks grew more common. My father would point to the block on Broadway where his cousin was said to work as a lady of the evening, around the clock. One day, he even introduced me to her at the Post Office Café. She was dressed in a bright pink skirt with an ivory ruffled slip.

She called me *hijito lindo* and I remember thinking how much she resembled my aunts, only more haggard as a result of her rough life.

Some of the old businesses survived the exodus: Paris Hatter's, with their windows full of stetsons: hot dogs and homemade root beer at Schilo's: the dark and sublime Esquire Bar, with a long bar that seemed to date back to the battle of the Alamo. For the most part, though, shuttered and bankrupt became the norm: El Winn's Five and Dime, Frost Brothers Clothing shop, and Joske's department store; the centro gradually grew seedier and seedier.

Sometime in the early '70s Uncle Lauro came into possession of a downtown diner as a part of eleventh-hour adjustments on a real estate deal he had brokered. The diner had been a greasy-spoon chili and Tex-Mex joint with a counter and twenty tables, named Eddie's Cocina #3, specializing in enchiladas, chili con carne, grilled cheese sandwiches, chicken-fried steak, and rice and beans.

Uncle Lauro, who had always wanted to run a restaurant, decided to rename it "The Alps." He said he wanted to see if San Antonio, Texas, was ready for something he called "continental cuisine," which none of us had ever heard of, but it sounded like it was likely to have a chalky flavor.

"No more combination plates here," he proudly announced, showing us around the slightly run-down dining room before its renovation.

By the 1970s there weren't many Mexican-run businesses left downtown. Over the centuries, especially after the war of Texas independence, San Antonio's mercanía, with its roots in the colonial era, had been taken over by the later Anglo immigrants. There were Mexican-owned restaurants, small Mexican record shops, fruit, vegetable, and curio stands at the mercado, and Penner's, the men's clothing store owned by a Jewish Mexican family from Coahuila.

Uncle Lauro was determined to bring the cuisine of great Europa to the old Texas city, and he saw himself as a part of a wave of new Hispano entrepreneurs whose day in the sun had finally come. He wasn't angry about the legacy of racism and exclusion that had kept Mexicans out of the business picture in San Antonio, or if he was he didn't show it.

He just felt like he deserved a shot.

He was a modern American businessman, even as he might've felt other entitlements as a part of his patrimony in his ancestral lands. He looked every bit the part of the man of commerce, less from the all-American stereotype and more in the style of Marcelo Mastroianni. Uncle Lauro was lanky, over six feet tall, fair and lean, balding in a distinguished European sort of way, always wearing elegantly draping business suits and shoes, with his pressed shirt unbuttoned at the collar. Like his brother, my uncle Lico, he wore his eyeglasses with a faint dark amber tint in the lenses, set in such sleek jet-setter frames as could give his long chiseled features a hint of a worldly mandarin élan, like Aristotle Onassis.

In another era he would not have looked out of place in full courtly regalia, with white ruff lace collar and gold-filigreed jacket, like the El Greco portrait of a *Hidalgo de Nota Elevada*. If Uncle Lico sought literal demonstrations and proofs of our Spanish lineages, Uncle Lauro was a broken-down knight lost in time. He radiated our old Iberian dust. His home was a proud, oak-shaded corner manse of limestone, built in the style of a medieval castle. It was on a street called King's Highway.

He and my aunt Ruth often looked as if they had stepped out of *La Dolce Vita*. She was glamorous and beautiful, a star debutante in the dazzling era of the Mexican society scene in the 1940s. Uncle Lauro was publishing, editing, reporting, and selling ads for *La Revistá Sociál*, his weekly social calendar of San Antonio's petit burguesía of Canario, Mexican, and Tejano families.

As editor, Uncle Lauro wisely featured a profile on Ruth Garza, his future wife, in the first edition of his newspaper, a journalistic gambit he swore he had only used once, in pursuit of his true love. But most issues included page after page devoted to pictures and profiles of the young ladies of San Antonio's Mexican American society scene.

"I've hired a chef who specializes in chicken Kiev," Uncle Lauro told my dad and I, standing in the Alps restaurant that was opened while it was still being renovated, ladders and toolboxes strewn between the tables.

"What's chicken Kiev?" my father asked.

"I'm not sure, but Chef says it uses blue cheese. That's not just for salad dressing, you know."

8. The inundation of Guerrero

Grandmother could have let all of the Lopez-Vela memories go underwater forever. There was a perfect opportunity that came along, and it was not even of her making.

It was 1954, and the past was being flooded out, under the streams of the Rio Grande. Irrigation water for the Rio Grande Valley was becoming scarce as the first large industrial farms began to encroach on the Texas side of the border. Soon, the last acres of small family holdings would give way to sprawling ranch kingdoms.

When the Texas government along with the backing of the U.S. Congress and President Eisenhower proposed a large dam project, it meant in principle that landowners in Texas and Mexico would benefit. The Falcon Dam would be built to dam up the Rio Grande between Zapata and Roma, Texas, creating a large reservoir that could be drawn from to baste the parched lands on either side of the border.

This meant that modern-day Guerrero, christened as Revilla by Colonel José Escandón, the first grand town of the Nuevo Santander *entrada*, the first true home of the Velas in the New World—already nearly two hundred years old—would soon be overtaken by the streams of the Río Bravo, as the dam was completed, holding back the great waters of the river's muddy course.

For a while, Grandmother and her sister Fermina were not prepared to let it be so.

Many of the descendants of the old families of Nuevo Santander were in revolt, all the way from Starr to Bexar counties. Appeals to the Anglo governor of Texas, Allan Shivers, would be futile. He advocated the dam project, and after leaving office became a businessman in the newly vitalized commerce of the Rio Grande Valley. Grandmother and her sister wrote letters of petition to the junior congressman from San Antonio, Henry B. Gonzalez, and to her old *amistad*, the young teacher from Cotulla, now a U.S. senator, Lyndon Baines Johnson.

Would America let historic Philadelphia be flooded? Or oldest Boston? The original Jamestown had been lost, but if we had known where it had been, would we allow it to be abandoned by history? Guerrero's story was older, one of a constellation of villages that held a secret tale about the beginning of everything that Mexico and Texas had become.

Why not let the dam be placed farther downstream, and far enough south to spare equally revered Ciudad Mier and Camargo?

Let an ample deep trench be dug around the old, historic settlements, let the border slip to the south, annexing the great patrimony of these old towns, for surely the Mexicanos there would consent to becoming Americans by means of this redrawn border.

Or couldn't the river just be made that much deeper, creating a basin that would provide abundant waters for the entire region of the Llanos Mesteños? That had been Fermina's idea after reading some research at the San Antonio Public Library about the building of the Panama Canal.

No arguments sufficed.

The old familias "de los Cuarenta," the forty original founding families of Guerrero that had come from the village of Cerralvo, either had no influence or they had thrown in with the developers of the vast project that would bring oblivion to their once-dear birthplace.

Congressman Henry B. and LBJ sent polite replies to Leandra's pleas. According to them, so great were the forces at play between both nations that nothing could be done. The town lay at the intersection of the Río Bravo and the important tributary known as Río Salado that would feed into the new reservoir. Farther to the south, the river was still used by riverboats taking on cotton and other cash crops for maritime shipping into the Gulf.

The old town's unique location, initially surveyed late in the seventeenth century by one of Alonso de León's expeditions, had finally come to spell its doom. The historic Vela homes of Guerrero, along with all the others, the picturesque plaza and its gazebo, the church devoted to La Virgen de San Juan de Los Lagos, all would soon go into the deep.

Though she had barely mentioned Guerrero in the decades before, when this irreversible death sentence became clear to

Grandmother, only one response was possible. Already in her early seventies, she would have to go there one more time to have a last look for herself at all that her antepasados had left behind.

Of course, her daughter Lucille would drive her mother the three hundred miles to the border crossing that would carry them back into the 1700s once more before it was all offered up to the nonpartisan river gods of the Rio Grande.

9. Out of the ruins, a long-lost cousin appears

There comes a point in time when memory can do little else but offer a ritual farewell to a world passing away. Remembering then becomes an act of resigned homage, a commiseration between ancestors and their progeny regarding the apparent inexhaustibility, and arbitrariness, of time. We remember all that was expected, all that was anticipated—and never manifested.

Late in 1953, after keeping them at a distance for decades, Grandmother was suddenly overtaken by her private memories. She had begun talking again about moving Leonides's bones from Cotulla to the Vela crypt in Laredo.

Mother doesn't remember her or Tía Fermina talking about Guerrero before, but when the news of the Falcon dam's imminent completion was reported in the *San Antonio Light* in 1952, predicting the inundation of Guerrero Viejo, the two old Vela sisters became agitated.

Perhaps they had been born there. Their birth certificates have disappeared, and Grandmother would only say that she had been baptized in San Diego, Texas; her age always remained a mystery— had she been born in 1880, 1883, or 1889? All of these appeared as her birth year in various documents after her death in 1975. And, as if preparing for some encroaching denouement, Tía Fermina prepared her final will, writing:

Know all men by these presents: That I, Fermina Ferguson of the County of Bexar, State of Texas, being of sound mind and memory

and in sound bodily health knowing the certainty of death and the
uncertainty of life and wishing to settle my worldly affairs while I
have strength to do so make and publish this my last will and testament hereby revoking all other Wills heretofore made by me.

In that testament from the spring of 1954, she left all of her
worldly goods, including her remaining share of the old Spanish
land grant, to her sister Leandra; just afterward, Mother drove
Grandmother and her aunt to Tamaulipas, Mexico, for one last
look at Guerrero. She took them to the border in the vast turquoise
Hudson my father had just bought, and crossed the Rio Grande via
a still extant hand-operated ferry at Los Ébanos, Texas.

Once they turned off of the frontera highway onto the dusty
road approaching the colonial town, Leandra and Fermina became
emotional with each other, pointing to the old houses and buildings along the way as their memories of a distant time began to stir.
By then, the town was already virtually abandoned, though police
remained to watch for looters. While the two sisters walked off on
their own through the empty streets, Mother remembers seeing a
plaque that listed all of the alcaldes of the town, showing literally
dozens of Velas who had served as mayor there since its founding
in 1750.

She later found the two sisters standing in front of the once
grand, now vacated Hotel Flores, the center of cosmopolitan culture in the heyday of Guerrero that regularly presented entertainers
from Mexico City and Paris and was owned and operated by one of
Grandmother's aunts, Eulalia Flores de Vela. They described how
elaborately decorated the hotel had once been, decked throughout
in red velvet with chandeliers that had been created in Hungary.

Now it was empty, like most of the rest of the old town, awaiting
the cleansing waters of the Rio Grande that would soon come.

On the silent road back to the border, Mother drove Leandra
and Fermina through nearby Camargo, another of Escandón's historic towns, where Grandmother wanted to see the location of
Leonides' Lopez land grant property, which she had recorded in a

small map that her husband had given to her before his death. What was once remote pasture was now at the edge of the town's environs, and fully built over with small houses, teeming with families. Grandmother had no idea when the Lopez had left it behind, and it would certainly never be reclaimed now.

Late in the nineteenth century the region was afflicted by waves of yellow fever and diphtheria epidemics, bringing many deaths, particularly among the young, and causing many families to flee. And then, beginning in 1905, another era of political instability returned as a rumor of a Mexican uprising called the Plan de San Diego, real or not, brought a new wave of political violence to the border, resulting in the killing of as many as five thousand Mexicanos in South Texas and north Mexico at the hands of the Texas Rangers.

The "Plan de San Diego," a document of mysterious provenance, called for the creation of an independent Republic of South Texas, a haven for Mexicans, Native Americans, African Americans, and Japanese. The ensuing spasms of violence caused still more families to leave the historic homeland behind, many making their way to Laredo, where Grandmother and her older sister Fermina spent most of their childhoods.

Fifty years after that last trip of Grandmother and Tia Fermina to their hometown, on the day I visited the ruins of Guerrero, exposed to light again by the onset of a great drought beginning in the 1990s, I sat in the plaza of Vicente Guerra as the late afternoon light turned a burnt amber, listening to the waters of river distantly lapping against the streets a few blocks to the north. I was the only person in the ghost town, and I had let no one know back in the United States where I was. These days, the whole region is scourged by narco-wars as rival drug cartels viciously battle over turf and control of their illicit trade.

The perpetual war that has haunted Nuevo Santander since its inception continues under a new guise.

I realized my truck alone was worth more than me, so I set out to return to the American side of the border before dusk, using the narrow two-lane road that goes over the Falcon Dam and leads directly into the U.S. customs station, which I found apparently empty.

As I pulled my truck into the checkpoint, a sole border agent looked out from his post, recorded my license plate into his computer, and came out to ask me if I was an American citizen. I showed him my New York driver's license and explained that I was driving my mother's truck for the research day trip I had just made into Guerrero Viejo.

"Please park your truck in lane number one, please, sir," he dourly responded.

On slow days in sleepy border stations, perhaps there's little else to do, but the stern unsmiling agent proceeded to execute a full search of the vehicle, entering the cab, checking the glove compartment, using a flashlight to look under the bench seat, extending a circular mirror on a long pole to inspect underneath the truck's chassis, and finally bringing out a dog for a full sniff test, while he knocked all along the body of the truck from every side.

Once he signaled that I could leave, I asked him about his name badge, having noticed he was a Guerra, and I told him that I had gone to Guerrero partly in search of my Vela and Guerra family roots.

"My Guerra family had some history there, but we came from Spain."

"Mine did too," I told him.

"But mine came over in the sixteenth century."

"Mine, too, from a village in Asturias, in the north. They were Guerra Cañamar."

Agent Guerra gave me a serious, skeptical look.

I opened the door of the truck and pulled out a genealogical book, *Thirteen Generations of Guerra in the New World*, that had been lying on the front seat, which he had apparently not seen when he searched the cab, because when I showed it to him, explaining that I had found my family's lineage detailed in that book, he lit up.

"Did you go to that reunion?" he asked.

"No, but I'm a descendant of the family."

"Well, I'm in that book!" he announced.

He invited me into the border station and showed me where pictures of him as a child with his father appeared and where he was shown with his own family in Brownsville, Texas. I showed him where my great-great-grandmother appeared in the family tree. Since I was descended from a Guerra woman who had married a Vela, we had "daughtered" out of the official Guerra chronicle.

He told me that the main Guerra family crypt was just down the road in Roma, Texas, and that the family organized large reunions, sometimes gathering thousands, every five or ten years. I told him I hoped that he appreciated that I hadn't brought up our kinship before he had a chance to fully search my truck, a gesture of deference between long-lost cousins. He laughed.

"And there's a family resemblance too," I said, pointing to our hair. "All salt and pepper," I noted, "but you have more salt than I do!"

"There's another resemblance," he replied, gently laying his index finger along his nose and pointing to mine. "You know we were Jews, right? We've got these noses, and we're all good at business."

"I'm useless at business," I told him. "But I am a devotee of the Bal Shem Tov."

I didn't tell him what I was really thinking.

As the centuries pass, a family's many paths radiate outward into a kaleidoscopic vision of humanity. Generations on, three hundred years since our ancestors first came into these lands of the New World, two estranged Guerra primos were still keeping a watch on the Río Grande, one who was sworn to enforce the border at all costs, the other who believed that eventually, inevitably, it would be erased and forgotten.

X

El Canto de Cenote Siete
(Con un autor anónimo)

Fourth Legajo

A note on these codices.

These documents should be regarded as my interpolations on the meandering course taken by the truth of ages. Our bodies have metamorphosed through eons so that they might remain vessels of this knowledge. This is a chronicle of time remembered after the end of ages. This is my mission. The things attested to I have witnessed with my own eyes, in one of the many bodies I have sojourned within. Once complete, it is my intention to render the entirety of my discoveries to some destination in the remote past where it can germinate and take root among my kindred predecessors, in the form of intuition or dreams, appearing as a vision of a fiery orb, sublimating knowledge through fire, apparently manifesting out of nowhere.

They have ascribed incontrovertible meanings to all manner of texts, purloined and spurious, redacted by charlatans, mutated by drunkards and manipulators, preached upon by the wounded and the conspiratorial. It truly is a wonder any flicker of truth has survived in the faltering candle of our times.

You may have received these documents in this way, or as a gift to an *unsuspecting progenitor courtesy of your ancestor from the future. You may be a reader in another age who has encountered them de pura casualidad.*

De los dichos de Cenote Siete.

We were inside the great machine of the universe, subject to all the forces of gravity, magnetism, and dissolution that always had bound and infused creation but were once beyond the reach of our senses. We suddenly felt all of these energies and affinities as palpably as touching our own bodies.

That was in the time of La Zona, a time we thought would last forever.

Then inexplicably, the machine was set in reverse in one unanticipated and frightful whirr that has sent many of us moving back through time, all the stars trailing behind in spiraling flares. El Fracaso de La Zona. I had steeped myself in stories of the past, discerning here and there faint imprints of a first and last book, an infinite compendium, the vast codex of the immaterial empires of man. The book was written in a universal language, embedded in so deep an encryption and so ubiquitously copied that it had become omnipresent but invisible.

I am living backward in time, sharing an interval of decades with you as we pass in opposite directions. I can traverse all ages, but I always return to this my same course; my momentum, my trajectory, my compromiso is into the past, connected through time and blood.

It becomes ever clearer that there is a story emerging, not of our making. It is a story our bodies are telling to time itself, the evolution of the human, the proliferation of cultures, and in ages to come, the demise of the masculine, the continuity of the feminine. The story can only be said to be emerging now because we are witnessing it. If we were not witnessing it, as we did not for so long, it would continue to take its course. For this is a story that has always existed implicitly, and so does not require our witness. We may have always been the instrument or vehicle of this story, but by witnessing it we enter into it fully as ourselves for the first time, thereby changing the old unfolding story forever.

For I am equally of the past as of the future.

And be assured that I am with you now.

We had not imagined the great setting aside, the one hidden and foretold in our blood. All of the worlds of the ancestors were to be left behind, even those that were only partly remembered.

There were many echelons of forgetting.

Of the first Spanish humans.

No one has a final account of the trace-lines of destiny that made España the portal through which the Old World would first encounter and fathom the peoples, natural bounty, and boundless geographies of the Mundo Nuevo. Serendipity hardly seems an apt word when so many cruel ironies were soon to abound. But an explanation of Spain's trials and triumphs in that era cannot fully encompass the peculiar way that Iberia's history had prepared its people for the fate that was to befall, or bless, them. Though Spain in 1492 was a relatively insignificant force in the emerging community of seagoing nations, its place in history as Europe's promontory into the Mediterranean and the Atlantic had long made of it a crossroads of humanity reaching back into the unplumbable recesses of the past.

For seven hundred years before the discovery of the New World, the loosely unified kingdoms of early Spain had been ruled over by Arab Muslim hegemons, while Christians and Jews alike participated fully in the society. Long before that, the peninsula had been one of the oldest places in Europe to be settled by early man, either arriving overland in a long diaspora out of Africa via Mesopotamia, or perhaps directly across the short stretch of water separating Africa from the mainland at Gibraltar. In that ancient age, the peninsula was densely forested, so much so that the Greek historian Strabo, in his Geography, *reported that a squirrel could traverse the entire span of that land simply by leaping from treetop to treetop. Strabo describes the people of northern Iberia as "sober," drinking only water, wearing their hair very long, "in the feminine style," and maintaining an austere lifestyle; they slept on the ground and subsisted on dry bread made from acorn flour.*

This millennial legacy of human occupation, exploration, settlement, and interaction, above all else, marked the way that the people of Spain would conduct their eventual discovery, conquest, and colonization of the vast dominions of the New World.

Old worlds were always displaced and supplanted by new worlds. Stories in the northern village of Zamakola told of a race of giants that had once

lived in those lands and left behind a monumental stone bridge called Jen-
tilzubi, "bridge of the Gentiles," in the forest of Dima. This was even
before the coming of the Basques. Villagers said this natural geological for-
mation was built by these legendary people, who were finally driven away
from their longtime home by the noisome sound of Christian bells.

The people of Iberia were descended from among the oldest lineages of
humans in Europa, including Neanderthals and Homo Sapiens, and then
later Celts, Romans, Africans, and Arabs. Some of the oldest human fos-
sils in Europe were discovered in the Sierra de Atapuerca in Spain, reach-
ing back one million years. Evidence of cannibalism was found there, along
with the discovery of of the most ancient ritual funerary practices, testify-
ing to a belief in the sacred body, and perhaps even soul.

Our blood testifies to the antiquity of these lineages. Once, in a warm epoch
127,000 years ago, hippopotami and lions roamed the peninsula. Later, when
it grew much colder and the world of ice came to southern Europa, reindeer
and mammoths roamed the same lands; all of their figures appear, chronicled
in the palimpsests of drawings our ancestors left behind on stone walls, deep
inside caverns, to vouchsafe the stories of what they saw and did.

By the time the ice disappeared, the Neanderthals were long gone.

But before that happened, there was a first mestizaje, the mixing of
peoples among our earliest ancestors; and through these encounters, the
survivors, our ancestors, were forever changed.

De los annales de los Niños Monstruosos.

Our greatest metamorphoses have always come from without.

We could forsake our birthright, change our home, leave behind for-
ests for savannahs, amble through deserts and plains, or climb high into
the thin, chilly air of the mountain worlds, but no human ever willed their
own body to evolve. No man or woman has made their legs grow lon-
ger, spread their shoulder blades farther apart, secreted enamel glaze over
harder, sharpening teeth. These are matters that take place according to
another clock, another compromiso entirely, que no? For millions of years,
our bodies changed their shapes and sizes as swiftly as shimmering light
through a perfect, clear prism.

Yes, gradually, los antepasados left behind the dark, wet selva that had nurtured us and made us strong enough to take in the great breaths through our noses that allowed us to stand upright straightening out the curving, concatenated vertebrae that had always straddled the ground, the air rushing in through our mouths. Henceforth, we would reach for the sun, perpendicular to la tierra.

We wandered out into the endless grasslands, no longer entirely apes, yet still uncertain how far to explore before returning to the refuge of the jungle. Gradually, we learned how to live anywhere. Gradually, we learned how to remember and dream everywhere, anywhere.

The subtlest things, beyond our control, could make a big difference. Suddenly, the hard enamel that began to coat our teeth meant we could eat something other than soft fruit, the crunch of roots and tubers, wild vegetables and stalks. Our jaws receded farther back into our heads, pushing back the tongue and the throat in an exquisite, inexplicable refinement, so that sounds could be controlled, words spoken, songs could be sung. Our faces became smaller, our brains bigger.

But dare I observe that often, metamorphosis has begun with the appearance of something ghastly, something totalmente inesperado, como la aparicíon de un Niño Monstruoso?

I have the body.

It is a small body, no larger than a child, a girl child put into her earthen cuna when ice still covered the lands of Iberia, near Abrigo do Lagar Velho, en la provincia that would come to be known as Portugal de los Portugueses. She was adored, her tiny frame tenderly decorated with an aureole of pierced shells and a dusting of red ochre.

Fijate que she was of us, and not of us—and still she was adored. For the line of her jaw was like our own, her bones as delicate as ours, her pelvis diminuitive, like ours. If you filled her calvarium with mustard seeds, you would find the cranial cavity left by her brain would contain precisely the same number of mustard seeds as our own. And her throat was beautifully curved, perfectamente encorvado, so that it might harbor the sounds to form words and speech, even song. But her legs were from another origin, strong and bowed, her shoulders sloping, so that she would have stood on the ground with the somewhat lumbering form of our primos, Homo

Antecessor, for I dislike the term Neandertales, and I believe that we should honor our ancestors, and their cousins as well.

Had anyone ever seen such as her before?

Perhaps she was one of many such humanos mestizos.

Indeed she was adored, and upon her death, she was adorned with precious totems that would last ages.

De los dichos de Cenote Siete.

Regarding the Requerimiento, with all due respect, I must pause here to pose a query to the great lawgiver: Why was there no commandment saying, "Thou shalt not enslave"? Why no injunction, "Thou shalt not conquer," or "Thou shalt not subjugate and exploit"? Why not "Thou shalt not disparage the gods of others," instead of "Thou shalt not put another god before me"? You must have known how many other gods were being worshipped, and how profound each tradition of devotion was in its own right?

What a different path history might have taken for the Mundo Nuevo desgraciado if upon any occasion when our dear brethren and sistren ancestor humans indulged these strange tendencies of our long-wicked species, their consciences were not extolled by dint of their faith, but rather called therefrom to account for themselves on the basis of this expanded and revised dodecalogue?

Why does everything spin? Was it ever so, or did things begin one way and then set to spinning off at some moment later in the story?

We story the void; we aspire to making our attention ubiquitous. The quest is always for the symphony of the inadvertent, the unseen legend, an act of redemption pursued secretly, of no importance to the apparent world.

Over Revilla Nueva, when the signs began to manifest again, a ship drifted in midair, floating north through a notch in the craggy mountain peak, well above the tree line, appearing over the bare hill horizon, heading off into the open sky of the valley. The caravela was floating, the great masts creaking as the shimmering sails fluttered and swelled on the mountain gusts. The flying barque passed above, silent as it went.

"Your triumph is nearing," I heard myself say.

Your search is nearly complete.

A Treatise on Memory.

The shadow of anything will fall directly away from the sun in precise measure of its form; the moon and the earth, thieves of each other's precious solar radiance, exactly mirror their gibbous and crescent phases, their cast shadows passing like veils across each other's face. This remains a part of the ordinary ratio of shadows in our home world of La Zona.

Forestalling any unforeseen interruption, every movement of these celestial bodies has been plotted, from farthest thence to the edge of fathomable evermore. And everything that casts a shadow will have a shadow cast upon it. And everything that passes into a shadow will eventually emerge from that shadow.

But what are the laws that govern the shadows cast across memory?

Can distant memory, darkened by long spells of forgetting, ever return to light? Must it not be so?

Whatever the Jovian cycle, whatever the vast periodicity.

Yet it was once told how the creator himself begat forgetfulness from within the womb of memory. An old poet sang of how Zeus lay for nine nights with Mnemosyne, goddess of memory, protector of Eleuthera's hills, and how later in Pieria she bore to him nine "like-minded daughters" who would bring the world "forgetfulness of evil, rest from pain," and above all Calliope, muse of history, who soothed all of the greatest lords so divinely that merely speaking her name would cause them to ejaculate. And thus all memory gradually disappeared into the ecstasy of history.

Life comes in a spark, molecules take shape, enabled by some hidden codex deep within to create mirror copies of themselves. Everything crawls out of the mud and walks out across the endless earth, and later trespasses into the heavens.

For millions of years, the human body changed its forms as easily as the transfiguring flame, changing its size and shape as swiftly as refracting light crisscrossing through the clear, perfect panes of a prism. We began to dream. The scales of men and women also changed, with the ratio of greater weight of male to female nearly evolving to equality. A male Australopithecus was 1.5 times heavier than a female. Later, we became virtually equal in size.

All borders are abominations in the eyes of our ancestors, every frontera a diabolical illusion. Then we remembered where we were. We discovered the phases of the calendar, the seasons of ice, planting, harvest, and repair.

Then the dolmens, pyramids, temples, cathedrals, mosques, and flying ships. Worlds are imagined and worlds are created, then destroyed, over and over again. How could such a story become so forgotten, so hidden, passing so everlastingly into dark ink shadow? This forgetting is our tender consolation, for if we carried all memory, we would only remember, forever.

Where would anyone find the beginning of the story that the Iberians brought to Mexico and sought to transplant there so deeply that it might take root and continue its true, final unfolding?

We will never restore the great story, never return to the place of beginning so that we might approach the full meaning of all that has unfolded, and continues to do so. Everywhere you look, within every recess of antiquity, there is another still more hoary antiquity hidden away, further multiplying the sources of the simple story we have inherited.

For this, there is no consolation, no completion except for history's unpronounceable providence.

> *There is only ever onward*
> *& every ghost is pompous*
> *though they may dissimulate*
> *a certain gauzy wistfulness*
> *powerful grief, vague forgetting.*
> *Remember: no solid ground anywhere*
> *for anyone now. Only ghosts know*
> *what comes after, hence their*
> *irrepressible pomposity.*
> *C7*

XI

Churrigueresco Helix

1. Following the winding Lopez path

"Why are you so interested in all of this?" my cousin Larry asks across his kitchen table. "Why does it matter anymore?"

After all these decades, dousing and delving around the branches and roots of the Lopez-Vela family trees, it's still not an easy question to answer. It is unfinished business in part, a quest handed off to me by Uncle Lico and Cenote Siete, an unexpectedly rare, labyrinthine family enigma that I discovered to be historical, geographic, and literary all at once. I've carried all the documents and manuscripts from place to place across the world, clippings, notes, books of quotations, and C7's historical wonders.

We are all bequeathed a mystery out of our family past, with no codebook for how to read it.

There are fundamental processes underlying everything that is alive and constituted by cells: division, migration, differentiation, and cell death—corresponding to birth, diaspora, inspiration, death.

My Lopez cousins and I grew up in a time of flux and abandonment, when the remedies for everyday complaints like a bad stomach or a nasty cut went from herbal nostrums to mercurochrome and 7-Up, and eventually penicillin. The fact that any trace of our old world has survived without the benefit of canonical imprimaturs until now, a hundred and eighty years on, says something about the indelibility of origins.

Despite appearances to the contrary, that world may yet linger in some remote library, echo in some undiscovered journals or repositories, even in the secret hold of our hearts; somehow, all our days, our every ancestral breath, have been vouchsafed, if not entirely remembered.

The sight of a peacock, tail in full fan, shimmering uncountable colors, was said to give Charles Darwin nightmares, challenging him to account for where all of that ostentatious variety and polychromatic specificity had come from. Among the Garcias and Santos of my father's family, our food, our gatherings, conversation, and storytelling in kitchens around tables kept the connections to our ancestors alive. We had inherited a delectable cuisine out of a history of poverty and austerity. And with every feast, in the city or in the countryside, it was as if our ancestors returned to be with us.

The Lopez and Velas left a much subtler, more elusive imprint.

There are stories of a grandfather clock that has the entire Lopez genealogy tracing back to the fifteenth century inscribed on the large glass door of the pendulum case, but for decades it has been in the possession of a reclusive octogenarian cousin who will not allow anyone to see it.

A person only remembers if they can remember what it is they need to remember.

To tell the story from the fragments I have gathered is a palpable way of offering an account of myself, of the origins of my own body, connected to the entire pageant of ancestral bodies that leads me back into our beginnings in most distant antiquity.

"I have the body," Cenote Siete ceaselessly repeats.

Perhaps, as he describes, the ageless spirit comes from a very different place, migrating through new bodies willy-nilly with each new incarnation. Maybe, before I was born Tejano, there was a

Tibetan incarnation, a lifetime in a Zulu body, an Armenian one, or Papuan, and on and on through the plethora of humanity's past. But one esoteric healer I know insists that we reincarnate within a narrowcast of specific related lineages, held together by bonds of genetic inheritance that shine when seen from eternity, like luminescent tribal markings. I can only vouch for this lifetime in my Lopez-Vela/Santos-Garcia body, entering the twentieth century in a long-delayed, somewhat calamitous birth, battered by caliper jaws, marked on the back with a large Mongolian spot, my small furry tail quickly and unceremoniously cut away.

That's enough to make you wonder where all of this began.

Cenote Siete says it is a compromiso, a troth with the ancestors that some of us are charged with deepening and protecting. He says it is a calling, a vocation, not for everyone. But there are always those who are carrying it on.

Over many generations, among many relations, the desire to maintain and understand a family's history can fade and disappear. If Uncle Lico hadn't gathered the documented history of the Lopez and Velas, I wouldn't have been able to tell this tale. Among all my Lopez cousins, only Bob in Baltimore harbored the same deep curiosity about the sources of our clans, and it only awakened fully when he reached adulthood and had a daughter.

My cousins otherwise set off in a myriad of life paths. Since my aunts or uncles never told it to them, they do not know the old story of our family I have sought to tell here, and it may not mean anything to them for it to be told now. My twin brothers know the antiquity and complexity of our ancestry, but it was never a central concern of their lives. Nonetheless, I tell them we are doing the same thing, by different means.

Along with my brothers, we have evolved a multivoiced phalanx against the inchoate darkness of our family's forgetting. We each of us use a different battery of tools and weapons, but we are all involved in the same project: mending human spirit, and perhaps sending it forward more whole into the still unknowable forms of humanity in times to come.

George always possessed an incredible power to discern the

pathologies of bodies, while his twin, Charles, tested the limit of bodies, his body particularly, gashing head and leg, breaking an arm as a child, and later, using dance to create stark images of the body set loose in an unstable world.

George, a psychiatrist in Houston, also runs a large psychiatric hospital. He was with me for a year at Notre Dame, overlapping his freshman and my senior year, so we've had a long conversation about the meanings of all our ancestral tales. Storytelling, especially about family history, always seeks some kind of healing, though its benefits aren't as immediate as those attained by prescription medicine or electroconvulsive therapy.

When I started wondering publicly about how genetics and family stories might intertwine or contradict one another, George thought the widespread presence of memoirs in the last twenty years was a symptom of the vanishing context of history or culture for fathoming who we are. Increasingly, he saw genetic science being embraced for the same reason.

"In the end, the need for context may be the driving reason for any memoir," he wrote to me.

With our broadening palimpsest of archaeological discoveries, recorded history, family stories, and genomics, context abounds— well out of our reach of understanding. Maybe a new religion will ultimately emerge to pull it all together.

George questioned some of my writing about genetics, referring to "a mystical presence of a shaping energy in the universe," referring to the work of the scientist Stuart Kauffman, who sees the presence of a force he calls "order for free" in the cosmos.

I had added the mystical bit.

For my brother, that idea could be seen as a consolation, to avoid reckoning with the real forces of creation as he identified them: "chance, probability, and chaos."

"I personally struggle with my own attraction and comfort in the reduction of science," he wrote to me. We had always maintained a convivial quarrel about the consolations of scientific inquiry, and I am his older brother; hence the self-consciousness about his Humean skepticism.

But telling the oldest family stories I could fathom only brought me to a deeper well of mysteries, of who we are, where we came from. Genetics isn't going to answer those questions.

"I feel somehow safer with increasing degrees of information and of details of physiology and genetics," George continued. "It gives me the ability to have a sense of understanding and prediction. At the same time, I tend to view the information as less worthy of note than the exploration itself. The accomplishments of man are less reflected in any code than the transcendent nature of any expression itself."

He ended the note to me on the question of how genetics and family tales intersect.

"I have to think more about the issue which is more or less transcendent and telling: the evolving information and science of genetics, or the racial, ethnic, cultural, and national difference which have emerged and been expressed through time in broader response to broader forces of 'natural selection.'"

Perhaps these obsessions do run in family lines.

In 1953, a distant cousin of ours, Antonio Maria Guerra, wrote a small book, *Mier in History*, offering an account of the history of one of the Villas del Norte on the occasion of the town's two hundredth anniversary. He presents his modest tome to the reader as his "one and only child, pure and bare, without proper and showy raiments," adding that "the act of being born with her face to the sky, her hair to the sincere wind of the province, with her feet rooted in a land of fire that burns her soles, makes her arrogant and proud; . . . she has the virtue of Truth."

He begins his history of one of our shared ancestral homes with latitude and longitude bearings, pinpointing Mier on the banks of the Río Alamo, three kilometers from where it pours into the Río Grande, which he refers to as the "Bravo del Norte."

Guerra tells how he has discovered fossils of prehistoric animals in the sand of the Alamo's banks, including human bones such as vertebrae and a humerus, the jawbones and molars of mammoths, and an enormous turtle; all of this "at the crossing of the Arroyo de las Conchas and the Río de las Conchas."

The Lopez-Vela tale reminds me that families are always a part of a human story that runs deeper than the story of any one nation or people. We migrate, venture farther out to the fronteras where we may settle in for a long spell, states come and go, and we are ever becoming something new, ever metamorphosing, gradually divesting ourselves of the untold ethnogony that brought us to where we find ourselves today.

2. A mestizo in New York City

You wouldn't know if the man or woman you met in the dusty plazas of one of Escandón's new towns was a second or third cousin, a secret half brother or sister, perhaps even an unknown, estranged sibling.

The consanguinity laws were introduced to prevent incest, but they were essentially unenforceable in Nuevo Santander. In cases where the possibility of shared parentage was a concern, a dispensation would be required to allow an amorous liaison to be consecrated with a church marriage.

There were so few women in the farthest northern reaches of New Spain that the common event of cousins marrying cousins was hardly even noted.

All lineages were blurring into the opening sky of the mestizaje. What mattered was whether a child was born male or female (preferably male), or born fair or dark (preferably fair), with Español, Indian, or black features (preferably Español). This was the calculus of Mexico's "castas."

In Mother's family, she was the darkest of the lot, and the last of the siblings to be born. The Cotulla barber Luisito would call out to her when she passed his shop in the morning on the way to school.

"Buenos días, Prietita, como estás?"

Good morning, little darkie, how are you?

To be "prieta" was to be very dark, the color of roasted coffee, toasted caramel, sweet, tawny membrillo. Even in the scorching summer sun, Mother was olive-skinned, café con leche, but in the castas of Cotulla she was still "prieta."

In the winter as she grew paler out of the sun's unstinting glare, she would become "morena," dark beige leche quemada. And Luis-ito would give a toothless shout from the door of the shop,

"Oye, Lucilita Morenita, adonde vas?"

Hey, little brown Lucille, where are you going?

Mother still remembers how she would secretly seethe.

A while back, I was invited on to a radio talk show in New York City, to talk about San Antonio, "Mexican America," and the South-west. I had been a long fan of this host, an august, crumpled, and bearded New York Brahmin who had begun his career decades before at the progressive Pacifica radio station—and I told him of my admiration with great enthusiasm as the show was about to begin, with an unheard of Tex-Mex *acordeón* tune already tinkling in the background as my musical introduction.

"You won't be a fan when we're done," he answered just before introducing me on the air as the broadcast light went on, " . . . and welcome to the show!"

He was right.

During the interview he variously disparaged Mexican and Chicano art and literature and then worked up a real lather disre-specting Tex-Mex food from San Antonio, comparing it unfavorably to the superior traditional sauces of Mexico City and central Mexico, themselves (truth be told) only approximations and reinventions of their French models, and he seemed primed by his producer's notes to attack me as a bloodthirsty multiculturalist, determined to insult European culture and deride the peerless Western canon of literature, philosophy, art—and culinary excellence. Not only was the border world of South Texas marginal to American culture, it was marginal to Mexican culture, an in-between world of no conse-quence whatsoever.

"I have to say you're a little misinformed," I managed to reply at one point, referring him to the juicy jalapeño pork tamales from Tellez's on General McMullen, to the smoky brisket plate with fresh habanero chile sauce at Garcia's on Fredericksburg, the caldo Xochitl at El Mirador on South St. Mary's Street, and the huevos ranche-ros at the Taco Donut Shop, not to mention the iced chocolate cake doughnuts there I'd been eating since I was a niñito and which had metabolized into at least eighty-five percent of my body mass.

I was explaining that a book I had written about my father's family and San Antonio was in part autobiography but mostly a meditation on the legacy and echoes of Mexico's indigenous and mestizo origins among the Mexican Americans I had grown up with in Texas. America was mestizo, always had been, but just didn't know yet how to embrace that history, that identity. On this matter, Mexico had a lesson to share with its northern neighbor.

The real revolution in twentieth-century Mexico, carried forward by the Chicanos, was the overturning of the Spanish conquerors' subjugation of the indigenous civilizations and the mestizo culture that had arisen in the aftermath, combining Spanish and indigenous blood. With my mother's Spanish family and my father's indigenous and mestizo ancestors, the conquest ran like a fault line right through the middle of the living room in the suburban house I grew up in in San Antonio.

"You don't look like you have a drop of Indian blood in you," he quickly retorted.

"And a drop is all it takes, right?" I replied.

He changed the subject, and the conversation moved on.

It was a strange moment that got me thinking of how the missing story of our ancestors might be in the blood after all, or at least a big part of it we've ignored until very recently, with the discovery of DNA fifty years ago. Geneticists tell us that not only does the genome contain a blueprint for each of our unique human bodies, it is also a failsafe "hard drive" of our ancestral past, a vast mestizo codex of our sublimely mixed origins and diasporas across the planet, going back to our very genesis as unicellular life. Additionally, the genome is time-coded, allowing us to identify specific relations to ancestors in specific periods of time, reaching back tens of thousands of years.

I contacted one of the many laboratories that now offer to scan your genetic codex, requesting tests that would reveal information about both my paternal and maternal ancestral origins. The request can be made via the Internet, part of the Web's obsession with genealogy, second only to pornography. Soon a kit arrives in your mailbox containing swabs you scrape against the inside of your cheeks, place in vials, and return to the labs. The tests promise a document that will establish your specific genetic lineage, correlated to thousands of others in an ever-expanding database, and charted in time according to periods of migration when a specific lineage is known to have become more widespread, leaving a record of its journey in the genetic record.

While this "document" is still directly legible only to trained scientists, geneticists tell us we'll soon be able to read our DNA in a vernacular version. For now, if we could read one letter a second from the 3.12 billion A's, C's, T's, and G's of this 3-D double-spiral text, it would still take a hundred years to read your own genetic code, a vast text of our personal and collective origins.

Author Matt Ridley puts it this way: "There is something hard, indivisible, quantum and particulate at the heart of inheritance . . . an unbroken chain of copyings over four billion years." Biologist Robert Pollack describes DNA as "a precise copy of our sole and complete inheritance, one that is more ancient than any human artifact." Geneticists such as Pollack, Luigi Luca Cavalli-Sforza, and Bryan Sykes tell us that our DNA, which is not only comprehensive in its recall, but chronologically coded, will reveal the full history of our ancestors and their million-year-long wanderings across the planet.

Forever into the past, always already, the story went on, always being added to, but without anyone to read it. Our generation is the first to begin doing that. What will we find there? Does it contain that missing story of ourselves?

There is a philosopher who believes he has found a code that reveals the exact words, *God Eternal, Within the Body,* digitally encrypted and inscribed within the codons of the human genome, though he doesn't explain why the message should appear there in modern English. Questions to the same philosopher: Does the same message appear in every species' chromosomes? All of the plants? In every living thing?

Nonetheless, suspicions will arise that there are quintessential, hardwired "codes of the self," hidden inside the body. Perhaps our breath counts out a prayer to the divine in Morse code. Our rest-less motions during sleep spell out some other cosmological truth in semaphore. As the biologist Richard Dawkins has noted, the codes we have discovered underlying the mirrored helix structure of DNA are eerily "machinic," like a difference engine deep inside of nature, digital, constituting an ongoing mutating algorithmic permutation on the human. But even if we can retrieve every numerical config-uration that constituted all ancestors ever, we would still only be at the gateway of the real mystery, only at the portal into the labyrinth of who we are.

In evolutionary terms, you have to wonder why all of our ances-try has been recorded. Now that we are beginning to read this blood codex, we are going to make some new story of ourselves out of what we find there. We will seek to reconcile the differences between the stories written in our blood and the stories of history, cultures, and nations.

Is not the story our blood is telling the first, true story of ourselves?

And yet, only fifty years into our ability to read the genetic code, we have already developed the ability to write over it, to change our own genetic legacy, going forward. Though it remains controver-sial, scientist Freeman Dyson believes there will soon be numerous species of humans, products of deliberate genetic recombination. For millennia, our genes were for reading only, at a level of our being well beyond consciousness. Our science changed that.

Henceforth, we will be able to revise and invent upon this ancient code of ourselves. The geneticist Spencer Wells, leading a global genographic project for the National Geographic Society, has pointed to the urgency of uncovering our genetic legacies, writing, "It is our single, unique human history and it would be nice to know what that is as we hurtle into the future and start to change our genetics."

And what we find at the level of our DNA is a history of our ancestral diasporas, the restlessness of our antepasados, always set-ting out, becoming something new, then setting out again. The way of understanding this history that emerged in Mexico after the Conquest was through mestizo identities, a way of seeing ourselves as the inheritors of numerous global cultures.

The genetic record of these wanderings, in a sense, is always being lost—it is being quickly overwritten in the rapid mestizaje that globalization has wrought, beginning in 1492, when the genetic circuit of humanity was closed once and for all, after perhaps forty thousand years when branches of humanity first traversed Asia, crossed the Bering Strait, and entered the lands that would become the Americas. Henceforth, from the late fifteenth century, humanity would become ever more mestizo, ever more mixed, combining the cosmic array of human cultures, becoming a *raza cosmica*, in the words of the Mexican philosopher José Vasconcelos, describing the Mexican nation. Virgilio Elizondo has a beautiful utopian framing of this in his idea of new humanity in Mexico emerging from the bedroom, where new life began, the kitchen, where the new bodies were nourished, and the sanctuary, where they were consecrated.

The first spark of mestizo consciousness is elusive, perhaps lost forever.

We can look to specific early biographies in this history, such as that of Gonzalo Guerrero, a shipwrecked conquistador who sided and fought with the Maya against his own countrymen, and allegedly saved his own mestizo children (among the first in Spanish America) from being sacrificed by making the case that the gods rejected the mixed blood of his offspring with a Mayan wife. Also, El Inca, Garcilaso de la Vega, in his *Royal Commentaries*, reflected on his own mixed origins and his complex emotional decision to leave Peru forever for Spain, bidding farewell to his Andean Inca ancestors.

These early voices are a part of the utopian strain of this identity, always questing after new understandings of self and society in the New World.

The dystopian side of the history is chronicled in Antonello Gerbi's *The Dispute of the New World*, where he traces the ways mestizo identity was regarded as a blight on a bloodline, mixing the exalted lineages of Europe with the stunted, inferior, if not outright devilish strains of the New World. Indeed, for centuries, the church and the academy sought to marshal natural history itself as prima facie testimony against mestizaje. In the Old Testament, Yahweh is seen repeatedly issuing injunctions to his chosen people against race mixing.

Of course, this chastisement failed miserably, not only ideologically but also historically. Rather than strictly observing racial boundaries, mestizaje bloomed from the very beginning of the human race. In fact, there's considerable debate right now among paleoanthropologists about the extent of mixing that took place in the most remote species past, especially concerning the fate of the Neanderthals and whether *Homo sapiens* still carries a genetic legacy of a distant, primordial mestizaje.

Ironically, for those of us who are inheritors of the Mexican epic, one of the places where this deep mestizaje is believed to have occurred is in the Iberian Peninsula, underlying all of our family histories out of that land. One of the most dramatic cases for the mixing of Neanderthals and *Homo sapiens* are the remains of that young girl's bones dug up recently in Portugal, which Cenote Siete put before me.

As he described it, her small body, showing the morphologies of both Neanderthal and modern human parentage, was ritually adorned with ochre and reverentially arranged and decked with beaded shells, as if she was prepared by those who buried her for some great debut in an unseen world to come.

3. A mestizaje in deep time

The Españoles who came to the New World were the progeny of this already ancient mestizaje that had been forgotten after multiple colonizations in antiquity and superceded by the seven-hundred-year-long period of the convivencia during which Christians, Jews, and Muslims from across the Mediterranean and African littoral mingled their traditions of knowledge, science, culture, and art. These were people who were unaware of how accustomed they had become to merging their celebrated lineages with those of others from vastly different worlds.

In my mestizo-Mexicano-Tejano lineage, I've wondered how mestizo identity came to be embraced and celebrated in Mexico, after a long history of being regarded as inferior or less than human.

The mestizo vision was present from the beginning of Mexico's epic in all of the mestizo craftsmen who created beautiful household objects, painted the churches with images derived from their Indian and European ancestry, and reflected throughout their world in hundreds of ways the many fruits of their mixed origins.

In the 1584 Mexican codex known as the *Historia de Tlaxcala*, there are arresting images that offer mute testimony to the birth of the mestizo mind. In one, there is a depiction of the erection of the first cross by a group of Franciscan friars, showing a host of the old gods flying off like banshees, fleeing their ceremony. In another image, two friars are blithely setting light to a bonfire of the Nahua gods. The drawings betray the hand of an artist who was rooted in both worlds, able to evoke the precise faces and masks of the old gods— Tlaloc's goggle-eyed stare, the curious horned profile of Quetzalcoatl in his incarnation of the wind god Ehecatl, the frightening skull grin of the old god Huehueteotl—while presenting the whole scenario through a Western perspective, recognizing the friars in profile, enacting their ritual of cultural annihilation. In a haunting third image, an Indio is discovered practicing the old religion, and then shown hanging from the gallows.

Transformation and metamorphosis were of great interest in early mestizo Mexico. The pre-Columbian civilizations were themselves the products of widespread mixing, Mexica with Zapoteca, Chichimeca with Tlaxcalteca, and the beliefs of the ancient ones of Teotihuacan, Tula, and Chichen Itza were broadly adopted by their successors who had come from myriad origins. In the aftermath of the Conquest, one of the earliest best sellers of a new Mexican reading public was Ovid's *Metamorphoses*, chronicling the changes of men into animals, gods into men, tales of transformations that seemed to parallel the mutability of the Mexican society that was beginning to take shape.

As these palimpsests of worlds began to accumulate and deepen, Greek myth over Aztec ornament, Mayan geometry over Iberian filigree, color upon color, refracting the diaphanous sources of mestizo conscience, a new artistic expression emerged in Mexico, with a super baroque style that came to be known as churrigueresco. The art of the churrigueresque brought a forest of detail and ornamentation, echoes of the plethora of mestizo identities that were emerging in the cosmic mixing of races taking place in post-Conquest Mexico. Churches became phantasmagorical copses, bristling with silver bàs-relief foliage. A Hapsburg double-headed eagle stands on a cactus, consuming a serpent in both beaks, adapting the emblem of Azteca patrimony.

In the vernacular world, the churrigueresque reaches all the way in to the present day. Surveying the sitting room of my mother's house, decked with purple-and-gold-upholstered sofas and chair, a gilded Adam and Eve are being expelled from the Garden of Eden next to a Wurlitzer organ; nearby, a sculpture of the Last Supper has Hershey's Kisses on the plates of each of the disciples, and in the middle of the Louis XIV–style coffee table, there is a small replica of Liberace's piano in eggshell-hued porcelain, complete with a tiny candelabra.

Amid this unabashedly delirious mixing of peoples taking place in colonial Mexico, the "castas" appeared in the seventeenth century as a system of classifying all of the possible combinations of races and ethnicities. If the process could not be curtailed, at least it could be given scientific order and rationale.

This system was encapsulated in the formulaic depiction of a nuclear family; mother, father, and offspring, often captured in the midst of everyday life, at a meal, in a market, rolling cigars to make a living.

Indio con Española produce Mestizo. Español con Mestiza produce Castiza.

There were as many as eighty-five different permutations catalogued in this taxonomy of human mestizaje, and once Spanish blood was muddied with the admixture of some other barbarous nation, it would take three successive generations of Spanish admixture before the progeny could be once again dubbed "Español."

Español con Negra produce Mulato. Mulata con Español produce Morizco.

And some of the descriptions took a strangely poetic bent.

Morizco con Española produce Chino. Chino con India produce salta atrás, a leap backward.

Ironically, though these "castas" paintings from Mexico's past depicted all of the various combinations of races and ethnicities and their resulting offspring in a scientific and objectifying manner, they also began to allow a deeper insight into this longstanding but repressed aspect of our ancestry.

In the 1757 census of Revilla, there were sixty-two families reported, with each husband and wife designated as Español, mestizo, or Indio. Among the families there were thirty-one servants, one mulatto, and one slave.

In truth, we are all mestizo.

For me, the nineteenth century Oaxaqueño artist Hermenegildo Bustos, himself of mixed origins, was the first to paint mestizo faces with all of their depth and dignity, a feature that Frida Kahlo and Diego Rivera adopted in their work; but this shift to mestizos testifying to their own innate human worth and beauty really only appears late in the nineteenth century. Bustos had begun his career painting *santos*, small narrative votive paintings that commemorate the intercession of a saint or a virgin on behalf of some desperate petitioner. In return for a healing, a stroke of fortune, or some other blessing, the petitioner would then commission one of the small paintings, usually executed on tin, that would then be hung in the church. Bustos later began to paint portraits, often echoing the convention of the "castas" paintings, with a father, mother, and child, but in his gaze the subjects were not taxonomic specimens; his mestizo subjects stare out from the canvases with depth, compassion, and dignity.

After the turn of the century, writers like Jose Martí and José Vasconcelos (alongside a host of other Latin American intellectuals) began to develop a literary-philosophical version of this shift of thought near the turn of the twentieth century, extolling mestizo identity and history, becoming a new crypto-nationalist ideology which was embraced by the revolutions that swept across Mexico and Latin America—and have also deeply imprinted the civil rights movements of U.S. Latinos.

Over time, these reflections "from within" on mestizo identity and meaning have been expressed in philosophy and art, theology and literature, and ultimately through activism and politics. In the last thirty years, this intellectual tradition has widened to address the gender and sexual identities of mestizos.

So this is an important lineage to recognize, undoubtedly one among many from mestizo communities around the world struggling to find a voice after a long history of marginalization, stigmatization, and oppression. Collectively, they represent efforts to discover and understand the historical experience of mestizaje from within oneself and our links to our progenitors and the worlds they lived in.

When it comes to mestizaje, humans are proving to be very slow learners.

But there's another shift under way in our understanding of mestizaje as a force shaping history, namely in the numerous ways we're being called now to reckon with the unseen, repressed presence of mestizo identity that was *always* present, giving the lie to historical myths of pure national identity. The recent discoveries (facilitated by genetics) that both George Washington and Thomas Jefferson were fathers of mestizos are examples of this large-scale shift in the macro perspective on mestizaje's role in societies from all over the world.

This is a context for understanding mestizaje that is just now coming to light, the one best put by French theologian Jacques Audinet, when he observed a few years back that mestizaje is "the human face of globalization." Linked to recent developments like the Washington and Jefferson mestizo forefather stories, this insight helps us also to illuminate retrospectively how pervasive and profound a historical force mestizaje has been, always already, so to speak, even if it has been kept hidden away. If we are to take this seriously, it requires us to reexamine and mount a sweeping critique of our histories, to discern and try as best we can to correct how they have been distorted by deeply seated presumptions about our presumed national and cultural identities.

This perspective also makes it possible to see the deeper aspects of mestizo identity, namely the profound human struggle between ways of being that are premised on who we believe we *were* as opposed to who we are *becoming*. Mestizo identity is implicitly the ontology of human *becoming*, of transformation into something new out of all that we and our ancestors have been.

We're confronted with a range of new questions, problems, and challenges to the way mestizaje will shape our individual, national, and global futures. While embracing a mestizo "ontology of becoming" might sound utopian, and though not so long ago it seemed we were on an irreversible march to a multicultural, multipolar global future, the last twenty years have seen those expectations dashed.

We don't really have a social form for this shift. If we're becoming something new, what do we do with everything we thought about who we were, everything we believed defined who we are? In times of transformation, how do we know what part of ourselves we want to hold on to, and how do we reckon out a litany of all of the historical identities we harbor within us?

If, as geneticists tell us, we will soon be able to read in our own DNA the story of our deepest origins in remote time, exposing our constant migratory histories, how will that affect the dearest senses of ourselves we've become so accustomed to, as Frenchmen, as Mexicanos, as Africans, Chinese, or Persians? The anxieties swarming around this historical force of "becoming" and the discovery of our infinitely mesticized past are behind the numerous instances around the world where we've lately seen religious and nationalist fundamentalisms surge, often propelled by murderous onslaughts, against anyone or anything perceived to be threatening their respective fortresses of identity.

The future may be inevitably mestizo, but in a world bristling with all sorts of plotlines of mass destruction and genocide, how will we get there? Incarnate mestizaje is the literal process by which peoples have encountered each other in history, for better or worse, and then mixed in with each other, again for better or worse, through love, coercion, or violence.

Spiritual mestizaje represents a higher struggle still, a profoundly compassionate human space that is fundamentally about "becoming the other." It is a beckoning that applies not only to those who identify themselves as "mestizos" but indeed to all humans living in our globalizing times. This mestizaje limns the form of the human in a cosmic context, a context in which we are truly "one." It is an understanding of the human that will be strongly suppressed by any number of separatist triumphalisms, whether religious, nationalist, or otherwise. How will we set aside any expectations that *our* group, and *ours alone*, will triumph in history, before we can embrace the totality of the human legacy of becoming, from all of the traditions and cultures of the world?

That's the impossible quest it has fallen to our times to undertake, postpone, or negate.

4. Imagining the república cosmica

"I propose that you seek in yourselves remembrance of the Before, and tell what you find, and believe your words."

That was what I had found written on an old note card, but couldn't remember where the quotation had come from. Were they from early dichos of Cenote Siete or the words of some prophet or a guru? At some point, a girlfriend had written the words "toilet bowl" on the other side of the card. Decades later, I found these words again, rereading Laura (Riding) Jackson's book *The Telling*. With that simple charge, Laura shared her compass for a search into ourselves that was both uncompromising and, despite her own avowed repudiation, poetic.

Whatever Laura had intended, this remembrance of a "Before," mysterious and formless, for me represented the search into my family's past. If we have any reach into the world of the Before, it is through our family lineages, elusive as they may be. Stories augmented by genetics, the emerging mirror of ourselves. It reminds me of the Hubble telescope; the way it has given us a lens into the early history of the universe. By peering deep into the recesses of the universe, it has also extended the human gaze into the recesses of time, the time of Creation, the cosmos, the time of the galaxy, our solar system, of the earth.

How was I, a humble Chicano scribe from South Texas who was

at that time in an extended exile in New York City, implicated in that story? What does it make of all of the stories of who we are that *have* been passed down, losing a little more each generation?

If someone could invent a Hubble telescope that could gaze deeply into the human heart, what might we see? Like the Hubble, it would have to be a subtle, perspicacious telescope, its powerful mirrors milled perfectly smooth and impeccably polished to gather the faintest of reflections, showing us greater detail than ever imagined, and, just as the Hubble has done in the material universe, capable of extending our gaze farther into our past than we can fathom.

How would what we see there change us? How could it not change us? The Hubble has shown us amazing sights, gargantuan luminous rainbow-colored dust clouds nurturing new stars and galaxies, neon spiral nebulae whipsawing into one another, black holes extinguishing starlight forever and the still adamantine light of primeval stars that were shining in the earliest eons after the Big Bang. We've all marveled at those pictures, but how have they changed our understanding of the universe we find ourselves in? How have they enlarged or transformed how we think of who we are?

Like the discovery of DNA at the molecular end of creation, these immense spectacles of the cosmos raise questions about how we think of who we are, and how those stories fit into the larger story of creation. How do we come into *that* story? Where are we in the story—how far along in the tale?

To put this differently, how long can anyone be Mexican? How long can you be Armenian? Uzbeki? Jewish? African? Perhaps one hundred years? Five hundred? A thousand? More? How much time do we need to begin to think of ourselves as irrefutably of a certain culture or national tradition? How much of that story does your family still remember and pass on?

I have a friend whose family can trace its lineage back to thirteenth-century Mongols from the Caucasus. But that remote a reach is uncommon.

For all of the talk of the culture wars, more prevalent among many Americans these days is the idea that they have no heritage. "I'm a mongrel," one black kid said to me in a class I taught some years back in a settlement house in the New York City neighborhood called Hell's Kitchen. "I don't come from anywhere," he added. "I'm from the Bronx."

In an old song of the post-punk band the Smiths, the Mancunian Morrissey, recently adopted as an honorary Chicano, captured this sentiment of urban-suburban American anti-identity perfectly, singing, "I am son and heir to nothing in particular."

To be mixed is to be from nowhere.

To be mixed is to be from everywhere. If we are from everywhere we have a right to be anywhere. And if we have a right to be anywhere, no borders will stand.

So, how long do we imagine remaining Chinese? Or Japanese? Russian? Persian? Indonesian? Will our offspring be Navajo like us in fifty years? Another hundred? Five hundred? A thousand? Can you imagine your progeny remaining culturally the same as you for ten thousand years more? Does it make a difference to you?

I'm not talking about assimilation, which is a historical process, one that comes and goes, ebbs and flows in the passing tides of nations, history, and politics. Through the lens of the imaginary Hubble of the human heart, there is a longer, more deeply embedded process of "becoming" that emerges as the real human mystery, the one that links our own species's past to the forces at play in the universe. How do we become something new and at what cost for all that we must leave behind?

This is really the crux of the so-called "culture wars," perhaps better understood as one part of the emerging worldwide enigmas of identity. Globalization, especially the human process of globalization—mestizaje—is changing all of us, and many choose not to change, or even seek to reverse change.

What is American? Our DNA will testify to the fact that Americans have always been mestizo, going back to the celebrated forefathers of the republic. Jefferson secretly kept his own mestizo children as slaves. We're just grappling with how such an identity might change the public sense of what it means to be American, and what kind of story we will tell about how we came to be this way.

The late Harvard historian Samuel Huntington wrote, "America was created by 17th- and 18th-century settlers who were overwhelmingly white, British, and Protestant. Their values, institutions, and culture provided the foundation for and shaped the development of the United States in the following centuries." He asked, "Will the United States remain a country with a single national language and a core Anglo-Protestant culture?"

And what is it that most threatens this legacy? According to Huntington, not radical Islam or ultra-liberal "One Worlders." Instead, the republic's future hangs in the balance due to the intractable Hispanics, who are set on keeping their language (did any founding father speak Español?), staking claim to their historical homelands, and populating too numerously in a short time.

"By ignoring this . . . Americans acquiesce to their eventual transformation into two peoples with two cultures (Anglo and Hispanic) and two languages (English and Spanish)." And even more ominously, "They could . . . eventually undertake to do what no previous immigrant group could have dreamed of doing: challenge the existing cultural, political, legal, commercial, and educational systems to change fundamentally not only the language but also the very institutions in which they do business."

Mexican writer Carlos Monsiváis pithily characterized Huntington's insight as, "The United States is planning to invade the United States."

In human terms, in genetic terms, the story of the United States is being written inside the larger story of the New World, of *América entre las Américas*. Ever since the arrival of the Europeans, and then everyone else, in these lands we have been on the path of becoming globalized mestizos, our destiny as a species, if we last long enough, to mix our traditions, beliefs, heritage, blood, and bodies.

If we endure, we will become beautiful.

Of course, mestizaje has always been a part of world history and culture, from the days of early man to Mesopotamia, to the Mediterranean foment of Greek and later Hellenic and Roman culture, and on and on. But, five hundred years ago, with the inception of the

Mundo Nuevo, mestizaje became the world's destiny. And in deep time, five hundred years in the past was ten minutes ago. We're just in the beginning of this, so it's no wonder there's so much confusion and contradiction and groping in the dark for the righteous way forward.

In addition to so many writers of color in our time, starting in the mid-nineteenth century in Mexico artists like Bustos and Kahlo and thinkers such as Jose Martí and José Vasconcelos transmitted this prophetic vision of mestizaje.

So did Walt Whitman, in "Song of Myself":

> I am of old and young, of the foolish as much as the wise,
> Regardless of others, ever regardful of others,
> Maternal as well as paternal, a child as well as a man,
> Stuff'd with the stuff that is coarse and stuff'd with the stuff that
> is fine,
> One of the Nation of many nations, the smallest the same and the
> largest the same.

The worldwide rise of murderous nationalisms and fundamentalisms demonstrates the sometimes destructive role that cultural identities can play in world affairs, especially lethal in an age of technologies of mass destruction. Our age has also offered the first chance to tell and celebrate many neglected or ignored heritage stories, in some cases after centuries of denial, exclusion, and oppression. At the very same time we are called to remember who we were, where we came from, and to go beyond, to transform ourselves and our societies, to become something new, a *república cosmica*.

So, in this vexed moment we prepare to read the codices of our blood, seeking the missing story of ourselves. But our DNA really tells us we are not who we think we are. We have no one true homeland, except perhaps Africa.

We are wanderers.

We must delve further, more deeply.

I'm not appealing for poets to submit themselves to the language of science. As biologist Robert Pollack observes, "Humanists shrink from a text constructed by natural selection and written in an invisible chemical medium." This is about claiming cosmology, DNA, and the quantum world as a medium for poetry, for vision, going beyond however we've been instructed to see the human genome as an exclusively biological and medical fact.

But can't we just tell more stories about our abuelitas?

That's a good place to begin, but there's a lot more to the story I want to hear, and the way things are going, even if it's indelible in our blood, the time to tell the story is now, and the sooner the better.

When the first of my genetic ancestry test results arrived, it was the Y-DNA scan, an analysis of the ancestral origins of my paternal DNA. The results, to say the least, offered a new story about my father's antepasados.

While I had always felt my father's family connecting us to the indigenous past of Mexico, an old mestizo lineage once known as "de los Santos" emerging out of the encounter between Europeans and Indians, the tests opened a window into the farther sources of the lineage, from among Ashkenazi and Sephardic Jews. Catholics for as long as anyone could remember, no memory of this earlier ancestry had survived among the Santos.

In maps that accompanied the test results, the "Cohanim" haplogroup that my DNA matched was shown to have originated in North Africa and the Arabian Peninsula, perhaps ten thousand years ago, gradually migrating into Eastern Europe, into the Balkans and the Caucasus, before journeying on into the Iberian Peninsula, from where they found their way to the New World. Further, this lineage was said to have been associated with the priestly caste responsible for the ritual obligations of the Temple in Jerusalem.

I had known that our family story was partly rooted in the stories that had originated in Israel, of the interactions between God and man that had taken place there, and the story of Jesus that had later been carried to Spain and eventually to Mexico, arriving finally in the hearts of the founders of Nuevo Santander who saw their lives and works as fulfilling long-held prophecies out of this tradition. I imagined a deeper pilgrimage in time, a long journey of many ancestors who carried these legacies by many paths out of the past, leaving their cherished homes behind altogether, setting out always for a farther horizon, perhaps never pausing again to remember the worlds that had been left behind.

Now I was planning another trip to Spain, to return to the Archivo and then to make my way north to Asturias on the Cantabrian coast, to the village of Llanes that my mother's ancestors had left for Mexico in the 1590s. Another journey would be necessary to finish this tale, a journey to the lands that were the source of the beliefs my ancestors had brought to Mexico, a journey it turns out, my ancestors from Israel had already made, in reverse, farther back in time.

I had a dream that I was walking with my father, somewhere in the narrow streets of Greenwich Village in a stormy autumn twilight. I was surprised and elated to see him, as he had already been dead nearly ten years, but I tried not to act as if anything was amiss. He had never liked excessive expressions of drama.

He explained to me that he was writing a song, and that he wanted my help with one of the lines. It was a song about my mother, he said, and he was having trouble with a section describing the beauty of her body. He was amused that I was slightly discomfited by the idea of opining on this lyric, but we soon agreed on the simple description *la poesía de tu cuerpo.*

"The poetry of your body," he repeated, beginning to sing it under his breath.

"That works well."

Suddenly, the winds that had already been gusting heavily really kicked up, and I began to notice that my coat was filling up like a sail as I began to hover above the New York sidewalk, able to maintain and slowly even increase my altitude by leaning to one side or the other. I looked over to see if my father had noticed that I was beginning to take flight, but he walked on into the wind, unimpressed, as if he was wondering why it had taken so long for me to shirk the pull of gravity.

XII

Zonas Santas

1. On the pilgrim's path

Any memory can return you to the prospect of a pilgrimage, and every pilgrimage is first and last a journey of stories. No matter where your journey takes you, no matter what sacred story you can recover, there is always an older story, always an older archive, beckoning to you from a still farther home of earlier ancestors. Any family story, followed back generation by generation as centuries pass by, will eventually bring you to the precipice of an unfathomable antiquity. You can be called to account for your ancestors, and also to account for the stories they carried with them from the world before.

Every mile of the pilgrimage leads you in that direction.

On a cool April night, it was nearing ten o'clock in the inky shadows of the great fifteenth-century cathedral of Sevilla, Spain, when the two grand doors of the cathedral creaked open and a large gilded palanquin with a statue of Jesus bearing the cross slowly began to emerge, parting a waiting throng. The figure was dressed in a golden tunic tied with an ivory sash at the waist, the crown of thorns cocked jauntily to one side of his head, and his pained but stoic expression glowed as if lit from within by a small lamp. The litter, decorated in gold and bordered with flickering lanterns, lumbered out, tilting from side to side like a ship going forward as its great weight was supported by an unseen host of straining porters underneath.

The statue was preceded by a solemn procession of clarion trumpeters and attendants, some in robes, others in purple gowns or black formal suits with white gloves, carrying candles or puffing censers through the gathered crowd, into the warren of cobbled Sevillano streets in the first of one of that city's legendary Easter rituals for the year.

The priests wore masks of simple fabric, with crude holes cut out to see through. The masked figures were like humans washed of their historical identities, the pure presence of human energies, stripped of particularity, following the prescribed rituals that imparted to any who witnessed their acts a deeper sense of their own meaning.

Here was the chorus of our ancestors, leading the way to a resurrection.

Christ and his throng of devotees, engulfed in a cloud of burning frankincense, passed through the Plaza Virgen de los Reyes, behind the Archivo de Indias where I had returned for one more visit the day before, and disappeared into the Andaluciano night trailing their fragrant smoke and divine racket, a clamorous waking dream in the middle of my last long journey in search of the ancestors' paths. It had already become a journey in time.

Ten days earlier, I was standing on the rocky northern banks of the Sea of Galilee on a crystalline morning, in the crowded and jumbled basalt ruins of Capernaum, the lakeside village where Jesus is said to have lived for a time with Peter and some of his disciples in the early days of his ministry. Recalling the rural simplicity of that setting, along with other places I had visited in Galilee and other parts of Israel and Palestine where Jesus's story had begun, I wondered how the story of events that transpired in those humble places in distant times could lead to such an elaborate pageant in our time, like so many that had been brought to Mexico in the time of the Conquest.

I've never been much for leisure travel. I have always gone to distant places with a mission, to make a documentary, to find a library, to research a book, to seek answers to questions I might not even be able to enunciate when I set out. But you get out onto the road so that something can be revealed—one of the central tenets of inadvertentism.

This monthlong journey, first to Israel then to Spain, was at least in part a pilgrimage. It was a *peregrinaje* to the origins of family and to the sources of ancestral faith, a way of seeking out the deeper history of my Mexican family's story by following the routes by which geography was marked by belief.

In the prologue to *The Canterbury Tales*, Chaucer speaks of springtime as the season when people long to go on pilgrimages, searching for saints, as he says, "on strange shores . . . in sundry lands." And like travel itself, making pilgrimage seems to be a deeply rooted human impulse. Whether to Jerusalem, Mecca, Varanasi in India, Santiago de Compostela in Spain—or Falfurrias, Texas (home of the shrine of the healer Don Pedrito Jaramillo), we visit sacred places in part to connect with the most profound stories of who we believe we are and who we believe our ancestors might've been.

The act of pilgrimage is meant to uncover new meaning in our lives, appearing out of the unpredictable itinerary of revelation.

I went to Israel with a group of *peregrinos*, or pilgrims, in this case an international circle of theologians, and two archaeologist guides, representing a host of universities in Latin America, the United States, Canada, and central Europe. Conversations on the bus, or late into the evening, might be in English, Spanish, French, or Italian. Several of the theologians were people I had worked with when I was making my documentaries about the liberation theology movement in Latin America.

My longtime friend and mentor Virgilio Elizondo, with whom I've made many other journeys witnessing this movement and carried on a now decades-long conversation about the meanings and ongoing prophetic unfolding of mestizo identities, had organized this trip. Taken together, these concerns make up the still unfolding legacy of Spain's culture in the New World.

Our journey through Israel and Palestine traced the life of Jesus in reverse, beginning in the old walled city of Jerusalem, the scene

of the drama of the crucifixion and resurrection, and then heading
west through the nearby Judean desert past Bethany, the place of
Jesus's baptism by John the Baptist, then to Qumran on the shores
of the Dead Sea, the dwelling place of the community of Essenes
who authored the Dead Sea Scrolls and may have had contact with
both John the Baptist and Jesus.

From there, we headed north through Palestine on the West
Bank highway, past Jericho, through the fertile Jordan River valley, stopping at the village of Bet Alpha, the site of an excavated
first-century synagogue—then continuing on into the verdant hills
and fields of Galilee, and finally stopping at a lodge run by Franciscan nuns on the summit of the Mount of Beatitudes, at the northern tip of the Sea of Galilee. After some days exploring Galilee and
the Golan Heights, we set off to return to Jerusalem, passing by
Nazareth, where Jesus spent his youth, and Mt. Tabor, where Jesus
is said to have transfigured himself before three of his disciples who
observed him speaking to Moses and Elijah.

We arrived back in Jerusalem as a freakish spring snowstorm
was just getting under way. On the map, the entire route spans
barely three-hundred miles—a day trip for a Texan—yet gazing out
the bus window you can feel ages passing by, observing a changing landscape humans have been traversing for countless millennia,
scattered with ruins from prehistoric, Mesopotamian, Egyptian,
Judaic, Roman, Byzantine, and medieval civilizations.

Virgil and I had been imagining and speaking about this trip for
many years, calling it a pilgrimage of theological reflection. Our
destination was to the "beginning of the beginning," meaning Galilee, where the drama of Jesus's life and teachings first took shape.
He reminded the group of a quote from Pope John Paul II in one of
his encyclicals: "Because of the incarnation, every detail of the life
of Jesus is part of the revelation."

The itinerary we followed was meticulously drawn from references
to places in the Gospels, so every spot we visited connected us back
to the paths that Jesus is said to have taken, his trips between Galilee and Jerusalem, and among the many places he traveled to within
greater Galilee, from Nazareth into Tiberias and farther north into

the Golan Heights. Virgil posed the fundamental question: "Why Galilee?" Why of all places, as the story goes, did God choose to take human form in this specific place on the planet? It is a question that echoes in many religious traditions. Why was the Buddha born in India? Why was Moses born in Egypt? Why was Mohammed born in Arabia a descendant of Ishmael, an illegitimate son of Abraham? At root, perhaps these were all family stories. Our evolution has been marked by these indelible incarnations that took place in specific times and geographies and at certain stages of our emergence, yet we give little thought to why it was so, and whether this is a process—divine incarnation—that is ongoing in human history.

In Jesus's time, the remote northern region of Galilee was regarded by the Temple-centered Jewish culture of Jerusalem as of lower caste, tainted by Syrian, Samaritan, Mesopotamian, and other exotic cultural influences. It was a depraved borderland. Why was it believed the God of the Hebrews chose this locale and time in which to incarnate and revise an ages-old covenant with humanity?

What could we discern about ourselves by traveling there today?

As is the custom among proper pilgrims, every morning began with a prayer drawn from the place we were visiting. The first morning we awoke in Galilee, the Beatitudes were read at the top of the hill where Jesus is believed to have first preached those powerful words. One or two of our group would also offer some thoughts for that day. And at the end of our adventures every day, there would be a mass and more reflections: how Jesus was an outsider in the world into which he was born, how he always identified with the poor, the insulted and excluded, and how he often retreated into the solitude of Galilee's idyllic natural setting.

Every day I gazed out on it, the Sea of Galilee loomed with an ever-changing, oracular presence. On a clear day, the water was iridescent as birds danced overhead in the churning gusts, swooping down to the water occasionally to pluck out a fish. On cloudy days with fishermen on the lake, the grey mist they sailed through made the whole scene seem part of a timeless netherworld where spirits walked among us.

Somewhat sheepish among a group that included many ordained,

I went more as a seeker than as a believer, perhaps even indulged as the circle's resident heretic or favorite infidel. Those were more masses than I'd been to in the last twenty years of Sundays put together. Though Catholic, the Lopez and Velas had never been pious. I don't remember Grandmother even having a crucifix, or any statues or images of the various important virgins around her house. Uncles Lico and Lauro might've been members of the Knights of Columbus for business purposes, but they weren't regularly practitioners of matins or evensong. Occasionally my parents took us all to church, and my brothers and I all were altar boys for a brief spell, but I much preferred tormenting priests and nuns in catechism class with denunciations of the belief in original sin or in the church as the only path to heaven.

I knew this belief tradition had been a part of my family's story. The church's story was now deeply interwoven, inseparable even, from the long story of Spain and its creation of the New World in the Hispanic Americas. Mexico was born in a spark of prophetic expectation that the work of the world was nearly done, realizing the Christian scriptures that promised a millennial paradise on earth and an eternity of divine union. All of this took seed in Mexican earth, largely superseding the beliefs of all earlier ancestors.

In the year 1501, imprisoned in Sevilla under suspicion of fraud and mismanagement in the affairs of the Indies, Christopher Columbus spent his brief incarceration assembling his *Book of Prophecies* for the monarchs, a miscellany of scriptural citations drawn from the Old and New Testaments he believed would exonerate him by expounding what he called the "secrets of the world," and irrefutably demonstrating his own role in the fulfillment of the Christian epic, writing, "I have already said that for the voyage to the Indies neither intelligence nor mathematics nor world maps were of any use to me; it was the fulfillment of Isaiah's prophecy."

> This is the beginning of the book or collection of auctoritates, sayings, opinions, and prophecies concerning the need to recover the holy city of Jerusalem, and Mount Zion, and the discovery and con-

version of the islands of the Indies and of all the peoples and nations,
for Ferdinand and Isabella, our Spanish rulers.

Two hundred and forty years after Columbus wrote these words,
the conversion of the Indios infieles of Nuevo Santander by José
Escandón was a furthering of the same project, even though Columbus had written his book in a time when he believed that "only 155
years remain of the 7,000 years in which, according to the authorities cited above, the world must come to an end."

By Escandón's time, Mexico had already lived well beyond the
time of the world's expected end.

In Israel with my fellow travelers, we were journeying to the
scenes of Jesus's storied life from which this whole cosmology was
born, going to the birthplace of this spiritual tradition that would
spread to virtually every precinct of the planet, reaching across
Mexico and creating the world out of which my ancestors sprang.

I was curious about seeking out these wellsprings of the faith
that would later be transmitted to Spain, in legend by Saint James,
and eventually to the New World, inspiring the colonization of the
lands that would become north Mexico, South Texas, and indeed,
San Antonio itself—where my family would be among the many
generations of carriers of the tale that began in Galilee.

When I received the first results of the scans of my paternal genetic
lineage, the accompanying maps of my ancestors' migrations showed
trails leading out of northern Africa, winding and clustering in knots
throughout the Arabian Peninsula, then tracking into Eastern Europe
and along the Mediterranean littoral, and finally into Iberia.

In Israel I was in one homeland, heading for another.

That's where I would pick up their story again, in Sevilla.

2. Pilgrimage to herencia

I arrived bleary-eyed early in the morning at Madrid's Barajas
airport via an overnight flight from Tel Aviv, after the weeklong

sojourn in Jerusalem and Galilee. After a time of close fellowship with the group of theologians, I was now facing nearly a month of solo wandering around España, la madre tierra incognita. Adding to my disorientation, the two a.m. flight from Israel had been delayed nearly two hours when all planes were held while a bird was shooed from inside the cabin of a nearby jetliner that had already been fully boarded. And like every time I visit Spain, I wondered what I was doing there yet again—what might be revealed by another quest in search of my family's forgotten ancestral Spanish past?

Where the trip to Israel and Palestine had been in part a pilgrimage to the origins of Christianity, this journey into Spain was to be a *peregrinaje* to the origins of me—specifically, the origins of my mother's Vela, Lopez, and Guerra families, based on information I'd already found in the Archivo de Indias in Sevilla, with another visit to learn more about the fate of the Escandón expeditions my families had participated in.

After this last spell of time at the Archivo, and a brief stay in Madrid, I planned to travel by train into the north via Bilbao in the Basque country, to Llanes, Asturias, the village on the rocky Atlantic coast my ancestors had left in the 1580s to seek their destiny in Nueva España, which became Mexico, and eventually Texas.

Historical records showed my family first came into the lands of Nuevo Santander in the middle of the seventeenth century. One of my ancestors, Santiago Vela, was a part of Alonso de León's (the elder) first expeditions in the 1660s into las tierras bárbaras, the barbaric lands.

I have made many trips into Mexico and across South Texas in search of family roots. But to really tell a tale of our history, I had to go back to the stirrings of our other origins, in Spain. I had been traveling there for nearly thirty years by then, since that first trip in my university days—when I was mugged on my very first night in Barcelona.

And I'd been back to Spain numerous times since, first to make the documentary about Pedro Arrupe, the Basque-born leader of the Jesuits, and later to the Archivo in Sevilla, seeking out traces of heritage, *herencia*, that still connect my South Texas familia to

Iberia. But I had never journeyed to Asturias. Gradually, though, unexpectedly, Spain had come to feel like a long-lost home.

This remains a quiet cultural curiosity in the Chicano community. Since the early twentieth century, when Mexican philosopher José Vasconcelos first celebrated Mexico's mestizo identity, mixing European and Indian ancestry, and later with the Chicano civil rights movement's embrace of Mexico's indigenous origins, it became unfashionable to explore the European, mainly Spanish, side of Mexico's mestizaje.

Hernán Cortés was the grandfather no proud Chicano wanted to admit to.

Ni la abuela Isabela. Solamete Malintzín, the Indian woman with whom the Conquistador fathered his mestizo children.

Spanish heritage was relegated to the relic shelf of Chicano consciousness, next to the Neanderthal jaws and conquistador helmets. In San Antonio, cultural organizations and genealogical societies such as the Canary Islands Descendants Association and Los Bejareños have remained interested in highlighting the Spanish cultural legacy of the city and the South Texas/north Mexico region. Many have made their own journeys seeking family history in Spain.

Recent years have also seen the publication of important new historical research, much by Latino scholars, about early Tejano society, illuminating the extent to which these lands were imprinted by their first Spanish and mestizo settlers. But Spain is engrossing, no matter where you come from. Today, the postmodern cosmopolitan urbanity of cities like Madrid and Sevilla belies the long history of these places, along with the great antiquity of human presence in the Iberian Peninsula itself. Paleoanthropologists have identified northern Iberia as the scene of many early prehuman and early human communities, with destinations such as the caves of Altamira or the Sima de los Huesos, a sinkhole full of Neanderthal bones in Atapuerca, for the curious heritage tourists interested in our deep species ancestry.

While traveling through Spain, you can see cave paintings by early humans, artifacts of early Celtic settlers, Roman ruins, masterpieces of Gothic and Mosarab architecture, as well as iconoclastic contemporary buildings, walled medieval towns in parched craggy valleys, well-appointed olive groves, and paintings and sculpture by *modern* humans from all of these epochs—the inexhaustible catalogue of human expression assembled over uncounted millennia of migration, invasion, colonization, and ancestry there.

But this last *peregrinaje de herencia*, my pilgrimage of heritage, had a principal subject and a principal destination. Perhaps the idea of another long journey just to visit a library and a remote homeland hardly seems worth considering. Could any more of our South Texas family story really be hidden away in the legendary Archivo de Indias in Sevilla, or in the craggy coastal terrain of Asturias?

I was in search of the story of the last Spanish conquistador of Mexico, the man who inspired my ancestors and the ancestors of many other South Texans to join him in settling the northern, uncivilized "lands of the infidel" in the borderlands of the new Spanish empire.

Sort of an abuelo to all abuelos Norteños, grandfather to the grandfathers of the north: José de Escandón, Conde de Sierra Gorda, Gran Fundador de Nuevo Santander.

3. A return to la vida archiva

When I asked the archivist how to tie the knot binding of the legajo of documents properly, he sighed at the query he must've heard thousands of times, prepared himself with a deep breath, and then swooped both hands over the canvas bale in complex origami swipes, leaving behind a perfect bow. I would never learn it properly.

"Now you must teach me," he said.

The diminutive, white-haired senior librarian at the Archivo looked up with a friendly smile from his desk and sheepishly asked me, "Por favor, Señor, donde era Nuevo Santander?"

Where was Nuevo Santander?

The elder librarian told me his sister had lived in San Antonio for forty years. Recently widowed, she had just returned to Sevilla. The day before, he had seen in the logs that I was researching the

early history of Nuevo Santander, a province of the northern hinterlands of New Spain. He had asked his sister where it had been,
and she had no idea.

So, where was Nuevo Santander?

"Even the Spaniards have forgotten," I thought. No wonder
we've forgotten.

It was three years since my earlier visit to Sevilla, when I had
surveyed the holdings of the Archivo for information relating to
the history of the earliest settlement of the Nuevo Santander and
my families' roles in that enterprise. For the most part, these are
documents and reports sent to the Consejo de las Indias, the royal
council charged with overseeing the affairs of all the viceroyalties
of New Spain.

There are also many documents, maps, and reports directly
relating to the earliest history of San Antonio. But the documents I
had come to see were in the catalogue as *Expediente sobre la Población
y Pacificación de la cosa del Seno Mexicano*, concerning the settlement
of Nuevo Santander, the region ranging north from Monterrey to
present-day Victoria, and from Brownsville west to Laredo. Many
of the older Mexicano families of San Antonio descend from the
families that originally founded these towns.

From eight in the morning to three in the afternoon, over two
weeks, I ploughed through this trove of history, following the story
of Escandón's remarkable campaign to establish a network of new
villages that would extend New Spain's reach to the far north, sup-
press the Indians, and prevent the encroachment of the wily French,
who had been making probes into South Texas. What emerges in
these documents is the tale of Mexico's last conquistador—a Knight
of the Order of Santiago who had outlived the age of the knight and
the conquistador.

Finding notes to myself I had left in these legajos during my last
visit, I traced my way through the Archivo's records of this whole
story, with my ancestors making appearances in some of the earliest
census records from the 1750s of Mier, Camargo, and Revilla, the
first two of which still exist, the last, which became Guerrero, having gone under the waters of the Rio Grande in 1954.

By the end of his career in the late 1760s, after a series of investigations commissioned by the Council of the Indies, Escandón was charged with being overly violent in his suppression of the Indians of the region; using many as slaves; failing to properly attend to their evangelization; neglecting to make mandated land grants to the settlers, my family among them; and improperly aggrandizing his own fortune through fraud and theft from royal coffers. One account reported that Escandón had ordered the beheading of many Indios, displaying their heads in the villages of their alleged crimes. His titles were suspended, his authority revoked during the period of the trial, in a court in Querétaro.

Then I found another scribbled note from myself, *Here begins the major collection of documents relating to the prosecution of José Escandón . . .*

Escandón's own defenses appear deep in the sediment of these records, in the fifth legajo, written in his own hand, answering the host of accusatory reports and dark assessments of the underpinnings of his once celebrated founding of the Villas del Norte. In his letter to the head of the Consejo de las Indias in July of 1769 he sought to recover his offices and denounced his prosecutors, "who seek to darken and destroy the merit of my works and service to the crown, to sacrifice it entirely with no regard for my honor or posterity, substituting authority for reason, affecting matters of great gravity concerning the common interest of the public and the royal service . . . for I received mounting reports of the total ruin of Nuevo Santander with all its Christians, intimidated by the hostilities, theft and killings by the Yndios." His fitful signature follows, as *Joseph* de Escandón, jagged and blotchy, shows his age and the stress of his predicament.

He died only a few months later in 1770 and was only posthumously acquitted of all charges, but the land grants that many families received (and some hold to this day) were made in 1767 as a result of this trial. It is perhaps a great irony that the records of those grants have been one of the most significant ways that Mexican Americans have been able to search out their lineages in Nueva España and Spain.

Still, there's a poignancy about many of our families being a part of this legacy, mostly forgotten, yet all of us still marked by the passing of the era of the Conquest, and the fitful birthing of what would become the modern border between Mexico and Texas. Already two hundred and fifty years years long, the first epic chapter of New Spain was ending, just as the United States was being born.

On the last day of my visit, I was finally ejected from the Archivo with the rest of the readers just past three o'clock in the afternoon, my eyes weary from hours reading classical Spanish calligraphy. I made my way down to the promenade along the grand Rio Guadalquivir and had a plate of al dente fideitos in a garlic basil sauce and pez a la plancha en salsa de nuez at the Bodega Santa Cruz.

Looking out onto the broad river that had carried so many ancestors down to Cadiz, into the Mediterranean, across the Atlantic and to the Mundo Nuevo, I imagined an old map in fading sepia ink that showed a wake stream of abandoned memories, all the ones that couldn't be stored away and catalogued in archives, the smell of ripe oranges in the trees along Sevilla's cobbled streets, a grey African parrot lighting on a windowsill of a mariner's room on the day of his departure for the New World.

I wondered what Uncle Lico would've made of the lineages of our ancestors that had come to light since his death, when so many had doubted there was any story of note to recover. There was no king of Spain as ancestor, but the story he had begun had led to a tale that continued to unfold before me.

In December of 1771, at a memorial mass for the memory of his father in the Iglesia de la Ilustre Congregación in Querétaro, Don Manuel Escandón y Llera offered a tribute and an impassioned defense of his father's career as the colonizer of Nuevo Santander, insisting that his work there had been a part of a divine mission, closing his oration with a citation from the Book of Maccabees:

> . . . be zealous for the law, and give your lives for the covenant of your fathers. Remember the deeds they did in their generations, and great glory and fame shall be yours.

4. Digging Jerusalem

"This is where it all started," our guide said, pointing across the Valley of Hinnom. On a glorious sunlit morning in Bethlehem, we were on a hill looking across the long, deep valley at the great walled city of stone-colored Jerusalem, nestled in the heart of a bustling, populous modern metropolis.

The remaining tower of King David's palace was visible, as well as the shining golden dome of the Al-Aqsa mosque, allegedly built on the site of the great temple of Solomon, perhaps the most contested piece of earth on the planet, especially as concerns the completion of the prophecies of numerous religious traditions.

By the time Jesus of Nazareth was born, the spiritual tradition of his ancestors was already thousands of years old, but the events of his life would mark a new beginning in a slowly unfolding tale about covenants between God and humans. Making a pilgrimage to Jerusalem is an elective part of Christian and Jewish faith. The earliest known Christian pilgrim was a fourth-century French nun. While pilgrimage to Mecca for a Muslim is a pillar of the faith with set destinations and rituals, Christians and Jews undertake a journey to Jerusalem for personal reasons, and itineraries can be planned according to the varying affinities and emphases of a pilgrim's faith.

Our journey was focused on the life of Jesus, so we enlisted the aid of Shimon Gibson, one of the most accomplished, and youngest, archaeologists of ancient Jerusalem. A British-born Israeli who has the aura of a hip Indiana Jones, Shimon had recently been in the news as the discoverer of the controversial Jesus ossuary, a stone burial box bearing an inscription said to refer to James, the brother of Jesus. But Shimon doubts it has anything to do with the storied Jesus of Nazareth.

Standing in the shadow of the medieval stone citadel at Jaffa Gate, Shimon explained how the Old City of today is a palimpsest of history, layer upon layer of epochs and eras, from the origins of the

settlement to the times of David and Jesus, to the Byzantine, medieval, and Ottoman periods of Jerusalem's past. All of them have left
their mark, but you have to go digging for them, or at least look
closely to discern them. Very little of what is visible today is as it was
in Jesus's time. We visited the ruins of the Bethesda pools where
Jesus is said in the Gospels to have performed healings among visitors to Jerusalem who were ritually purifying themselves in the deep,
spring-fed mikvahs. Shimon believes he has established the place
where Jesus was tried, a broad marble plaza that still contains the
paving stones he is convinced are the same ones Jesus would've trod
on. From there, we walked the legendary Via Dolorosa, unlikely to
be the true path Jesus followed on his walk to Golgotha, but still
possessing the power to transport many pilgrims in sad wonder
as they walk along the narrow streets, touching the stone walls as
they go.

For Jews, the sacred center of the Old City is at the Wailing Wall,
the last remnants of the Great Temple of Solomon. For Muslims, it
is the Haram Al-Sharif, the site of the Dome of the Rock, sacred to
Muslims as the place from which Mohammed began his storied visit
to heaven. For Christians, the center is undoubtedly the Church of the
Holy Sepulcher, which houses both the tomb in which Jesus's body
was allegedly laid and Golgotha itself, the purported scene of the crucifixion, thronged today by spellbound pilgrims gazing at a rock said
to be cracked from the earthquake that erupted at the moment of
Jesus's death. Between these two there is a rose-colored marble slab,
venerated by believers as the place where Jesus's body was prepared
for burial. As at so many places in Jerusalem, pilgrims bustle over one
another to reach and touch the stone, or to place rosaries or other sou-
venirs against it that they will carry home to friends and family.

Shimon explained that this church, in which a host of various Catholic and Orthodox sects offer masses throughout the day,
evolved over many hundreds of years, but he wanted to take us to the
oldest remaining part of the sanctuary. To get there, we had to exit
the church, winding our way through the streets until we came to
a small Arabic bakery, deep within the Old City. After offering the

baker a few shekels, we were led into a storage room behind a door in the room where locals were enjoying small plates of sweets.

There, amid bags of flour and a jumble of stones, was an enormous stone arch, keeping its silent witness of the centuries, thought by Shimon to be the original entrance to the Church of the Holy Sepulcher that welcomed the first Christian pilgrims to Jerusalem sometime in the fourth century.

Despite these secret exalted spaces you might find in Jerusalem, it's hard not to be deeply affected by the tragic nature of the place, how even though humans have crossed paths and gathered in the city for so long, and treasured its many legacies, it is today the seat of some of the most tireless discord that humanity harbors.

Every stone is counted. Every discovered tomb brings a new controversy. Everything is contested. How will the strife among us be retired forever? What will we have to become to let that be so?

Current political circumstances make that hard to imagine, especially when considering the difficult question of the nature of returning to places of ancestral origins, all the fervent yearnings that are felt by people in every part of the world for some dispossessed homeland.

How does anyone ever harbor a hope for truly returning?

As I entered the Old City through the Jaffa Gate, an uncanny lyric came up on my iPod Shuffle, from the opening of a moody demo version of the Beatles' "I Am the Walrus":

"I am he as you are he as you are me and we are all together . . ."

But walking to and from Bethlehem in the West Bank, near where I was staying, through the labyrinthine security cordons and video surveillance system of the recently constructed wall, gives an outsider a taste of the dunning everyday experience of Palestinians who commute to work in Israel. Can this be what may yet emerge from the wall that is under construction on the U.S. border with Mexico?

Often, without warning, the checkpoint can be closed and the workers have to seek another entry from distant Ramallah, or simply lose a day's work.

One young female Israeli soldier with an American accent expressed frustration at the spiraling violence and paranoia that has ensued over the last several years, leading to the Israeli decision to build the barrier.

"Maybe this wall will come down someday," she said, though she didn't seem very hopeful.

Beyond Jerusalem, the seat of early Judaism's temple-centered culture, you begin to see more of the various ancient traditions that helped shape the beliefs of the world in which Jesus was born. This long-traveled land is under contention in every direction, Israeli flags flying even over villages in the Palestinian lands, and history and archaeology are often employed to claim primacy over territories.

These were the lands through which all ancestors passed in their journey out of Africa. Peoples met peoples, and soon their gods were appearing in many forms, directing the destinies of their nations. It's no wonder no other spot on earth is so disputed.

On the road to Galilee through the West Bank, in the village of Bet Alfa, there are ruins of a sixth-century synagogue that have been excavated and restored, including an extraordinary mosaic that covers the floor of the sanctuary. There, you find images of a menorah and of the Ark of the Covenant, as well as a tableau of the Abraham and Isaac story, illustrating the deep, archetypal power of the story of a father's sacrifice of his son that profoundly inspires both Jewish and Christian faithful. How long have we been imagining these scenarios of sacrifices, of expiation, redemptions, and resurrections?

But reflecting the multiplicity of antecedent beliefs that shaped ancient Judaism, the central image of the large mosaic, taking up most of the floor, is an elaborate zodiac disc, common in early synagogues, testifying to another of the sources of early Jewish belief in Babylonian culture and civilization.

5. A new world pilgrim in the museos de Madrid

I had only a few days in Madrid, in between my journeys to Sevilla in the south and Bilbao and Asturias in the north. The museums there run the gamut from the cutting-edge contemporary Centro de Arte Reina Sofía, which was exhibiting a survey of early video art and a Chuck Close retrospective, to the museum at the Convento de la Encarnación, which features a vast *reliquaria* that includes skulls and bones of saints, splinters of the True Cross, and a vial of the beatific dried blood of St. Pantaleón that mysteriously liquefies every year on the saint's feast day.

I was still thinking of the Archivo librarian's question: *Donde era Nuevo Santander?*

Where was Nuevo Santander?

If it still seemed imponderable that our families could forget their roles in the Spanish epic story in Mexico, it seemed equally strange that Spain's own memory of its onetime prophetic enterprise in the New World would be forgotten. In the short time that I had, I wanted to visit museums that could show me two things: how Spaniards saw themselves, and how Spaniards saw the New World. How much of the heritage story that I was searching for in Sevilla and Asturias remains alive in the Spanish conscience?

If we have forgotten Spain, how much of us is remembered in Spain?

The answer is complicated, but essentially—not much.

The Museo Arqueológico Nacional, founded in 1867, tells a panoramic story of the emergence of Spanish culture and society, beginning with an account of prehistoric origins in Neanderthal and early human communities nearly eight hundred thousand years ago. Exhibits then chronologically trace the gathering chronicle of deep Spanish identity, detailing the many pre-Christian peoples from north, south, and east who colonized the Iberian Peninsula in antiquity, making ancient mestizos of the Spanish long before they arrived in the New World.

The most celebrated of these ancient objects there is La Dama de Elche from the fourth century BC, reputedly a funerary bust of a woman wearing an elaborate headdress with two mysterious discs on either side of her head and a series of thick necklaces with hanging shells; she reminded me of the images and effigies of the goddess Diana from Ephesus in Turkey. Throughout the long history of Iberians and the culture they brought to the Americas, these images of female demigods, from the Dama to the Virgen de Guadalupe, have remained a powerful abiding presence.

While later exhibits show some of the influence of the long period of Moorish rule in the peninsula's history, the unabashed splendor of Christianity's triumph after the Reconquista is on full display in the later halls. With these dazzling artifacts—golden chalices, jewel-encrusted altars, even gilded confessionals—the museum embodies the sense of victory and exalted destiny familiar from some of Spain's representatives in the early history of the New World. But you'd never know that Indios in Peru or Mexico dug up much of the gold and silver adorning the crosses and other church ornaments on display. That is never mentioned.

The trove of greatest import for any New World *peregrino* is the Museo de America, tucked away in the University City in the Arguelles barrio of Madrid. Established in the 1750s as the Real Gabinete de Historia Natural, the museum gradually evolved to become the principal showcase for objects, codices, and artifacts gathered from across the empires of New Spain.

Again here, the Conquest goes virtually unmentioned, perceptible only as a shadow cast over the inventory of objects housed in the museum. It is the unspoken preamble augured in a litany of "Primeras Noticias," listing the names of the first rapporteurs of the unimagined world: Colón, Vespucio, Martír, among the earliest. One display includes the makeshift pens made of reeds along with the stiff papers that constituted the writing kits of these explorers.

And when the Conquest is pictured in one room, it is a glorious epic figured in an exquisite mother-of-pearl mosaic across a series of screens representing Cortés's entry into Tenochtitlán. In another series of romantic lithographs harkening to a Mexican version of Orientalism, Cortés's storied career is pictured—the rebellion of his men in the Yucatán, the presentation to him by the cacique Zingari of Malintzín, his Indian consort and translator, and another scene of him reclining in a tent as she serenades him with a harp.

There are golden Moche figurines and elaborate geometric weavings from ancient Peru; a stele from Palenque, Mexico; a sculpture of Xipe Totec, the Aztec god who wears a suit of flayed human skin; and a full copy of the brilliant polychromatic pre-Conquest Mayan Códice Tro-Cortesiano.

One room contains a miscellany of the hombres monstruosos of the New World, a headless man with his face in his chest, bird men, a horse with a human face, a dog man, giant Patagonas, a many-headed beast bearing a trident, and other hybrid human-animals such as a wolverine with a man's face and a hairy woman with monkey feet.

If everything is combinable, then eventually everything will be combined.

The Museo de América could just as easily be called the Museo del Mestizaje, as the museum's collection indirectly chronicles the mixing of races and cultures that took place across Spanish America. Some nations were vanquished, as other nations were overtaken by the rising tide of mestizaje, mixing generation to generation until earliest origins became cloaked in mystery.

Along with some superb examples of the Mexican "castas" paintings which sought to classify the taxonomy of racial combinations, the Museo owns perhaps the paradigmatic work of mestizo art from New Spain, the portrait known as *Mulatos de Esmeraldas*, showing an island king and his two sons, the descendants of shipwrecked slaves who had mixed with indigenous ancestors and come to rule among the Esmeraldeño Indians of northern Ecuador. This group portrait from 1599, the oldest known in the Americas, and painted by an Indio artist, Adrián Sánchez Galque, shows the three black-skinned Afro-Indian figures, Don Francisco de Arobe, and his sons, Domingo and Don Francisco, with their faces ornately pierced in indigenous fashion, but dressed in *gorgueras y puñetas*, ruffed Spanish collars and sleeves under bright Chinese silk robes, each one bearing a spear of noble authority, proudly gazing forward into posterity. Commissioned for the occasion of celebrations observing the coronation of Felipe III, the painting still electrifies, a prophecy of America's mestizo destiny.

Finally, I spent a long afternoon at the Prado, combing the permanent collection in search of any painting that might contain a reference to the New World, without success. There are stunning works by Velazquez, of course, and El Greco, and the dumbfounding prescience of Goya's vision in his haunted series of images on war—but no images alluding to the Conquest, no scenes from the Americas, or the experience of Spaniards across the Atlantic Ocean.

Except one.

It was in a semi-lit hallway to the men's room on the third floor.

There, I found an exquisitely carved marble bàs-relief from the eighteenth century, entitled *El Consejo de las Indias*, by the sculptor Juan Antonio de Padua, a lintelpiece that once adorned a doorway in the royal Spanish palace in Madrid.

In this ornately carved piece, the Royal Council of the Indies that figured so prominently in José Escandón's story is shown as a host of august caballeros convened around a horseshoe-shaped table. A Herculean figure in a loincloth is dragging an Indian in before them, his fist clutching a large bundle of the man's hair, arms flailing, his face racked with an expression of abject fear.

The assembled throng of Spanish nobles looks on, pulling back from their council table aghast, spellbound, and slightly terrified themselves.

6. The spell in Galilee

A drive up the Jericho highway through the Jordan Valley where the Jordan River runs in the distance took us past the ruins of the ancient Roman city of Scythopolis, an important town of the Decapolis, the influential league of ten cities of the region during Jesus's times. It's an area that has been settled since the fifth millennium BC, where you can see the remnants of an imperial Roman metropolis including a grand columned avenue, amphitheater, and expansive bathhouse complex. An earthquake in 749 CE destroyed the city.

Although it is not referred to in the Gospels as a place that Jesus visited, some New Testament scholars believe he must have visited the important cities of the Decapolis. They suggest that the prominence of the cult of Bacchus, god of wine and revelry, in places like Scythopolis and Tiberias, a Roman town on the Sea of Galilee, led to the early association of Jesus's movement with the profligate wine-worshippers of these northern cities of Galilean Samaria.

Galilee remains gloriously rural, and arriving in early spring, it was in full bloom, with large fields of goldenrod and stands of pink bougainvillea alongside the roads. Lodging at an inn on the northern edge of the Sea of Galilee, I walked through a dense copse past a family of staring marmots to the stony shore one early foggy morning and watched fishermen in a small boat first casting out their nets, then circling back while beating a low bass drum slowly to herd their day's catch into those nets.

This is the epicenter of the geography of the Gospels: the Mount of the Beatitudes; alongside is Capernaum, the village where Jesus lived with Peter and his family; Tabgha, where the miracle of the loaves and fishes is said to have taken place; and another site on the banks of the Sea of Galilee known as Peter's Primacy, where the Gospel of John says the resurrected Jesus charged Peter with the leadership of the new church.

Strangely, when the disciples and some of Jesus's friends first saw him on the shore, they did not recognize him: "But when the morning was now come, Jesus stood on the shore: but the disciples knew not that it was Jesus."

Jesus was naked in his resurrected body, shouting to them in their boat where to cast their nets to catch fish, and only Peter is said to have recognized him, coming ashore to wrap him in his coat.

But still none of the others dared to ask, "Who are you?"

Running through the accounts of Jesus's appearances after his resurrection, there is this strange motif of something unworldly but unexplained about his pale new body, cautioning his mother not to touch him, allowing others to feel his wounds, going unrecognized by others, as if in this metamorphosis his body was shedding its human biology, becoming as rare and forbidding as uranium.

Wandering this countryside, you quickly get a sense of how peripatetic Jesus's teaching ministry was, perhaps auguring all those evangelist travelers to come, all the walking about, always on the road between many locations in Galilee and farther north, and then the fateful journeys to the seat of empire in the south where he encountered Roman authority and the priestly Temple elite in Jerusalem.

The final stop on the journey was Mt. Tabor, believed by many to be the place of the Transfiguration of Jesus, when during the climb of the hill he reluctantly revealed himself as the Messiah to two of his disciples, and they later observed him transformed into a radiant light body, in conversation with Moses and Elijah. Mt. Tabor dramatically rises up eighteen hundred feet from the flat plain of the Jezreel Valley. The Church of the Transfiguration is on the top of the mountain, reachable only by minibus shuttles helmed by bold Arab drivers who carom up the narrow road barely negotiating hairpin curves, which can leave a visitor preparing for his own transition between worlds.

As we arrived at the church on a bright early afternoon, thunderclouds were gathering, and a wintry storm was beginning to churn great curtains of dust through the swaying olive trees. Within an hour, the skies had darkened and an icy rain began to fall, and for a long spell everyone wandered off into corners of the dark basilica with their own thoughts. Later, we assembled in a small stone chapel, and an Italian priest among us offered a quiet mass with the storm gusting and thundering outside, after which each member of our group of pilgrims reflected on their impressions of the entire journey we had made.

There was talk of Jesus as a border-dweller, an illegitimate child of unknown ancestry, a child of the poor who became a country prophet seeking justice from a crossroads of cultures and civilizations of great antiquity—a place from which it was believed nothing good could ever come. This was the landscape of events that would echo out across the world and through time, the story told over and over, pictured in countless paintings and sculptures, numberless retablos hung on Mexican chapel walls.

The journey brought unexpected revelations, leaving more questions at its end than I began with, as befits a proper pilgrimage. I went looking for the source of the beliefs, the faith, the prophetic anticipations that some of my ancestors brought to the New World and planted in the lands that were to become north Mexico and South Texas. And this was its second transplantation. It was a belief tradition already once transplanted to the land of Iberia from its birthplace in that land known in ancient times as Syria. By legend, it was one of Christ's disciples, Saint James himself, who brought the story of Jesus to the peninsula, itself already a longtime crossroads of cultures and civilizations.

Catechism and conventional theology classes had taught me the Christ story as something that was lived and revealed by Jesus, complete, preeminent, and conclusive, a final triumphant and inviolable revelation. My journey complicated that story for me, illuminating a Jesus who was born into and nurtured by a radically heterogeneous cultural world and a numinous natural setting. On the final leg of the trip back to Jerusalem, we passed the field of Megiddo, the prophesied scene of the battle of Armageddon. A small lumbering tank, clanking on its treads, passed us heading north toward the Golan Heights. With all of the strife that continues to haunt the Holy Land, it can seem we are accelerating down the path to that prophetic appointment.

But passing by Megiddo today, it is all birdsong and blooming flowers.

It would be a shame to blight such natural beauty with another war just to have a go at bringing on the end of the world.

7. Uncovering Indiano roots

The night train to Bilbao was a slow moonlit crawl north into the jagged mountains of the Basque country. Trains from Madrid to Sevilla are high-speed junkets, traversing virtually the same distance in two and a half hours. By contrast, the train from Madrid to Bilbao, on narrow-gauge rails winding up into the mountains, takes all night, leaving Madrid at ten-thirty and arriving in the Basque capital at seven in the morning. It's no wonder a gulf remains between the people of northern Spain and the rest of the country.

I was finally on my way to my last destination on this journey—Llanes, Asturias, the village my mother's Vela-Guerra ancestors left sometime in the 1580s. I had been through the Basque country and into Asturias one time before, making the documentary in the late 1980s about Father Pedro Arrupe, leader of the Jesuits.

I hadn't known then how close I was to one of the scenes of my family's distant origins in Iberia. We had even passed through Llanes on the way to an interview in a nearby coastal village with an aged surviving friend of Padre Arrupe named Señor Afanes. I felt an inexplicable sense of recognition as we talked near the lapping docks of the little fishing village, the jagged peaks of the Cantabrian mountains in the distance on one side, the shimmering waters of the Atlantic on the other.

Señor Afanes, a distinguished, long-retired doctor who had attended medical school with Arrupe, joked with me that I looked like a typical Asturiano, asking if there were any crazy fishermen among my ancestors. But he grew serious later, and said to me, "You will return here someday, *vas a ver*, you will see." The Asturianos are still proud of their history fighting off the Moors in the eighth century, led by their king Pelayo, and they will remind you that Castellano Spanish began in their region, gradually finding its way south into central Iberia. I hadn't thought of Señor Afanes since, but after many years and much research, I was indeed returning, now knowing that those lands had always secretly held a part of the story of my ancestral roots.

After arriving just past dawn, it would be just a short transit through a rainy Bilbao, scheduled to catch another train out to Asturias early in the afternoon. I recalled walking the streets of the historic Casco Viejo section of the city on my earlier visit, finding the quaint, flowerbox-decked building where Arrupe had been born, and Bilbao still had an almost medieval feeling. My layover on this trip was long enough to pass the morning at the Bilbao Guggenheim, the inspired monumental vortex of glistening titanium waveforms on the Rió Nervión that has helped to remap the once sleepy and reclusive city into the twenty-first century.

The mist-shrouded trip to Llanes via Santander, the birthplace of José Escandón, was another six-hour excursion, the slow little rural commuter train stopping at every village and town along the way: *Cicero. Orejo. Heras. Astillero. Valle Real. Valdesilla.*

As each village's railway signpost passed by, I wondered if my ancestors might have traveled through these places in their every-day lives or on their path to the Mundo Nuevo.

Looking out the windows of the train, wide-mouthed caves pock-marked the looming steep mountainsides, sturdy workhorses stood motionless in the soggy valley fields. It was such caves that sheltered the Neanderthals and first modern humans in those lands, begin-ning the long story of Asturias. In the caves of Altamira, farther west, they painted scenes from their lives, showing woolly mam-moths and reindeer that wandered the region when the ice shelf reached well into central Europa.

For part of the last stretch of the route, the train ran along the rugged verdant coast, with endless craggy, rocky cliffs ripping the waves of the Cantabrian Sea.

Llanes is an old fishing village that, as it turns out, has long been a place from which people have set out for the New World, from the sixteenth century to the present day. So much so, they came to be known as "Indianos," the émigrés who set out for las Indias, creat-ing a subculture among the many families whose ancestors jour-neyed to the Mundo Nuevo. Many made their fortunes there and returned to build elaborate, colorful houses that dot the Asturiano village landscape and are widely referred to as *los palacios Indianos*. The town, which is a popular beach resort haunt during the sum-mer season, is sleepy in early spring, all winding cobblestone streets bisected by a canal that fills up at high tide when the fishermen come in with their catch. The people there see themselves as Astu-rianos first, Spanish second, but above all—Celtic.

Celts are known to have colonized the western and northern regions of Spain in 700 BC, only giving way to Mediterranean cul-ture with the Roman conquest of Iberia in 19 BC. The deeply rooted Celtic identity never died. Rather than wine or frosty draft beer "cañas," fermented apple cider remains the Asturiano libation of choice. And I heard the traditional song style of the region, known as *la gaita*, riotously performed one night in a community center in Llanes: sounds of Flamenco shout-singing, accompanied by bag-pipes, as if you were hearing the fervent plaints of Spanish gypsies lost in the Scottish highlands.

As the roughneck singer in a threadbare suit boomed and trilled his sad story of betrayed love to a droning bagpipe accompaniment, the audience of Llanes denizens whooped and shouted him on, reminding me of a late-night tumult at Saluté bar in San Antonio, with Esteban Jordan riffing psychedelic variations on Tex-Mex standards with his accordion.

Later that evening, in numerous taberna conversations, bar denizens told me that my ancestral family, the Guerra Cañamars, who married in Nuevo Santander with the Velas of my mother's lineage, still abounded in the region. Earlier researchers such as fellow San Antonian Raul J. Guerra Jr. had already journeyed to Llanes, uncovering much of their history. But several folks urged me to visit the Archivo de Indianos, an archive of the history and artifacts of Indiano émigrés that was housed in a storied *palacio Indiano* in the nearby hamlet of Colombres. One especially informed barkeep who knew Colombres told me the palacio had been built by a certain Señor Noriega, a late-nineteenth-century Indiano who had made a fortune as a farmer and rancher in Puebla, Mexico, and that he had built this extravagant house in his tiny Asturiano home village expressly as a refuge in exile for his close friend Porfirio Díaz, Mexico's turn-of-the-century dictator, deposed in the Mexican Revolution.

The next morning, when I took the only train of the day that went to Colombres, I arrived to discover the town was two kilometers away from the station, atop a formidable hill. Just then, another wintry storm was commencing, and there was no taxi stand, only cattle farms in every direction. Knowing it would be my only chance to see the Archivo, I zipped up my raincoat and pulled its rain hood over my head to begin the steep uphill trudge.

But as I was rounding the first bend in my soaking climb, a small, beat-up car passed and stopped just ahead of me, and the passenger door flew open. Through the sheets of rain, I could see the driver, an old man, gesturing for me to get in.

"What the hell are you doing walking in the rain?" he asked, laughing, as we started up the road. The lanky old man had a long, unshaven, and haggard face, but his white shirt was freshly pressed under his canvas jacket, and when he smiled endearingly, several teeth were missing.

I told him I was going to Colombres to visit the Archivo de Indianos, and that I was working on a book about my family's Spanish family roots. He said he'd still be at his farm but for the fact that his burro had kicked him in the hand that morning and he was just coming back from the doctor with a thickly bandaged left hand.

"Well, I have papers from my family that go back to the twelfth century!" he shouted, laughing. "I keep them between the seed bags so that the rats won't eat them!" He guffawed as he clutched the steering wheel with his good hand.

It would be too uncanny if he were related to me, I thought.

But the truth was even wilder when I asked him his name.

"My name is Francisco Escandón," he replied. "I have a little farm here, beyond Colombres, en Santilla del Mar."

I asked him if he knew of or was related to the Mexican conquistador, whose career and fate I had just been studying in Sevilla at the Archivo General de Indias. I told him my ancestors had been a part of José Escandón's expeditions to settle northern New Spain in the eighteenth century.

"Claro que sí! He was a great-great-great-great tío or something," he answered, and proceeded to tell me how some of the Indianos Escandones had gone to Mexico, others to Colombia, and his line just stayed there in Asturias because they were the lazy and poor ones.

He told me his ancestors had originally come from Scandinavia in the twelfth century, "en un barco de trigo," a wheat boat, and they had fallen in love with Asturiana women, and remained behind when the boats returned home.

It had never occurred to me before, Escandón from Scandinavia.

I asked if he knew where the palace was that José de Escandón was reported to have built near Santander, allegedly with royal funds, one of the charges that had been leveled against him during his trial in Querétaro in the late 1760s.

"Mira hijo," he said, "todos tuvimos palacios, solo que ya nos olvidó donde fueron."

We all had palaces, we just forgot where they were.

Winding to the top of the road, we entered and rounded the small village square in Colombres and Señor Escandón pointed to a bright turquoise building sitting on top of a little hillock and announced that it was the Archivo de Indianos.

It had a touch of the churrigueresque about it—cerulean blue with elaborate yellow curlicue ornamentation around the windows and eves, a massive four-story wedding cake of a building that appeared to have dropped out of the sky into the Asturiano landscape, while the rest of Colombres's buildings were made of grey stone and mortar. And above the entrance flew a Mexican flag, and another banner with an image of the Virgen de Guadalupe, befitting this *palacio Indiano* that had been dubbed la Quinta Guadalupe by its creator, Colombres's proudest son, Iñigo Noriega Laso.

Señor Escandón dropped me off at the Archivo and I spent the day wandering the exhibits there, documenting the long-intertwining destinies of Asturias and the New World.

Inside, the palacio was even more phantasmagorical, each level built around a vast indoor atrium reaching up to the ceiling. There was a floor devoted to Indianos who had gone to Cuba, one for those who had gone to Colombia, another for those who had journeyed to Mexico; cabinets with keepsakes of their journeys, suitcases and journals, letters home to their loved ones, New World personal effects like armadillo-shell musical instruments, and a re-created dining room from Noriega's Puebla home, complete with bas-relief decorative sculptures of Mexican Indians decking the walls.

A plaque devoted to Noriega described him as "conquistador mas que Indiano," and chronicled how virtually his entire fortune and vast landholdings in Puebla and Morelos had been lost in the Revolution.

In the library, the book collection ranged across the span of the Spanish empire in the New World, including tomes on Inca art and the architecture of Cuzco, Colombian history, and a book that lay open inside a cabinet—*San Antonio, Tejas en la Epoca Colonial*.

When I left the Archivo, the day had became sunny and beautiful, and I wandered the narrow cobblestone streets of the village, eventually finding an inn where I ate a traditional fabada asturiana, a white bean pork stew, while some of the locals were smoking and sharing ample ciders and watching a noisy DVD of Antonio Banderas in *Zorro*, swashbuckling his way through old Spanish California.

But as I was preparing to return to the train station down the hill for the only train to take me back to Llanes, it began to rain heavily again. Hoping the rain might subside, I stopped in at a little church near the town square where a crowded village funeral was under way, as I'm always curious about the way people bury their dead.

The pastor was delivering a moving sermon about the meaning of friendship when I decided I had to set out if I wasn't going to miss the train.

On the front steps of the church, an old man's voice called out to me, "Listen there, caballero, aren't you even going to say hello? Don't you remember me from this morning?"

It was Señor Escandón, and he insisted on taking me back to the train station. We laughed all the way down the hill about the way families can run into one another over centuries, and we wondered if we might meet again.

Earlier in the morning, he had admired my burgundy Tony Lama half boots with zippers on the sides.

"Bien finos y elegantes," he had described them.

"Del estilo cowboy," I'd answered him.

When it turned out we wore the same size shoe, I told him he must have them.

After some convincing, I put on his muddy lace-ups that were mostly falling apart from their soles, and as the train came into the station he waved goodbye, standing next to his car in the light rain, in his pointy Tony Lama boots.

An old Escandón was finally going to walk in the boots of a child of the New World, while a latter-day Tejano was wandering farther into the madre tierra in the shoes of ancestors.

Epilogue

Imperio de Fuego

A testament of Lucas Guerra, scribe of Revilla Nueva: Regarding the matter of the fate of the man who called himself Cenote Siete, having dwelt here for a period of nearly four years, two witnesses of unimpeachable integrity have submitted the following account, observed from a riverside hill where they were seated a fortnight ago in the early evening hours: Guided by a swarm of bees, following his pair of chihuahuas, Cenote Siete was dressed in his robe of mirrors as he walked toward the riverbank and stepped into a nebula of teeming fireflies that glowed brilliantly around him for some time and then faded completely into darkness. The witnesses attest how thereupon he had entirely disappeared with only the sounds of night birds and the river currents remaining, and he has henceforth been lost to our company, leaving behind no notice or *despedida*, only his papers and the few effects in his dwelling, and it was as if he had never been with us at all. His companion Caracól has also vanished without a trace. Their possessions have been gathered for safekeeping in the event that either should return to our settlement in the near or distant future . . . L.G.

That was the last dispatch in the trove of C7 materials, appearing long after I'd last received any direct missives from Cenote Siete, the last of which read simply:

Every writer has at least two books in them—the book they write and the book that is impossible to write. In the end, it is only the impossible book that is worth writing, the one that is always out of reach for the writer. That is the book we await.

That impossible book, the book titled *Immaterial Empires*, remained unwritten. The signs had been everywhere for some time, but there was always the sense of waiting for some further signal, some affirmation that the time to proceed had arrived. So much for inadvertentism. What would it take to signify true permission to tell the story?

Was it not enough to learn of the family's descent through history, going back almost five hundred years? Wasn't that the original curiosity?

Was it not always evident that it was the women in my family who kept alive, if ever so faintly, our troth to distant ancestral origins?

Was it not enough to be led to the story of José de Escandón and his exploits?

What of the discoveries and wonders? Did they not require investigations as to how some stories were manifesting themselves in the world that had previously only been secret ruminations in the hold of my heart?

An Olmec head was discovered in Brooklyn.

Evidence unearthed of a Neanderthal-human mestizo in Portugal.

How was it that the light permanently changed from iridescent silver to dusky amber in the skies over New York City in the time after the attacks of September 2001? Then later, a blood-red eclipse moon hung over the city like a gory shield, followed by an aurora borealis that appeared as a shimmering vortex pulling streams of pearly light into the black night sky.

Sometimes the storytelling is postponed so that you may put off the end of the tale. But the impulse to write this impossible book had run long in the family. My distant elder primo, Antonio Maria Guerra, undertook his history of Mier on the occasion of the town's celebration of its two hundred and fiftieth birthday in 1953. He introduced his book with a citation from another work on the history of Nuevo León by Davíd Aloberto Cossia: "If history is a true narration of the happenings that are worthy of remembering, it is unquestionable that the historical truth would be the highest virtue to which a historian can aspire." Antonio Maria said he was writing Mier's history to tell the story of deeds "probably unknown to our children."

"In this compilation I shall consign only that data which I have found to be perfectly authenticated, or consigned by authors of known veracity, without giving credit to fables or legends, which only lead to confusion, altering the truth."

In his dedication he wrote, "To thee comes my one and only child, pure and bare, without proper and showy raiments that would make her attractive: she does not even wear the paints that would cover her defects; I have not sought an expert human hand that would model her body and align it, so that she may come to you polished and presentable. The act of being born with her face to the sky, her hair to the sincere wind of the province, with her feet rooted in a land of fire that burns her soles, makes her arrogant and proud . . . she has the virtue of truth."

But who knows where we began? In truth, the story is only unfolding now, and no one knows where it will end. Was it not long ago already time to return to the task of completing the impossible book, the illimitable chronicle of our heritage in the immaterial empires of las Américas?

Then, after a long spell without mortality among us, the Lopez of my generation began dying. First it was querido primo Bob, who I was able to visit in his home in Baltimore the week before he died.

After more than twenty years pursuing this untold family story from New York City, I returned to San Antonio in 2005 to be closer to my family, to be with the poet who has become my wife, and to spend more time with Mother, who was entering her eighties as a widow living alone in our old family home, struggling every day with diabetes, Parkinson's disease, and chronic back pain.

She still keeps an active schedule of outings, meetings, organizing, and politicking, but she feels the weight and limits of her Lopez-Vela body as never before. Sitting in a chair in her dimly lit bedroom on an evening after my return when a plunging blood sugar count had given her fierce chills and shivers, she wearily looked up at me and said:

"I just could never imagine that my body would ever do this to me."

Weeks before, as I was packing my apartment to leave New York City, I received news that Bob's cancer had arrived at its final stage and that he had returned home from the hospital to await the end. Almost a year had passed since he had gone public with his fateful diagnosis, bringing an outpouring of sympathy, well-wishes, and prayers from his radio listeners in Baltimore. When his condition increasingly kept him from making it into the studio, he would broadcast from home, after the station set up a studio for him there in his study.

After learning that caring listeners had formed prayer circles to beseech the Almighty on his behalf, he unleashed vituperations. As a long and famously self-confessed ardent atheist, he warned them that if they did not immediately desist from delusional intercessions with divinity petitioning for his health, he would find the most effective Vodoun priest in Baltimore and have them all irrevocably cursed.

By the time I was able to make the trip to Baltimore, he was unable to get out of bed but he had a glow and tranquility about him, every now and then punctured by his irrepressible ironic spirit. As his wife, Jean, took me into the bedroom and left me with him, he was sleeping. I watched him for some time, taking fitful breaths, his face fixed in an expression of bemused contemplation.

When he opened his eyes and saw me, he immediately put on his most mischievous grin, mustering a faint, "Hey, cuz."

And then after a pause, staring at me at his bedside, he grumbled, "Come on now, John Phillip, come on, just come clean and confess it."

"Confess what?"

"Yeah, right. Act all innocent, like I didn't see you."

"You saw me? I just got here."

"Two nights ago? Right there where you are now? A full 3-D number, all shimmery like an Obi-Wan Kenobi hologram. And you told me everything's gonna be alright. Come on! I saw you. Hmmph. You're the mystic one, cuz, and now you're denying it?"

Jean brought in some water for him and he called out to her, "Hey, Trixie, JP's denying he was here the other night in his space-suit, can you believe that?"

I wondered whether Cenote Siete might be widening his circuit of visits among the Lopez-Vela descendents.

Bob had lost a great deal of weight, making him look more like our uncle Lico. "Man, cuz, you've really got the Lopez nose," he said, staring at me. "Roman nose, aquiline, and cleft at the tip like Grandmother and my dad." He dozed off a bit and then opened his eyes, cloudy at first, then perfectly clear again. He fixed me in the long stare of a thousand-year-old cousin, taking in a long, deep breath.

"I wonder what I might have done if I'd had a life like yours."

As he sighed, those words hung like an accusatory benediction, and all I could say was, "You have had the great Lopez life, Bob. A real stranger in a strange land, and all those people wanting to hear what you'll say next."

"Howard Stern still sucks, and Art Bell never met an alien he didn't love," he replied, mocking my radio heroes, laughing until he coughed.

I asked him about his home broadcasts, and if he wasn't periodically tempted to just go on the air, interrupting a Van Halen or Bachman Turner Overdrive song, just to offer some top-of-the-head musings about what a crock religion is. He chuckled, then got serious.

"You know, JP, the only thing about having a transmitter in your home studio is that there is a transmitter in your home studio. It makes you really wonder what there is to say, really." He laughed once more, drawing me in with him, something about the way he put that, so limpid and true. He fell asleep. When he awoke, I gave him a foot massage and he told me that if there is an afterlife and he has any capacity to be in contact, he'll send me a message, not in code or hieroglyph, but "a *real* message," he emphasized.

We embraced and started to weep almost unnoticeably, until he said, "Can somebody turn down the bagpipe music, please?" Just then, his sister, my cousin Lola, arrived and brought him a lamb-kin doll their father gave her when she was in the hospital as a little girl.

"It's good you got here in the nick of time, sis. John Phillip's getting all gay with me now."

I read Bob the story about our grandfather Leonides's secret love child and his prolonged delay awaiting his final Laredo burial, and he chuckled one more time.

"Hey, John Phillip, now let's eighty-six that one!" he shouted between chortles, coining a phrase for suppressing information from his archnemesis of all time, Richard Nixon. "No reason to hang out all our dirty laundry, especially after all the time that's passed. Whaddaya say let's give Grandpa a pass on that one, huh, cuz?"

Bob died a few days later, and Baltimore gave him a grand farewell, with signs all across the city announcing, "We'll miss you, Lopez," and, "Have a good journey, Lopez." He was fifty-two years old, the age at which his father, my uncle Leo, and our grandfather Leonides had died. It has been four years since then, and primo Bob still hasn't checked in.

And just a few months after Bob's death, my cousin Linda, eldest daughter of Uncle Lauro, died on a July Fourth evening, after a sudden and unexpected heart attack and stroke. My mother was keeping vigil with her in her hospice room, and she called me at three in the morning to tell me that Linda had just passed away. Before me and my brothers were born, Linda had been like a daughter to my parents, later like a sister to us, and she had joined us on several family vacations, and we visited her when she lived in California and Massachusetts.

When I got to the hospice, I entered the room and found Mother with a stoic expression on her face, calmly sitting in a chair alongside Linda's body in the hospital bed as if she were keeping some ancestral compromiso to accompany our dear relations in the time of their leave-taking from this world, and she was determined that the lives of our surviving Lopez clan were especially mandated to her regard, as a witness, a consoler, a silent companion elder.

She was incredulous that there was any story of note to be told about our family's past, always reminding me that her father, Leonides Lopez, died when she was a child, so that the Lopez story was lost—and that her mother, Leandra Vela Lopez, had revealed little of the history of the Velas, preferring instead to go to her death in the mid-1970s with her family's story hidden away in her heart.

If someone was interested, anyone could go in search of their family's place in Tejano history; but historians are just beginning to write that history now. We are only now emerging out of the fog of our unwritten past. And gradually, we are discovering we are not who we thought we were.

Españoles, Mexicanos, Tejanos, Americans.

We were always someone else before we came to be whoever our ancestors thought us to be. And by the time we had a sense of being one identity or another, we had already become something new. This is why genealogy is so poignantly fragile and incomplete as an exercise in understanding ourselves.

Not too long ago, the Velas of South Texas organized a reunion in McAllen, Texas, across the border from the historic Villas del Norte of Mier, Camargo, and Revilla/Guerrero, and nearly three thousand people turned out to remember that family's history. The Vela story is very much alive. When one elder Vela lady approached a family historian and told how she was the descendant of a widow whose Vela husband had been killed in an Indio uprising in Mier late in the eighteenth century, he knew the exact episode in detail and commended her for her great-great-grandfather's courage, as he had volunteered for the small delegation of townspeople consti-tuted to defend the settlement.

"Your grandfather was a legendary Vela, ma'am, you should be proud," he told her.

Even after a long time as Texans, another Vela tía told me, "We were Mexicans, and we had to sit separate from the Anglos in the church. And her mother said, 'Que digan lo que digan, hay un Dios que sabe todo." Let them say what they will, there is a God who knows everything.

She recited the names of her relations: Estanislado, known as Tanis, Cleofas, Faustolio, Bandilia, Aveldia, Marcofa, Philemon, and three separate Uvaldos, one of whom never married and was accidentally shot.

When I asked her how she remembers so much into her nineties, she replied, "Lo que temprano aprende, nunca se olvide." What you learn young you never forget.

And then she told me something else her mother told her.

"If we endure, we will become beautiful." Cenote Siete had written the very same words years before.

In his public lecture, the family historian located the origins of Vela's ancestry fifty thousand years ago, when, he explained, *Homo sapiens* managed to extinguish the lineages of "Eurasian Adam." He had organized a broad genetic sampling of Velas and found the DNA evidence of the family demonstrated the lineage's sources in the Balkans, Italy, and later Spain, where he said the surname first appeared in the twelfth century. There was evidence of earlier origins in the Basque Pyrenees, the name recorded in the *Codex Albedensis seu Vigilanus*, which had been donated to the Escorial Library of Philip II by the count of Buendía.

He traced the earliest appearance of Velas in Mexico to 1513, cited the participation of Velas in the Chichimeca War of 1547, and how the first of the Velas, Jorge Vela, made his way north to San Luis Potosí in 1548. By 1626, the Velas were in Cerralvo in what would soon thereafter become Nuevo Santander. Though I was a distant cousin of the Velas of that reunion, our common ancestor likely came from Cerralvo—today in Nuevo León—Mexico, around that time in the seventeenth century. From Cerralvo, they made their way with the Escandón expeditions to Mier, Revilla, and Camargo.

But when I did the genetic test of my matrilineal origins, despite all of the documents I had uncovered showing my grandmother's family origins in Asturias, Spain, the results came back showing indigenous pre-Columbian origins. The Lopez-Vela tale reminds me that families are always a part of a human story that runs deeper than the story of any one nation or people. We migrate, venture farther out to the fronteras where we may settle in for a long spell as states come and go, and we are ever becoming something new, ever metamorphosing, giving little thought to the untold ancestral journeys and transformations that brought us to the present time.

As an inadvertentist, I have sought none of this. But it has all found me, slowly, inexorably, gradually, but ever unceasing. Less than a year after I had returned to San Antonio, the death portrait of Colonel José de Escandón y Helguera, Conde de Sierra Gorda, the last conquistador, made a surprise visit to the city. I was already deep into my investigations about my ancestors' roles in his historic expeditions into the terra incognita of New Spain. The painting was a last-minute addition to *Retratos*, a touring exhibition of portraits and self-portraits from Mexico, the Caribbean, and Latin America, spanning three thousand years. I was allowed to visit the galleries of the San Antonio Museum of Art alone on the evening before the opening of the show, where I found a single lamp illuminating the portrait at the end of the first long hall.

It seemed to smolder, like an apparition of the ghost of a forgotten grandfather.

In the midst of his efforts to settle and pacify Nuevo Santander, Escandón is said to have come to San Antonio in the 1750s. Now he had returned.

Painted in 1770 by Andrés de Islas, a student of the great Mexican painter Miguel Cabrera, the portrait shows Escandón lying at rest on satin pillows with lacy black florettes that overflow the silver-filigreed ebony coffin, perched on a little stool, set upon a platform draped in a brilliant red silk with an undulating floral pattern.

Escandón is wearing black velvet pantaloons, with his expeditionary suede boots pulled to his thighs, necessary to fend off the thorny brush on horseback in the sierra; and he is dressed in the elaborate attire of the Order of Santiago, the fraternity of knights formed in Galicia in the twelfth century to protect the pilgrims en route to the shrine to Saint James of Compostela.

His scarlet tunic is trimmed with gold-embroidered borders and hems, over which a buttoned white surplice bears the distinctive Red Cross emblem of the order that looks like a haunted fleur-de-lis dagger. This unremembered grandfather shows a tranquil mien, the legendary works of his epic life completed, his tricorned hat set upon his head for the last time. Escandón's white-gloved hand gracefully cradles the top of a long wooden cane, his small finger lifted slightly in a mudra of expectation, and it seems he might put it to the ground, open his eyes once again, and step once more out of his hoary repose.

The inscription calls him *Conquistador, Pacificador, y Poblador* and says his age was exactly seventy years, six months, and six days.

Conqueror, Peacemaker, Creator of pueblos.

It did not say *Creator of Worlds*, but that's what it meant. And perhaps, "keep me in your heart for a while."

You would never know that this man died precisely in the moment of greatest anguish in his life, after a lifetime of exploits and accolades, under the shadow of the trial against him in Querétaro that threatened to reverse all his fortunes and good name. Was he the last conquistador? Born in 1700 in Santander, Spain, and in Mexico by 1715, he actually outlived the heroic age of Nueva España.

Would all future conquistadores be brought to trial and consigned to infamy?

There were so many Mexicano families in San Antonio whose ancestors had come into the region during Escandón's empire-building missions, but few would come to see their old grandfather lying in repose in the Museum of Art. Escandón, the knight, the founder ancestor, the flawed hero of Nuevo Santander, who had found his place in the revered cavern of oblivion, settled in for his months-long sojourn in the old river city he had known in its earliest years.

Recently, on a visit to the home of Raymond and Alicia, old family friends, Alicia told Mother and me that she had just made a videotape transfer of the old film of her parents' wedding in the late 1940s, and she remembered that the footage included some sequences with my grandmother Leandra.

In the film that had been beautifully shot by a professional cinematographer, the radiant couple being married were shown holding hands and wearing the traditional *lazo* rosary, encircling both of them; they were kneeling under an arching trellis of lights before the altar of San Fernando Cathedral. You see the faces of the people gathered in the congregation, fancily dressed Mexicanos from the old families of San Antonio, pausing briefly on the smiling faces of the bridesmaids and the demurring groomsmen. After the camera followed them in the processional out of the church and greeting the assembled family and friends outside, the scene switched to the dinner and reception afterward, held nearby at the Gunter Hotel in downtown San Antonio.

Panning across a group of standing young women, my mother, a young woman here, smiles with a few of her friends, waving at the camera. And as the cinematographer then moved to a large dining table and began slowly tracking across the faces of all of the older guests, he stopped on my grandmother, wearing a silky emerald-colored blouse with a white lace collar. In her late fifties by then, she looks up from a conversation with her neighbor and stares into the camera with a wry grin, exuding a confidence that she was keeping all of her secrets safely to herself, forever.

Acknowledgments

This book was written during a six-year spell of investigations, wanderings, and migration, so I'm especially grateful for the host of people and institutions who gave me shelter and support along the peregrino's camino.

I began these writings during a residency at the American Academy in Berlin, with great thanks to its executive director, Gary Smith, who has managed to create and sustain a vibrant global community of inquiry and creativity on the banks of the Wannsee. Mil gracias also to President Elaina Richardson of Yaddo, in Saratoga Springs, New York, where I spent one frigid early winter witnessing a lunar eclipse, a churning, opalescent aurora borealis, while chronicling the empire of fire. Mentor and co-adventurer Virgilio Elizondo, along with University of Notre Dame's Institute for Latino Studies, and its executive director, Gil Cardenas, were a godsend, making the final trips to Israel and Spain possible. My cousin Larry Lopez and his wife, Rosemary, let me finish the book in the Casa de Sueños, a limestone cottage on their Lopez Ranch in Bergheim, Texas. It was edited in marathon sessions amid innumerable pints at Flying Saucer Draught Emporium in San Antonio.

Ricardo Romo, president of the University of Texas at San

Antonio, generously provided me with an office there, as later did vice president of Trinity University, Michael Fisher, with the intercession of el gran maestro, Dr. Arturo Madrid. My inveterate and ageless conspirator fellah James Der Derian included me in an inspiring and still-expanding operational base in the Global Media Project at the Watson Institute for International Studies at Brown University, whose founding executive director, Tom Bierstecker, first supported our vision of combining documentary media with teaching international relations theory and history. Susan Beresford and Alison Bernstein and my colleagues at the Ford Foundation also offered invaluable support during my years there, when this book was germinating.

The mestizo hermeneutics that provide the underlying code for the stories I've told here were interrogated and refined during innumerable conversations and tale-spinning sessions with a coterie of great minds and hearts that form the corps of our periodically convening Licéo Mestizo, especially Antonia Castañeda, Arturo Madrid, Tomás Ybarra-Frausto, David Carrasco, Miriam Bujanda, Gerry Poyo, Ben Olguín, Javier Rodriguez, and Homero Vera. Aida and Guadalupe Martinez offered their counsel, and peripatetic boxes of birth, marriage, and death records, in seeking out genealogical origins of my Lopez and Vela families. Gracias to them all.

My research was greatly assisted by the librarians of the Archivo de Indias in Sevilla and in San Antonio by the uniquely Tejano erudition of Tom Shelton at the library of the Institute of Texan Cultures. Many thanks to my musical collaborators, Ray Tamez for his guitarra churrigueresca and Leonardo Ferraro, who revealed Cenote Siete's encrypted electronic voice.

I'm grateful for the numerous publications that published earlier versions of some of this writing: *Bomb* magazine, *San Antonio Express-News*, *¡Tex!*, and the *Langdon Review of the Arts* in Texas. Thanks to my agent, Janis Valley, and editor, Jane Von Mehren, who first advocated publishing this book; it was then patiently encouraged and brilliantly edited by Paul Slovak, gracefully designed by Nancy Resnick, and exquisitely shepherded by Beena Kamlani.

I give great thanks for my loyal companions who over the years have endured endless improvisations and rehearsals of these tales, an essential part of my writing process, particularly Tom Levin, Adam Ashforth, Carina Courtright, Pamela Cadwallader Ilott, Rolando, Briseño, Angel Rodriguez-Diaz, Leah Gitter, Pedro Luján, Rafael and Sandra Guerra, and my great ally sister, Sandra Cisneros. I'm thankful for the time and extensive travels I shared with the wise and intrepid Lene Hansen, who accompanied me through the sometimes fitful beginnings of this book in Berlin and Copenhagen.

Though it may not be exactly how she would have written it, this family tale wouldn't have been possible without my mother, Dr. Lucille Lopez Santos, whose stories of her ancestors kept alive the legacy of a great story that remained untold. She is an inspiration, a source of boundless affirmation, and her support was invaluable, along with that of my two brothers: George and sister-in-law Cindy and Charles his partner, Rick Bond. Mil gracias to Aunt Lydia and all of the Lopezes who gave me their stories, and to Jean and Leandra for letting me share their precious time with my cousin Bob in Baltimore.

Along the way of telling this tale, I met my wife, la gran poeta Frances Treviño, for whom I left New York City and returned to our shared homelands, where we have created a life together in the hinterlands of onetime Nueva España. This book is dedicated to her, and to our child, Francesca de la Luz, whose arrival we await in the spring. The story continues.

Casa Dos Chihuahuas
San Antonio de Béjar, Texas
December, 2009